Cosmos as Creation

Cosmos
as
Creation

Theology and Science
in Consonance

Edited by
TED PETERS

Abingdon Press / Nashville

COSMOS AS CREATION

Theology and Science in Consonance

Copyright © 1989 by Abingdon Press

Second Printing 1990

This book is printed on acid-free paper.

Library of Congress Cataloging-in-Publication Data

Cosmos as creation: theology and science in consonance / edited by Ted Peters.
    p.   cm.
  Bibliography: p.
Includes index.
    Contents: Theology and science today / Arthur R. Peacocke—Cosmos as creation / Ted Peters—Creation and cosmology / Ian G. Barbour—The doctrine of creation and modern science / Wolfhart Pannenberg—Cosmology, creation, and contingency / Robert John Russell—The evolution of the created co-creator / Philip Hefner—Does prayer make a difference? / Nancey C. Murphy—Scientific creationism and biblical theology / Roger E. Timm—The future of the cosmos and the renewal of the church's life with nature / H. Paul Santmire.
  ISBN 0-687-09655-3 (alk paper)
    1. Religion and science—1946- 2. Creation. 3. Cosmology.
    I. Peters, Ted, 1941-
BL241.C59   1989
231.7'65—dc19   88-39258
                                                              CIP

MANUFACTURED IN THE UNITED STATES OF AMERICA

This book is dedicated to the ongoing work of the Center for Theology and the Natural Sciences at the Graduate Theological Union in Berkeley, California.

Since its founding in 1981, the Center has pursued questions of theological import that arise from studies in the natural sciences. It is both an ecumenical and academic organization which focuses on the methods, concepts, and history of the interaction between science and religion. It develops research programs, sponsors conferences, holds forums, and leads workshops involving scientists, theologians, clergy, students, and the general public. Among its programs is the J. K. Russell Fellowship, through which the most creative scholars in the field of religion and science are invited to come to Berkeley to carry on dialogue. Many of the past J. K. Russell fellows are contributors to this book.

CONTENTS

Preface   *11*
Ted Peters

1. Theology and Science Today   *28*
Arthur R. Peacocke

2. Cosmos as Creation   *45*
Ted Peters

3. Creation and Cosmology   *115*
Ian G. Barbour

4. The Doctrine of Creation and Modern
Science   *152*
Wolfhart Pannenberg

5. Cosmology, Creation, and Contingency   *177*
Robert John Russell

6. The Evolution of the Created Co-Creator   *211*
Philip Hefner

7. Does Prayer Make a Difference?   *235*
Nancey C. Murphy

8. Scientific Creationism and Biblical
Theology   *247*
Roger E. Timm

9. The Future of the Cosmos and the Renewal
of the Church's Life with Nature   *265*
H. Paul Santmire

Index   *283*

Cosmos as Creation

Is the natural world just that, natural? Or is it more than natural? Can we speak of it as a creation, as the product of a divine intention? If the natural world is the province of the scientist, how can the theologian justify describing it as the domain of God's activity? This is the problematic of the present book, How can we speak of the cosmos as creation?

.One of the unpredicted and astounding trends of our time is the reasking of the God-question within the orbit of scientific discussion about the natural world. The God-question arises primarily in the form of the argument from design. It is the incredibly well-tuned constants of the cosmos discerned by modern physics that have made human life possible. Had the gravitational force of the cosmos been slightly greater or slightly smaller, for example, the universe would then consist of either red dwarf or blue giant stars. Either way, life as we know it would have been impossible. Given the possibilities, the odds against life having ever appeared at all are in the billions to one. Yet life has appeared. It is worth asking whether or not there is a design built right into the history of nature. And such questions are in fact being asked within the scientific community. Freeman Dyson at Princeton asks if the universe in some sense just knew that we were coming. Thus, physicist Paul Davies says that science has advanced to the point where formerly religious questions can now be seriously tackled. Another physicist, Alan Lightman, describes scientists as people of faith, as people with a deep faith in the unseen world and its mathematical rationality. Everyone involved in the discussion recognizes, of course, that we are not at the point of proving the existence of God on the basis of scientific evidence. Yet the significance of what is going on is that the God-question is reemerging as an intelligible question within the context of the study of nature. James Gleick, writing in the January 4, 1987, issue of *The New York Times Magazine*, says that "God's turf" now belongs "not to the theologian, but to the scientist."

It seems that the time is ripe for theologians to step back onto this turf. We need to ask what possible implications new scientific discoveries and theories might have for our understanding of God's relationship to the world. *How can we understand our cosmos as God's creation?* Or, to put it in the form of a challenge, How can theologians at this point in time continue to speak intelligibly of creation without taking modern natural science into account?

That the time is ripe for harvesting the opportunity to rethink the relationship between science and theology is further evidenced by a new openness on the part of church leaders. In the last century, Pope Pius IX's *Syllabus of Errors* of 1864 said it was "an error to believe science and philosophy should withdraw from ecclesiastical authority." But a hundred and one years later, in 1965, the Second Vatican Council declared the natural sciences to be free from ecclesiastical authority and dubbed them "autonomous" disciplines (*Gaudium et Spes:* 59). Pope John Paul II has gone even further. He has said that the church should take responsibility to defend the free pursuit of the secular sciences. And, still further, the pontiff has asked that we seek a new reconciliation between faith and reason, a rapprochement between theology and science. We are currently living in a time when the opportunity is ripe to make a move in this direction.

Which brings us to the task of this book, What should be the relationship between theological knowledge and scientific knowledge about the world in which we live? Since the Enlightenment we have pretty much assumed that they represent separate domains of human knowing. We have erected a high wall of separation between church and laboratory. Yet this is most unfortunate, because we all assume there is but one reality. So sooner or later we will become dissatisfied with consigning our differences to separate ghettos of learning. We will then look for parallels, points of contact, consonances, crossovers, and conflations. This will be exciting. In fact, this dissatisfaction and this excitement already exist. The search for a shared domain of knowledge—for rapprochement—is underway. And the excitement is rising.

How to Understand the Relationship Between Science and Theology

How best should we proceed? How should we understand the relationship between science and theology if we are to move in the direction of rapprochement? Here we will suggest that we begin by pursuing *hypothetical consonance*. By consonance we are looking for those areas where there is a correspondence between what can be said scientifically about the cosmos and what the theologian understands to be God's creation. Consonance in the strong sense means accord, harmony. Where we find accord or harmony between the disciplines, let us explore them further under the hypothesis that they are speaking about the same reality. In a weak sense, consonance may refer to common domains of question asking, i.e., situations where asking the question of God—whether answerable or not—is the reasonable thing to do. In the forthcoming essays on Big Bang cosmogony, for example, we will see that it is quite reasonable for both scientists and theologians to ask about the possibility of a divine role in bringing the cosmos into existence. Whether in the strong or weak senses of the word, the concept of consonance reflects an important underlying assumption, namely, there is one God

and one world so that, in the long run, science and theology are
attempting to understand one and the same reality

Not everyone would agree with this assumption. Consequently, there are numerous alternative proposals for understanding the relationship between science and theology. But,
in this writer's judgment, hypothetical consonance is the best
road to follow because the alternative routes lead into blind
alleys. Let me mention some of the more popular blind alleys.

The first blind alley is *scientism,* sometimes called "naturalism" or "secular humanism." According to scientism, science
provides all the knowledge we need to know. There is but one
reality, the finite reality of nature, and the natural sciences
provide the only methods for giving us the truth. Religion does
not provide us with knowledge of reality. It provides us only
with pseudo-knowledge, that is, false knowledge about
nonexistent fictions. Earlier this century, the British philosopher and atheist, Bertrand Russell, told a BBC audience that
"what science cannot tell us, mankind cannot know." In short,
the scientist allegedly gives us truth and the theologian gives us
delusions. Because it denies any validity to religious experience or insight, scientism is a blind alley; it assumes the
impossibility of rapprochement between science and religion.

The second blind alley is ecclesiastical *authoritarianism.*
This is the theological position of assuming that if there is a
conflict between faith and reason that reason must be wrong. It
assumes that special revelation constitutes the highest truth
and, therefore, should exercise authority in evaluating and
arranging the discoveries of natural reason and science. The
Syllabus of Errors promulgated by Pope Pius IX in 1864 sought
to make a strong defense against the encroachments of the
modern world. As we mentioned above, error number 57 held
that it is an error to believe science and philosophy should
withdraw from ecclesiastical authority. The assumption here is
that scientific knowledge and religious knowledge share the
same domain, so that in the event there is a contradiction one
must be right and the other wrong. The further assumption is
that the church knows what is right and has the right to direct
the course the sciences take. The problem with ecclesiastical

authoritarianism, of course, is that science cannot function unless it functions freely. It requires academic autonomy if it is to advance. This independence is just what Pope Pius IX denied and what Vatican II affirmed. Without academic freedom we cannot have genuine science, and without genuine science rapprochement is a sham.

The third blind alley is *scientific creationism*. Today's creation scientists are the heirs of yesterday's fundamentalists. Both take a strong stand for the literal truth of the Bible. There is a marked difference, however. Whereas the fundamentalists of the 1920s stood on the authority of the Bible, today's creation scientists are willing to argue their case in the arena of science. They assume that biblical truth and scientific truth are of the same sort; they belong to the same domain. When there is a conflict between a scientific assertion and a religious assertion, then we allegedly have a conflict in scientific theories. The creationists argue that the book of Genesis is itself a theory that tells us how the world was physically created: God fixed the distinct kinds (species) of organisms at the point of original creation. They did not evolve. Geological and biological facts attest to biblical truth, they argue.

What is good about scientific creationism is that it seeks a common domain for both scientific and theological discourse. There is a problem, however. Scientific creationism fails to recognize the historical distance that separates the mind-set of the ancient world from that of the modern world, the world view of biblical times from that of scientific times. The originary symbols of the Christian faith first came to articulation in a time when our language was dominated by myth, symbol, and nuance, and pointed to transcendent mysteries. The language of modern science strives for univocity, mathematical precision, and the elimination of mystery. Things have changed so that we need hermeneutical principles to move from the Bible to the modern world. The scientific creationists fail to recognize the full width of the gulf that separates antiquity from modernity and the length of the bridge we need to build.

The fourth blind alley might appear to be the right way to go, because it is advocated by highly respected scientists and theologians; but, nevertheless, it leads to a dead end as well. It is the *two-language* theory. Recognizing the point I just made against the scientific creationists regarding the ancient language of religion and the modern language of science, many scholars in the twentieth century have argued that scientific theory and religious faith represent two separate and distinct domains of knowing. Albert Einstein, for example, distinguished between the language of fact and the language of value. "Science can only ascertain what *is*, but not what *should be*," he once told an audience at Princeton; "religion, on the other hand, deals only with evaluations of human thought and action." Note the use of "only" here. Each language is *restricted* to its respective domain.

Perhaps the most articulate contemporary advocate of the two-language theory is Langdon Gilkey. When he testified against the scientific creationists at Little Rock in 1981, it was the two-language argument that convinced Judge Overton to rule Arkansas Public Act 590 to be unconstitutional. The Arkansas law had decreed that evolution and creation were both scientific theories and, therefore, both should be studied in the public schools. But, argued Gilkey on the stand and in his book *Creationism on Trial: God and Evolution at Little Rock*, evolution speaks the language of science while creation speaks the language of religion; and one does not translate into the other. Science deals only with objective or public knowing of *proximate* origins, whereas religion deals with existential or personal knowing of *ultimate* origins. Science asks, *How?* while religion asks, *Why?* What Gilkey wants, of course, is for one person to be able to embrace both Christian faith and scientific method without conflict. To do so is to be bilingual, so to speak.

The problem with the two-language theory is that it prevents any rapprochement from the outset. It separates by definition. It assumes there is no connection whatsoever between what Christians believe about God's act of creating and the observable creation that is the result. It assumes that there is no connection between the ultimate question, *Why* did God create? and the proximate question, *How* did God create? In actual parlance, however, one cannot even say *that* God creates without in the very formulation say something about *how* God creates. The two can overlap. The lines between ultimate and proximate questions and causes are much more blurred than Gilkey assumes.

The real problem with the two-language theory is that it forbids cross-disciplinary conversation. Even if we should find points of consonance between scientific understanding and theological understanding, it would have to be considered nothing more than a coincidence. We could not explore the possibility that the language of one might serve to illumine the other. We could not develop the assumption that both are speaking about the same reality. Conversation would come to a dead end, even if it did get started. In sum, the two-language theory is a blind alley for those who are hoping for any kind of rapprochement between natural science and Christian theology.

I like the idea of hypothetical consonance better. It recognizes where we are at the outset: theology sings one song and science another. Nevertheless, it gives us something to listen for. We can listen for those measures where both make sound at the same frequency, where we hear a momentary bar of harmony. Then we can at least ask if this might some day lead to a shared melody. In this book we audition with a couple of examples: creation out of nothing and continuous creation. The reader will soon see that most of the authors contributing to this book advocate going beyond the two-language theory toward some sort of consonance.

Where we need to go to say we have arrived will be a situation in which knowledge gained from theological resources will actually contribute to scientific knowledge and, conversely, one in which scientific inquiry makes a substantive contribution to the theologian's knowledge of God's relation to the world. We are not there yet. Anyone who says we have arrived at this point is either mistaken or pretending. Nevertheless, it is a goal worthy to be sought.

The Four Themes of This Book

This book tries to move us toward this goal. Our particular task here is to draw out possible theological implications from current scientific knowledge. Therefore, this is not exactly an instance of general dialogue between disciplines. It is not a sharing back and forth. Rather, what we are engaged in here is primarily theological reflection. Although the methods and data and theories of the natural sciences provide the material content of much of what we discuss here, the questions we pose will be primarily *theological* questions, raising concerns regarding our understanding of God and of God's relation to the world. Although many of the authors have credentials in one or more of the sciences—Ian Barbour and Robert Russell are physicists, Arthur Peacocke is a biologist—we are asking them here to deal initially with a theological agenda, How should we try to conceive of the world of nature in light of what science has to say about nature and in light of the Christian concept of creation?

The reader will soon see that there are four uniting themes that run through this book. First, the world of nature is dynamic. It is changing. We can expect new things. To understand the cosmos we must understand it temporally. This is the indisputable implication of Big Bang cosmology and of biological evolution. It is also the implication that we draw from the biblical picture of the historical acts of God. God has done new things. God promises yet another new thing, namely, a final act whereby the whole history of nature will attain its eschatological consummation.

This leads directly to the second uniting theme: the need for a doctrine of continuing creation *(creatio continua)* to complement the traditional doctrine of creation out of nothing *(creatio ex nihilo)*. This is not an either/or situation. Curiously enough, contemporary scientific cosmogony is reviving interest in the Christian notion of *creatio ex nihilo*, because the Big Bang theory seems to correspond roughly to traditional notions of a singular beginning to the world. This will be explored in detail. But in addition, the epigenetic appearance of new forms of reality in natural history does not permit the notion that everything was created all at once. Creation is ongoing. What Christian theologians had traditionally thought of in terms of divine preservation *(conservatio)* needs rethinking. We need

to consider God's ongoing relation to the world as one of
continuing creativity.

The third theme has to do with the interpretation of scripture
in light of modern science. What most of the contributors to this
volume tacitly agree on is that our understanding of God's
relation to the creation comes from the broad sweep of the
biblical drama. It does not come from a literal analysis of the
first two chapters of Genesis. The book of Genesis is vitally
important, of course. Yet the mode of interpreting it includes
its context in the Bible as a whole and its meaning for
contemporary thought forms as well.

The fourth theme focuses on the place of the human being in
the cosmos understood as God's creation. The existence of the
human race may be contingent upon the course of natural events,
but we cannot help but wonder if it is only an accident. There
seems to be a purpose for our presence, a purpose that is part and
parcel of cosmic history as a whole. We are participants in the
ongoing story of creation. We are created, to be sure, but we are
also creators. We participate in the dynamism of nature. We,
along with everything else, cross the thresholds of time at the
advent of new and novel things. What this means ethically—to
understand ourselves as created co-creators—is that we should
care for the world just as God cares for the world.

What Our Theologians Are Saying

Our first essay, "Theology and Science Today," was
originally an address which Arthur Peacocke delivered at
Pacific Lutheran Theological Seminary in Berkeley in February of 1986. Trained in both biology and systematic theology,
Professor Peacocke is director of the Ian Ramsey Centre at St.
Cross College, Oxford University and was the 1986 J. K.
Russell fellow at the Graduate Theological Union Center for
Theology and the Natural Sciences. Peacocke holds that both
natural science and theology presume to be dealing with
reality, with the same reality. It therefore behooves theologians to pay attention to what is going on in the sciences and to
reconceive our notions of God accordingly. What is going on in

twentieth-century cosmology is key here, especially the theories of an expanding universe and of biological evolution through chance selection. It is through the dialectical movement of chance and law—the movement that is constantly producing new things—that God works, says Peacocke. God is creating continually, and we can see the result of continuous creation in the emergence of new forms of reality. And all of this is happening *within* the life of God, he adds. This makes Peacocke impatient with traditional theism and its masculine images of God, because the traditional view places the world external to God. Rather, suggests Peacocke, reflection upon science leads the theologian toward a panentheistic conception of God and toward feminine images of a divine mother where the world is pictured as emerging from within the divine life proper.

The two essays that follow, my own and that of Ian Barbour, assess the importance of the Big Bang theory of the origin of the universe for the Christian doctrine of creation. Both chapters contend that astrophysics along with evolutionary theory evoke a picture of a dynamic world with a long history of change and development that yields the continual appearance of novel forms. What this means for the theologian is that we must understand God's work in terms of *creatio continua,* as a creative activity that is continuing. Hence, we can no longer limit the term "creation" to a single divine act that occurred at the beginning and is now over and done with. Rather, creation is ongoing. New things are expected yet to come. This does not mean, however, that we need to jettison the more traditional view of *creatio ex nihilo,* according to which God creates out of nothing. We can and should have both. Furthermore, both understandings of creation seem to make sense in light of what we are learning from the natural sciences.

Chapter two, "Cosmos as Creation," appeared first in the fall 1984 issue of *Word and World* and has been adapted for use here. The central thesis of this essay is that the Christian doctrine of creation is itself an expression of the gospel, i.e., it proffers an understanding of the cosmos implied by an understanding of God's saving work in the cross and resurrection of Jesus of Nazareth. The Big Bang theory of the origin of the universe is examined with some care, showing how its inherent commitment to the idea of a history of nature should excite theologians into thinking in new ways about the ongoing creativity of God. Entailed in the Christian view of salvation as well as in the Big Bang cosmology is the notion of epigenesis, i.e., the notion that genuinely new forms of reality appear at various stages in the history of nature. Extrapolated into the future, this means we can expect still more new things. It is not scientific nonsense, then, to think theologically about eschatological newness.

Ian G. Barbour's chapter, "Creation and Cosmology," was originally an address he delivered in the fall of 1985 to the Isthmus Institute in Dallas. He has revised and updated it for this volume. Barbour is retired from a professorship at Carlton College. He served as the J. K. Russell fellow at the GTU Center for Theology and the Natural Sciences 1983–84 and will deliver the Gifford Lectures of 1989–90. Here he wrestles with the problem of conceiving of creation out of nothing, asking whether or not the idea necessitates the notion of a temporal beginning to the universe. He suggests that the notion of an absolute beginning is not required, that the concept of creation from nothing can be sufficiently accounted for by acknowledging the contingency of the particular world we have considering the array of other possible worlds that might have come into existence. Barbour invokes the anthropic principle within the context of chance and necessity so that we can see with dramatic force how cosmic evolution has brought us to this significant yet fragile point in the history of the universe. God is continually at work, he argues, guiding the world process toward divine and human ends. In sum, *creatio ex nihilo* is affirmed for its religious value—for its value of locating human consciousness within a relationship to God—yet conceptually it is absorbed into the much more heuristic concept of *creatio contiua*. Barbour then closes by identifying four post-Copernican and post-Darwinian elements in modern cosmology which might be reconcilable with the message of the biblical creation story.

In his chapter "The Doctrine of Creation and Modern

Science," which was initially an address given by Munich theologian Wolfhart Pannenberg on an American lecture tour in 1986 and then published in *Zygon* 23:1 (March 1988), Pannenberg argues that what the natural sciences and theology hold in common is the concept of contingency. This is not immediately obvious, he says, because scientists appear to be concerned with natural law. However, both nature and history are fundamentally made up of contingent events. If we understand law as a measure of the continuities or regularities within the ongoing natural process, then we can see that law is an abstraction from that which is the prior or more concrete reality, namely, the actual course of contingent events. This opens the door to asking about God's role in the contingency of the universe as a whole, i.e., we recognize that it could be the case that this universe might not exist. It also opens the door to asking about God's role in the contingency or accidental character of the parts, i.e., of the events within the history of the whole. The traditional doctrines of creation, conservation, and governance are reassessed in light of both creation from nothing and in light of a continuing divine creativity.

At this point Pannenberg introduces a startling hypothesis: field theory in physics can be used to explain God's action in the world. He asks us to consider the possibility that the concept of the force field in the work of Faraday and Einstein could explain how the Holy Spirit and perhaps even angels work in nature. He goes even further to suggest that the concept of a universal field comprising space, time, and energy may provide the framework for describing creaturely participation in the eternal presence of God, a participation that is granted to us in the experience of temporal duration. Finally, Pannenberg concludes that we have considerable room for confidence that both the theologians and the natural sciences are speaking about the same reality and with complementary conceptualities.

The chapter by Robert John Russell, "Cosmology, Creation, and Contingency," follows nicely on the heels of the Pannenberg essay. Russell, both a physicist and a theologian, serves on the faculty of the GTU and directs the Center for Theology and the Natural Sciences. Although he does not want to tie theological commitments too tightly to scientific commitments so that if one falls the other falls with it, he nevertheless wants what we say theologically to be as "consonant" as possible with what we say scientifically. Russell first argues that the concept of contingency is central to the doctrine of creation, both as *creatio ex nihilo* and as *creatio continua*. What is significant for theology, Russell says, is that all *scientific* cosmological models must include elements of contingency as well. Hence by examining the meaning of contingency in science we can both augment and shape its theological meaning for our time. To do so Russell turns to questions about the origin and finitude of the universe, the Anthropic Principle, and the eschatological future, suggesting several hypotheses that explore the potential for consonance between scientific cosmology and creation theology.

In chapter six on the evolution of the created co-creator, former J. K. Russell fellow Philip Hefner takes up the question of how evolutionary theory should influence the Christian doctrine of creation, especially Christian anthropology. Whereas Barbour and Russell had dealt with the question in terms of physical cosmology, Hefner's matrix is biological evolution and the theological problems posed by the principle of natural selection to the ethic of altruistic love. A systematic theologian at the Lutheran School of Theology at Chicago and director of the Center for Religion and Science there, Hefner formulates what may be the most valuable idea of the present book, namely, the conception of the human being as *created co-creator*, i.e., both dependent upon the God who creates from nothing yet an active participant in God's work of continuing creation.

God cares for the earth and has a purpose yet to be actualized in the future. That purpose, says Hefner, is the preservation and fulfillment of all of nature. So we, if we desire to align ourselves with God's overall purpose, will find ourselves caring about what happens. We might even say we care about caring. So, now we need to ask, Can care be expressed by God through the matrix of natural causation? Somehow we need to answer yes to this if we are to think that our care within and for the creation emulates or participates in God's caring. One way to get at this knotty question is to ask about the nature of prayer.

This is just what Nancey Murphy does. Professor Murphy holds both a Ph.D. in Philosophy of Science and a Th.D. in Systematic Theology. In her essay, "Does Prayer Make a Difference?" she affirms that the whole network of created causes is supported by the action of God. But, she argues, this does not preclude God from acting in specific and identifiable events. In fact, she says, it was the ancient Hebrew experience of God intervening in specific events that led the Hebrews to posit that God was the world's creator and hence responsible for all events. Without a revelation of God in a particular instance, we would never have known that God is the creator of the cosmos. This understanding of the cosmos is of decisive importance for our understanding of prayer. When we engage in petitionary prayer, we presuppose that God listens and is able to respond. God is not simply saddled with a closed causal nexus over which he cannot exert any influence. Christians are theists, not deists. We should go ahead and pray, assuming with good reason that there is a God who indeed answers prayer.

The chapter by Muhlenberg College professor Roger E. Timm, "Scientific Creationism and Biblical Theology," provides us with an excellent summary and update of the current controversy over *scientific creationism*. His essay, now revised and expanded, appeared first in the April 1986 issue of *Currents in Theology and Mission*. In it Timm takes the creationists to task for focusing on the issue of the supposed literal truth of the opening chapters of Genesis. What this misses, he argues, is the broad sweep of the doctrine of creation that appears throughout the Bible. If we look at scripture as a whole, we discern the message that our world was created good by a loving and gracious God and, further, that this creative activity of God is of a piece with his continuing saving and liberating activity. In his own way, Timm too advocates a combination of original creation and continuing creation. Of special importance, he goes on, is that this understanding of God implies that we humans have considerable responsibility toward the created order, toward caring for the earth.

This brings us directly to the last chapter. H. Paul Santmire's essay, "The Future of the Cosmos and the Renewal of the Church's Life with Nature," was originally published in the fall 1984 issue of *Word and World*. Santmire is a Lutheran pastor in Hartford, Connecticut, and author of a 1985 book, *The Travail of Nature: The Ambiguous Ecological Promise of Christian Theology*. Here he presupposes the kind of cosmology developed in the preceding essays of this book. He proceeds then to develop the paradigm of hope based upon a vision of reality that is fundamentally temporal rather than static. He deals with the whole of cosmic history and attempts to conceive of things wholistically and ecologically. This means we need to get beyond the traditional anthropocentric-soteriocentric line of theological reasoning to a wholistic hope that envisions the human drama within the wider and more comprehensive cosmic history. Although the human race is fallen, Santmire argues, the realm of nature of which we are a part is not fallen. "There is no cosmic fall," he says. This makes salvation, understood as the antidote to human fallenness, only one facet of the divine activity with the creation. Consummation, then, becomes the larger term. Eschatological consummation takes human history up into cosmic history at the point where God's goal for all is accomplished.

Now, Santmire asks, what does such theological thinking mean for the ministry of the church? It means a couple of things: first, we need to engage in righteous cooperation with nature and, second, we need to care for the earth. Finally, it means we should live with hope, cosmic hope.

How to See Cosmos as Creation

As the reader will shortly discern from this collection of essays, we do not want to take it for granted that the cosmos is a creation. We want to know *how* it is we know that it is a creation and, further, *how* we should understand it in light of the current thresholds of scientific thinking.

The situation is that we Christians are accustomed to

speaking glibly of the natural world as God's creation. On what grounds do we do this? Is it immediately obvious from observing the natural realm that it is the product of a divine hand or the object of divine care? We in the modern scientific world have been assuming that it is not. For some time now we have been assuming that if we study natural processes with the intention of learning the laws by which nature operates, what we will end up with is just a handful of natural laws. If we study natural processes with the intention of wondering about the magnificent mysteries that surround us, what we think we will end up with is an imagination full of spectacular puzzles. If we study nature for her beauty, we will see beauty. If we study nature to see her violence, we will see her as did Tennyson, blood "red in tooth and claw." Nature, we have been assuming for a century or so now, does not seem to take the initiative to disclose her ultimate foundation or even her existential meaning. What natural revelation reveals is simply nature. If we want to know more, we have to ask more questions. And we have to go beyond our natural relationship with nature to find the answers.

Where we as Christians need to go is to the historical events of the death and resurrection of Jesus Christ, the events that stand at the heart and center of God's revelation. Good Friday and Easter do not reveal that God is the world's creator for the first time, of course. But these events do confirm what had already been suspected in ancient Israel, namely, that the creation of the world was the necessary first act in God's continuing drama of salvation. The world in which we live is not merely a conglomeration of natural laws or puzzles; it is not merely the realm of beauty or violence. It exists because it plays a part in the divine scenario of redemption. It is on the basis of what we know about the God who raised Jesus from the dead that Paul can perceive how creation has been "subjected to futility," that it "has been groaning in travail," and that God has furthermore "subjected it in hope" because it "will be set free from its bondage to decay and obtain the glorious liberty of the children of God" (Rom. 8:18-25).

We have to look to special experiences of God that reveal

God's creative intentions before we see clearly that the world around and in us is in fact a creation. It is primarily on the strength of Israel's experience with the liberating God of the Exodus that the Old Testament writers could depict the world as God's creative handiwork. It is on the strength of our experience with the incarnate Lord that today's Christians can say, "God so loved the world" (John 3:16). Appealing to the Reformed doctrine of the decrees, some contemporary theologians express this by saying that God first decides for the kingdom, and then for creation. Consequently, it is the kingdom that determines creation, and creation is the promise of the kingdom. Whether we interpret nature through the symbol of the Exodus, the incarnation, the kingdom, or some other similar religious symbol, we find that we are dependent upon some form of revelation of God's purposes if we are to put nature into proper theological perspective, i.e., if we are to think of nature as a creation.

Thus, on this basis we might consider the possibility of a reversal in natural theology. The aim of natural theology traditionally has been to ask what our study of nature can contribute to our knowledge of God. But we could work with a somewhat different aim, namely, to ask what our knowledge of God can contribute to our knowledge of nature. To know that God is the creator is to know that the world in which we live and move and have our being is *creation*.

Of course, we need not have to choose between the two methods. We could begin with nature and then ask about God; or we could begin with what we think we know about God and then ask how this influences what we think about nature. Or, we could do both. Both is what we do here.

Ted Peters
Berkeley, California
January 1, 1989

ONE

Theology and Science Today

ARTHUR R. PEACOCKE

In spite of doubts and skepticism in certain circles about the long-term value of science, I do not need to tell you that our contemporary world is in fact a world of science in the sense that science is generally thought to command the heights of the cultural landscape. Science is a dominating force, a universal viewpoint that is reshaping the outlook of humankind everywhere, especially that of the young. It even modifies the language and images that most readily come to mind. Science simply cannot be ignored by anyone concerned with the plausibility of Christianity or indeed any other religion.

What about religion? Ever since the emerging species *homo sapiens* buried its dead with rituals, human beings have displayed an awareness of the tragedy of the ephemeral, the reality and yet the unacceptability of the cycle of life and death. The religious quest of humankind is one of the characteristic features of human societies at all times including

This chapter was originally an address at Pacific Lutheran Seminary on behalf of the Center for Theology and the Natural Sciences at the Graduate Theological Union in Berkeley, California, February 5, 1986.

Arthur Peacocke is director, Ian Ramsey Centre, St. Cross College, Oxford, England.

our own. Even in the twentieth century, there are rooms in the interior castle of the modern soul waiting to be filled, though unfortunately a plethora of twentieth-century devils is also attempting to fill them.

The relationship between these two claimants on humankind's loyalties, science and religion, is I think one of the most fundamental challenges that faces the mind and spirit of humanity today. To repress the problem to a level of the subconscious where it is ignored is to engender and enhance the psychosis of Western civilization which we see so much today.

What I want to do here is to consider some of the interactions between religion and science. It is really religion in the form of theology that I am talking about, of course. Theology is the intellectual reflection on the religious experience, the attempt to give it conceptual and propositional form. I will be urging basically that the scientific and the theological enterprises are interacting and mutually illuminating approaches to reality. That they are investigating reality is the instinctive intuition of scientists. As scientists, we would give up research if we did not assume we were learning something about the real world. So also with the theologian. We could not go on being "religious" unless we thought there is something real to which we address our prayers and which is important in our lives. Although science and religion may appear to speak different languages, what they share in common is that they speak of reality in their distinctive ways.

What this means is that our religious affirmations cannot be affirmed without taking account of the best knowledge we have of the world today, and that means the world as described by the sciences. Theology, I am presuming, will have to listen to and adapt to, but not be subservient to, new understandings of the natural world provided by the sciences. Both religion and science seek intelligibility within a framework of meaning, and I am presupposing that both are concerned with reality, the understanding of which is articulated by means of models and metaphors. Any affirmations about God's relation to the world, any doctrine of creation if it is not to become vacuous and sterile must be about the relation of God to the creation, and this creation is the world that the natural sciences describe. Theology really has no other choice unless it wants to retreat to a ghetto where people just talk to themselves and not to the rest of the world.

The scientific perspective on the world affords the currently most reliable answers—not complete, and always provisional, but the best we have for our generation—to such questions as, What's there? What's going on? How did it change? How did it get there? How did it come to be the way it is? So I want to consider certain features of the contemporary scientific perspective and then ask what implications that perspective has in influencing our choice of models of the way in which we might conceive of God's relation to, and action in, the world.

The New View of the Cosmos

First of all, what about the transformation of the scientific world view through twentieth-century physics and cosmology? By the end of the nineteenth century the absolutes of space, time, object, and determinism were apparently securely enthroned. We then lived, it was thought, in an unmysterious, mechanically determined world which was basically simple in structure at the atomic level and, statistically at least, unchanging in form. Yet within the first few decades of this twentieth century there was a veritable "twilight" of these gods of absolute space, time, object, and determinism. This has to be taken into account if we are to understand the reality of which we are a part.

Another distinctive feature of the scientific world view coming from twentieth-century cosmology is the idea that the world as a whole, the universe, is in process of change and evolution. The cosmologists and the astrophysicists have shown us how from a time in the order of 10 to 20 billion years ago, a primeval, unimaginably condensed mass of fundamental particles and energy could have been transformed by exploding and then expanding to the present observable universe with its billions of galaxies and stars. Cosmic evolution has been attended by a great increase in the richness and diversity of forms. This is certainly true on the surface of this planet earth; and the whole process has the aspect of being a creative process. As matter has coalesced into more and more complex forms, new and very different kinds of behavior and properties have emerged.

Looking back, we now see that the beginning of the twentieth century initiated a series of fundamental changes that amount to an unparalleled leap in the expansion of human consciousness of the world. And curiously enough, our awareness of our ignorance grows in parallel with, indeed faster, than the growth in our knowledge. Nevertheless, as John Polkinghorne, an Anglican priest and a former mathematical physicist at Cambridge, says, one is struck by the fact that mathematics, which is essentially an abstract free creation of the human mind, repeatedly provides the indispensable clue to the understanding of the physical world. At root it creates the possibility of science within the human mind so that we can understand the world.

This leads us to the observation that there is an inextricable connection between the grand sweep of the cosmos and the human organism. It turns out that if, for example, the interaction constant governing the forces between protons were only slightly different, then all the protons in the universe would have turned into inert helium at the early stages of the expansion of the universe. As it happened they did not. Had they done so, no stars and no life would have emerged. The material units of the universe are the fundamental entities constituted in matter, energy, space, and time, and as such they have built in, as it were, the potentiality of becoming organized in that special kind of complex system we call living systems, and, in particular, in the systems of the human brain and the human body. In human beings, in *homo sapiens*, the stuff of the universe has become cognizing and self-cognizing. This expresses in a new way the old assertion that the universe in which we exist is contingent. Moreover, far from the human presence in the universe being a curious and inexplicable surd, we find we are remarkably and intimately related to those events in the galaxies that produce, say, the iron that makes our blood red and the hemoglobin of our bloodstream. Every atom of iron in our blood would not have been there had it not been produced in some galactic explosion billions of years ago and eventually condensed to form the iron in the crust of the earth from which we have emerged.

So it is we come to stress the particularity of our universe. There are certain basic given features, fundamental constants, particles, and laws that limit what can eventually be realized through its processes. Even though these limitations are not necessary in the sense of being features of all possible universes, yet for us they constitute the givenness of our existence, of *its* necessity. And this givenness does not confine the open future in a universe in which dynamic processes lead to the emergence of new complex entitites of distinctive qualities and activities that include not only biological life but the whole life of *homo sapiens*. Moreover, it is the very givenness of the parameters of the milieu of human life that makes human freedom and human perception possible. So in this more general sense too, the cosmic order is a necessary prerequisite of conscious personal existence as we know it in human beings.

I believe we have to take this perspective on the world afforded by physics and cosmology seriously, though not too literally. This means that in thinking how it might influence our models of God's relation to and action in the world, it is the broadest general features that we must reckon with. It will be to the world so described by these sciences that theological questionings must refer. And it is in the world so described that we ourselves seek meaning.

Within the framework of twentieth-century cosmology the theologian needs to reaffirm that "there is God" and that this cosmos is "God's Creation." In doing so, however, I must be clear from the outset that in saying that "God is," and that "God is creator," I am not affirming that God is in any ordinary sense a cause in the physical nexus of the universe itself. Otherwise God would be neither explanation nor possible meaning. He— to exclude for a moment the feminine personal pronoun, which

I shall discuss below (page 36)—cannot be the old "God of the gaps." *Ex hypothesi* God's uniqueness and distinction from the world assures that nothing in the world itself, such as might fill one of its causal gaps, can ever be a totally satisfactory and true image of that all-embracing reality that we name as "God." The doctrine of creation affirms that any particular event or entity would not happen, or would not be at all, were it not for the sustaining creative will and activity of God. This fundamental otherness of God in his own inscrutable, ineffable, and ultimately unsurpassable being, is essential for what we mean by God. It is this that is referred to by the word "transcendence," and the predicate "transcendent": it is an inexpungible element in the Judeo-Christian and, indeed Islamic, theories of God.

Transcendent and Immanent Creator

Let us look now at some of the implications for our models of God and the world that arise from the aspects of the scientific world view I have so far indicated. The sense of God's transcendence is itself reinforced by the demonstration through physics and cosmology that vast tracks of matter, energy in space and time have existed, and probably will exist without any human beings to observe them. The excessively anthropocentric cosmic outlook of our medieval and Newtonian forebears is thereby healthfully restored to that more sober assessment that characterizes the Psalms, the Wisdom literature, and the Prophets. The creation exists for God's enjoyment.

What about time? Time in modern relativistic physics is an integral and basic aspect of nature. Space and time have to be mutually defined in interlocking relations and both are related to definitions of both mass and energy, themselves interconvertible. So matter, energy, and space-time constitute together the created order. Hence, on any theistic view, time itself has to be regarded as owing its existence to God, something Augustine long ago perceived. It is this "owing its existence to God" which is the essential core of the doctrine of creation. This concerns the relationship of all the created order including time itself, to its creator, sustainer, and preserver. Thus the fundamental otherness of God must include the divine transcendence of time. Nevertheless, there is an important feature that the scientific perspective inevitably reintroduces into the idea of creation. It is the realization, now made explicit, that the cosmos which is sustained and held in being by God, is a cosmos that has always been in process, producing new emergent forms of matter. *God creates continuously*. God's continuous creative activity is itself a creating in time.

The scientific perspective of a cosmos that manifests emergence of the new reemphasizes that dynamic element in our understanding of God's relation to the world which was always implicit in the Hebrew conception of a living God. The scientists now see no breaks in the causal and temporal nexus of the evolution of the cosmos or of life on the earth, and thus rule out any "God of the gaps." Thus we must conceive of God as creating within the whole process from beginning to end, through and through, or he cannot be involved at all. It is not so much a question of primary and secondary causes, as classically expounded by Thomas Aquinas, but rather that the natural causal creative nexus of events *is* itself God's creative action. It is this that the attribution of immanence to God in the creation of his world must be taken to convey. God is not some kind of diffuse spiritual gas permeating everything. Rather, we wish to say that all that is in its actual processes is God manifest in his mode as continuous creator.

This also makes intelligible that striking rationality of the created order that makes it amenable to mathematical interpretation. For if God is least misleadingly denoted as personal (indeed as supra-personal), then he is rational, and his creation in its ultimate depths will be the embodiment of that rationality: it will bear the stamp of his inner being. We might even go so far as to say, as did Kepler and Newton, that when we think mathematically, we are thinking God's thoughts after him. So a new stress is required, I think, on the immanence of God as creator in the light of the scientific understanding of the world, an understanding that demands to be reconciled with our profound intuition of God's otherness in himself, in his transcendence.

Panentheistic, Musical, Sacramental, and Feminine Imagery

In order to bring together these two conceptions—of transcendence over and immanence in creation—one could resort to various spatial models. I believe we should posit a "panentheist" position, meaning by that simply that the world is in God but there is more to God than the world.

I believe we must take seriously Paul when he was said to speak of the God in whom "we live and move and have our being" (Acts 17:28). We must recall that the Old Testament talks about God being closer than one's breath and closer than one's heartbeat: If we ascend up into heaven he is there; if we make our beds in hell he is there too (Ps. 139:8 paraphrase). There is no aspect of space or time or matter or energy including ourselves to which God is not present and sustaining the present. So God is not something added as an extra "x" to what's there, the "x" that is the world. The stuff and processes of the world as we know it are embedded in an expression of God in his modality *as* creator.

An analogy I would like to give here is a musical one. It is this: Suppose you are listening to a concert, to a Mozart quartet. The music is coming *to* you, but you are deep *in* the music and your mind is moving according to those musical forms. You are then meeting Mozart as he wrote the music. If you ask, where is Mozart now, *qua creator*, one must answer that he is nowhere except in the music. The music is Mozart, *qua creator*, in the modality of being creator. Do not look for him in the conductor or the musicians. And if you listen to that music and really absorb it so you are reliving the music deep within you, then you are meeting Mozart as composer. God's creation is that kind of activity, where that which is created is the very vehicle of the One who does the creating.

Now this is actually, precisely, what the Johannine and

sacramental traditions of the Christian Church say. The Word
was present in the universe, being made explicit and manifest
in the Word-made-flesh, in the person of Jesus, who was of the
stuff, atoms, and molecules of the universe. When we talk
about God as creator, we mean that in the processes of the
world we are witnessing God's creation as he is creating.
Moreover, this Word was made flesh (John 1:14), this
Word-of-God-Incarnate, is now present to us in, with, and
under the sacramental acts of that community, the Church,
commissioned to continue to enflesh that presence in the
world.

However, the concept of God as creator has, at least in the
recent past, been much too dominated by a stress on the
externality of God's creative acts. *He* is pictured as having
created something external to himself, just as the male fertilizes
the ovum from outside. But mammalian females, at least,
experience creation within themselves, and the growing
embryo resides within the female body. Therefore, female
images of the divine are more helpful in this context than male
ones. We should work with the analogy of God creating the
world *within herself*. God creates a world that is in principle
other than himself, but creates it within herself.

Biology and Continuing Creation

This brings me to the world view of biology, where some of
what I want to say simply reinforces what I said previously in
relation to physics and cosmic evolution. The continuity, for
example, of the biological processes of evolution, follows the
cosmological processes that produce stars, that produce the
sun, and that produce its satellite planet, Earth. The
continuities of biological evolution extend now to the molecular
domain, where increasingly the principles that govern the
emergence of self-reproducing macro-molecular systems are
well understood both kinetically and thermodynamically. I will
not present here the overwhelming evidence for the intercon-
nectedness through time of all the living organisms originating

from one or a few primeval simple forms. I will take it for granted as the agreed view of informed professional biologists of all creeds. Again, the gaps in the scientific account of this biological evolution that scientists yesterday thought they detected continue to have the habit of being closed by the work of scientists today—and those of today will no doubt share the same fate. The gaps where any "god" may be inserted keep diminishing. For we see a world in process that is continuously capable through its own inherent properties of producing new living forms. This inbuilt creative potentiality of all-that-is is, I believe, actually God at work. God is continuously creating in and through the stuff of the world he himself, she herself, has endowed with those very potentialities. So again, we find cause to stress God's immanence in the created order, or rather, the creating order.

I referred above to a certain looseness in the causal coupling that physics describes. And this feature of the natural world becomes even more noticeable in the open-ended character of biological evolution. In retrospect, each emergence of a new form of organization of living matter is in principle intelligible to us now as a lawful consequence of a concatenation of random events. This involvement of randomness means that although in *retro*spect the development is intelligible to modern science, yet in *pro*spect it would not have been strictly predictable. The processes of the world as a whole are not unfolded as predetermined sequences of events, like the development of a mammalian embryo from the ovum. The chief characteristic of progressive evolution is its open-endedness. Conquests of new environments create opportunities for further evolutionary development. As one goes up the scale of biological evolution, the open-ended character—the unpredictability and creativity—of the process becomes more and more focused in the activity of the biological individuals, and they become increasingly conscious. This aspect of the process reaches its apogee in the self-conscious creativity of human beings.

Such a perspective on evolution therefore attributes a special significance to human emergence in and from the material universe while recognizing that human beings have arrived by means of an open-ended trial-and-error exploration of possibilities, an exploration that is devoid of either false trails or dead ends. The emergence of consciousness is by no means immune from pain or suffering or struggle. If we could tentatively see God, as it were, *exploring* in creation and exploiting opportunities, then we could begin to get a hint of the nature of God's involvement in creation. God's own involvement in creation includes putting his purposes at risk. It is an involvement that for human beings we might well describe as "suffering."

The mechanism, of course, of biological evolution is well known—the mechanism cryptically denoted as "natural selection." All organisms past, present, or future descend from one or several other living organisms, and species are derived from one another by natural selection of the best procreators. So the process by which new species appear is a process of new life through death of the old. It involves a degree of competition and struggle in nature which has often offended human moral and aesthetic sensibilities. Modern biologists may restore the balance in our view of the organic world by reminding us, as G. G. Simpson puts it, "that struggle is sometimes involved, but it is usually not." Advantage in differential reproduction is usually a peaceful process in which the concept of struggle is actually irrelevant. The death of old organisms is a prerequisite for the appearance of new ones. There is indeed a kind of logic about this. For we cannot conceive in a lawful, non-magical universe of any way for new structural complexes to appear, except by utilizing structures already existing, either by way of modification, what we call evolution, or of incorporation, what we call eating. Death, pain, and the risk of suffering are intimately connected with the possibilities of new life in general, and the emergence of consciousness and self-consciousness, that is human life, in particular.

It seems hard to avoid the paradox that what theologians have, I think mistakenly, in the past called "natural evil" is in fact a necessary prerequisite for the emergence of free self-conscious beings. But if it is necessary, and if God is involved "in, with, and under" his creation, can we not say again that here we have a hint of God's suffering with his creation to bring it to its fulfillment?

Chance, Law, and the Divine Composer

The role of chance in the processes of biological evolution has also sometimes offended the sensibilities of many and led to atheistic conclusions or, at least, baffled Christian theists. The position here is, briefly, that we have to recognize that the process by which permanent changes in the material carrying the genetic instructions to the next generation of an organism, i.e., the DNA, is entirely random even though such changes may prove to be necessary for the survival and evolution of the species. It is the occurrence of such changes, i.e., mutations, which provides the variations on which natural selection by the environment favors some changes rather than others and so produces new species with the accumulation of change. So chance has a creative role in this context. The role of chance is what one might expect if the universe were so constituted as to be able to explore all the potential forms of organization of matter, both living and non-living, that it contains. It is this that I find significant about the emergence of life in the universe.

The existence of life and perhaps also of our actual universe is, then, the result of the interplay of chance and law. Indeed, recent theoretical studies in thermodynamics and macromolecular kinetics have shown how the mutual interplay of chance and law, the operation of chance in a lawlike framework, is creative. It is the combination of the two that allows new forms to emerge. On the one hand, if all were lawlike and regular, then the system would be ossified. It would always repeat itself. On the other hand, if all were chance, then we would have chaos. In fact, strictly speaking, we would have *nothing* at all. For no thing would be identifiable long enough to know it was there, even to be named by us. It is chance and law *together* that produce a universe in which new forms emerge, a universe that has creativity built into it.

Furthermore, the character of this interplay of chance and law appears now to be of a kind that makes it inevitable that some kind of living structure should emerge. It now appears that the universe has potentialities that are becoming actualized by the joint operation in time of random time-dependent processes in a framework of lawlike properties; and these potentialities include the possibility of biological, and so of human, life.

But what can the assertion that there is a God who is creator really mean in relation to this scientific context? We need to rethink our models of God's action in the world. Here is precisely one of those points where our new perceptions on the natural world, the role of chance, pose a question to the theologian who wants to go on affirming God's creative action in the world. The potentialities of the stuff of the world with their particular given properties to elicit life and so human beings, seem to be written into creation by the Creator's own self.

Using another musical analogy, we might see God the creator as somewhat like a composer. The composer begins with an arrangement of notes in an apparently simple tune—which of course is one of the elements of the genius of a Bach or a Beethoven. It may be the most banal, ordinary, and undistinguished tune, but the composer sees its potentialities. With an arrangement of notes in an apparently simple tune he or she takes those notes and then elaborates and selectively expands them into a fugue by a variety of devices. Thus does a Bach create a complex and interlocking harmonious fusion from his original material. The listener to such a fugue, with the luxuriant and profuse growth that emanates from the original simple structure, experiences whole new worlds that are the result of the interplay between an expectation based on past experience, law, and an openness to the new. It is the result of chance, in the sense that the listener cannot predict or control it. So perhaps we might envisage the Creator as unfolding the potentialities of the universe, which he himself has given it, selecting and shaping by the redemptive and providential action those that have come to fruition. God is a musical composer of fugues, an improviser of unsurpassed ingenuity.

In addition to this image of the writing of the fugue, one could bring in other images, such as the idea of God enjoying or playing in creation, one not new in Christian thought. The idea of God playing in creation is to be found in the book of Wisdom, and Harvey Cox has developed this notion in his book *The Feast of Fools*. The creative role of chance operating upon the necessities that are themselves created leads us, then, to accept models of God's activity that express God's gratuitousness, joy, and play in creation as a whole, and not in human beings alone. The created world is an overflow of the divine generosity.

Summary: Reconceiving the Doctrine of God

Let me summarize the picture now in a few tightly phrased sentences. How do we see our understanding of God's action in the world, in the world described by the natural sciencies? From the continuity and creativity of the processes of the natural world I inferred that God's creative relation to the world must be conceived of as a continuous, sustaining, creative action within these natural processes. This is what we mean by saying that the creator is immanent in the creation. This is why we look for meaning *within* the world of which we are a part. The natural processes of the world have led to the emergence within it of human beings who possess a sense of transcendence over their environment and this serves to sharpen the quest for the One who makes intelligible the fact that there is anything at all, the One who is ultimate being and who gives being to all else. So, we still postulate that the Creator is also transcendent over matter, energy, and space-time, over all that is.

However, the concepts of God the creator as both immanent and transcendent are not easily held in focus when applied to the One who is the Creator of that in which she is immanent. So the traditional models of God as *Logos* and God as Spirit, I would suggest, need supplementing today in the light of our new perspective on the world. This is again an example of how science raises a question for theology to ponder. I said earlier that the world must be seen as being within God, but the being of God is regarded as not exhausted by or subsumed within the world. And in that connection, the feminine image of God as creator proves to be a useful corrective, as I said, to a purely masculine image. The feminine image allows us to have the concept of God creating within her own being.

I would also say that as a consequence of the idea of continuous creation, we do not want to say that God is *more* present at one time or place. Rather, God is present in all of God's own universe, in all times and all places. All is of God at all times. Nevertheless, human beings find that in some sequences of events within created nature and history, God unveils more meaning than in others. Just as with each of us, although we are present all the time in our bodies and to other people, there are some gestures, some mannerisms, some phrases that reveal us better to one another. So God has written meanings into the universe. There are meanings of God to be unveiled, but not all are equally read. Some events will be more revealing than others, and this opens the way for understanding the possibility of revelation.

I venture the idea of God, as it were, exploring in creation, of actualizing all the potentialities of his creation. God is, as I said, unfolding as it were, fugually, all the derivatives and combinations inherently possible. This is where we humans come in. The meanings of God unveiled to and for human beings will be more partial and broken and incomplete the more the level of cosmic creation departs from the human and personal. Moreover, it is the personal level at which the transcendence of the "I," the ego, is experienced concomitantly with its immanence in our bodies. And so we could say that the more personal and self-conscious is the entity in which God is immanent, the more capable it is of expressing God's supra-personal transcendent characteristics.

My stress on emergence in cosmic evolution is one-sided without a balancing emphasis on the continuity that is required by the scientific perception of natural processes. So, from a theistic perspective, any new meaning that God is able to express in a new emergent should not be discontinuous with the meanings expressed in that out of which it has emerged.

Thus it is that the transcendence and immanence of our human experience raises the hope, or conjecture, that in a human person adequate for the purpose, immanence might be able to display in a uniquely emergent mode a transcendent dimension to a degree that would unveil without distortion the transcendent Creator. But is this not precisely what Christians aver concerning "Incarnation"? Furthermore, from a consideration of the character of the natural processes of suffering and death, and from a recognition that God has put the divine purposes at risk in creating free and self-conscious persons, I arrive at the idea that God suffers with creation and in the creative process; that, indeed, in this aspect we begin to discern God the Creator as love.

In such ways, I would urge, the two ways of discerning reality, science and religion, are consonant and begin to converge in our personal perspective as each points to a depth of reality beyond the power of model or metaphor, in which all that is created is embraced in the inner unity of the divine life of the Creator—Transcendent, Incarnate, and Immanent.

Cosmos as Creation

TED PETERS

Of the two families of theories regarding the origin and organization of the cosmos, the Big Bang proposed by George Gamow and the steady state advocated by Fred Hoyle and others, the Big Bang in one version or another currently seems to command the greatest attention among working astronomers and physicists. What is quite significant is that the Big Bang cosmology presupposes unilinear or historical time and suggests the possibility of an original beginning with an accompanying eschatology. What is even more significant is its mood of contingency, i.e., our universe just did not have to become what it is. Because of this it appears to raise important issues for theologians. Upon closer examination, however, we will find that they are mostly pseudo issues and that even with the staggering breadth of new scientific knowledge we today must take the same point of departure for the Christian

This chapter is an adaptation of a previously published article, "Cosmos and Creation," appearing in *Word and World* 4:4 (Fall 1984), pp. 372-90.

Ted Peters is professor of systematic theology at Pacific Lutheran Theological Seminary and convenor of doctoral studies in systematic and philosophical theology at the Graduate Theological Union in Berkeley, California. He is author of *Futures—Human and Divine* (Atlanta: John Knox, 1978), and *Fear, Faith, and the Future* (Minneapolis: Augsburg, 1980).

doctrine of creation taken by our ancestors, namely, the point where the Beyond made itself known in the saving gospel.

This is an important topic because Big Bang thinking has raised anew the question of the relationship between science and religion. Could we be moving beyond previous open hostility and present detente toward a new consonance on the doctrine of creation? Some say yes! Astronomer and religious agnostic Robert Jastrow startled the public a few years ago by arguing that "the astronomical evidence leads to a biblical view of the origin of the world." In a moment of sardonic wit and inspired eloquence, Jastrow penned the now oft-quoted lines:

> At this moment it seems as though science will never be able to raise the curtain on the mystery of creation. For the scientist who has lived by his faith in the power of reason, the story ends like a bad dream. He has scaled the mountains of ignorance; he is about to conquer the highest peak; as he pulls himself over the final rock, he is greeted by a band of theologians who have been sitting there for centuries.[1]

Pope Pius XII anticipated Jastrow's enthusiasm in a 1951 allocution to the Pontifical Academy of Sciences in Rome when he praised scientists for testifying to a creation in time and thereby postulating the creative work of "an all-wise God."[2] *Time* essayist Lance Morrow says we now have the equivalent of the Montagues and Capulets collaborating on a baby shower.[3]

In this chapter we shall ask, What should be the proper relationship between scientific cosmology and the Christian understanding of creation, especially *creatio ex nihilo*? What is needed to work on the answer is some understanding of how the ancient theologians actually climbed atop Jastrow's mountain in the first place. After an examination of the admittedly thrilling discoveries relating to Big Bang research, we will proceed to draw a contrast between mythological and historical cosmologies. This contrast is important because it is within the framework of emerging historical consciousness that the gospel revelation occurs. It was reflection upon God's saving work—the gospel—that led the Christian theologians of antiquity to make a commitment to *creatio ex nihilo*. It is this that provides the clue for unraveling the complex entanglement between scientific and religious apprehensions of the cosmos and its meaning.

Big Bang Cosmology

At the simplest level Big Bang theorizing about the beginning of creation appears to be an analogy based on the explosion of an artillery shell. According to this analogy about 15 billion years ago (plus or minus 50 percent) an explosion took place at a small epicenter and the entire universe today represents fragments still flying out through space. The universe is blowing up before our eyes. We earthlings are at the moment riding away from the point of origin on a chunk of shrapnel.

In addition to this simple analogy, the last three decades of scientific research have produced startling data that have confirmed and refined considerably the theory of an expanding universe. What has been learned recently has advanced our knowledge to a time as small as 10^{-35} or perhaps even 10^{-43} seconds after the very onset of the bang. Furthermore, the complementary research in both astronomy and physics has led to the strong hypothesis that at the point of the bang the universe was completely simple, completely unified. Now this marks the end of the line for strictly scientific research, because astrophysicists cannot within the framework of their discipline talk about singularlity or what was going on before there was any time $(t = 0)$. Nevertheless, it is scientific theory itself that has brought us to this exciting end of the line.

According to the Big Bang cosmogony, our universe started out very hot and has been in the one-way process of cooling off ever since. When the temperature decreases past a certain threshold a so-called freezing out takes place. Each freezing out involves the appearance of new forms of matter and energy. At the hot beginning we did not have such things as molecules, atoms, or even nuclei. The things (and laws of nature that govern the things) of our universe were produced not rapidly but gradually and unpredictably. When a volume of water freezes and expands, we know for certain that it will crack. Where it will crack cannot be predicted. What exists now is largely accidental, i.e., it is not simply the working out of principles already present at the point of origin. Let us take a brief look at this process of freezing and expanding by going backward or bangward in time toward the beginning.

The present era is characterized by molecules and atoms. This became possible due to a freeze at approximately the 500,000-year mark after the beginning, where for the first time the electromagnetic force permitted the binding of nuclei with passing electrons. Prior to that it was not possible. The cosmos was too hot and too dense for atoms. We had only plasma made up of simpler particles and nuclei.

Going back further, the heat prior to the three-minute mark prevented the formation of nuclei, because any nucleus that happened to form would be destroyed by collisions of speeding smaller particles. At three minutes, when the temperature dropped to a mere 10 million degrees, the strong subatomic interaction force became effective, making the formation of nuclei possible.

If we ask about the freezing out prior to the advent of particles, we find that at about 10^{-4} seconds into the bang these particles condensed out of a sea of still hotter quarks, of particles still more elementary than protons and neutrons. There seems to be no change in the fundamental forces during the quark era. But prior to the quark era, in the period from 10^{-35} to 10^{-10} seconds, we have the electroweak era, a period in which the interactions between particles are governed by only three—not four—fundamental forces: the strong, subatomic electroweak, and gravitational interactions. Thus the 10^{-10}-second freeze marks a critical transition at which the weak subatomic interactive and electromagnetic forces become distinguishable in their present form. In other words, the now distinct weak interaction and electromagnetic forces were previously unified or, perhaps better said, unborn.

If this is the case, and if we press our inquiry backward or bangward in time, would we arrive at a point only dreamed of by Albert Einstein, namely, the point where the four fundamental forces are unified? This is just what contemporary cosmologists are pursuing.

Figure 1
AT THE MOMENT OF CREATION

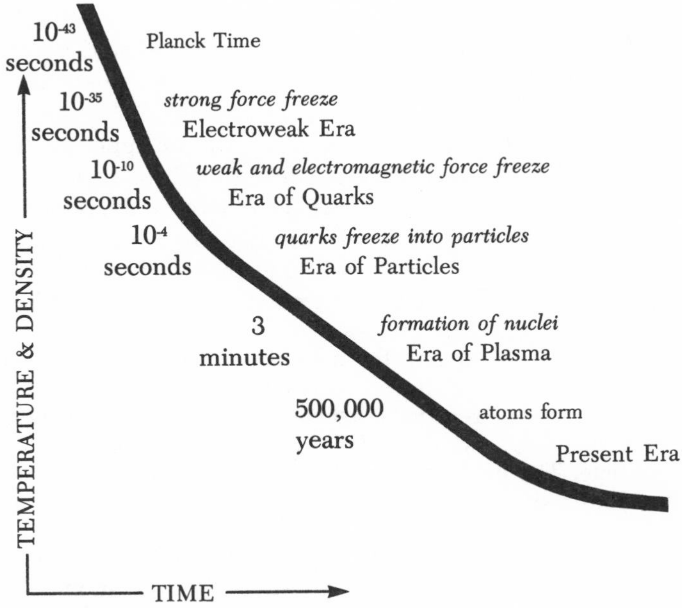

This brings us to GUT, an acronym for Grand Unified Theory. Einstein had pursued a unified field theory by attempting to reduce all four fundamental forces into one force, namely, gravity. What is happening now is that the quest for a unification theory is being sought in cosmology, in the study of past history rather than in the present state of things. Even though the four forces are at present fundamental and independent, could there have been an earlier time in which they were one?

Going even further bangward in time, then, we find that before the 10^{-35} second mark the strong subatomic and electroweak forces were unified. Going back still further to the 10^{-43} second mark and a density of 10^{90} tons per cubic inch when the entire universe was packed into the space of an atomic nucleus, we begin what is called "Planck Time," named after the German physicist Max Planck. This marks the first freezing out, whereat the gravitational force split off from the others. Planck Time lies between the original singularity and the Big Bang. Thus, when we speak of the beginning, we could refer to one of two things, either the onset of the bang or the existence of the singularity.

What was it like before Planck Time? Can we apply a grand unification theory and obtain ultimate singularity at point zero? Here cosmology gets highly speculative because the opportunity for laboratory experimentation at such enormous temperatures is simply inconceivable. Yet the eros for the truth that drives the human intellect leads James Trefil to write:

> The first 10^{-43} second in the life of the universe would have been an extremely simple and extremely beautiful period. There would be reactions that converted bosons to fermions and vice versa, so that there would be only one kind of particle. The unification of all four forces would leave only one basic kind of interaction. The universe would therefore show the ultimate simplicity: all the particles would be of one type, and they would interact with each other through one kind of force. To a physicist, such a situation is so inherently beautiful and elegant that the idea simply has to be right. Whether nature feels the same way remains to be seen, of course.[4]

Let us pause for a moment and ask why the sought-after unified field theory would appear "inherently beautiful" to a physicist. Why is there an aesthetic, almost romantic, appeal to the notion of cosmic unity? Perhaps there is much more than just the voice of the astrophysicist speaking here. The astrophysicist has an active mind and participates in the wider intellectual tradition of which we are a part. That tradition lives. In fact the voice of the effective history of the Western mind is whispering in our ears: find *the* truth! Find the one simple yet universal truth about all things! Trefil is responding to a built-in drive—Plato called it an "eros"—that is always carrying our inquiry toward the unity of truth, toward ultimate simplicity. Plato brought it to our attention by saying that everything that is composite, i.e., made up of two or more elements, necessarily finds the ground of its being outside itself, therefore, it cannot be the ultimate origin. The ultimate origin of all things must be simple, i.e., unified. It is this that constantly drives the astrophysicist as well as the philosopher to stretch if not go beyond the frontiers of empirically verifiable data to theorize about the ultimate beginning, to imagine a state of comprehensive unity. To do so, however, is to knock on the door of God. But we will return to this later.

Returning to our scheme and working our way outward from the Big Bang, the cooling matter eventually condensed and collected into galaxies, stars, and smaller units such as the planet Earth. We on earth today are still riding one piece of shrapnel out and away from the point of initial explosion. But where are we going? What does the future hold?

As we indicated before, the universe is walking a one-way street from hot to cold. As if we had not paid our utility bill, our cosmic house is moving from centralized heating to decentralized freezing. Our sun is currently halfway through its expected life span of 10 billion years, after which it will have expended its hydrogen fuel, burst into a red giant swallowing up the earth, and then extinguished itself. Whenever a star goes through its life cycle, it uses up a certain amount of raw material. Such material though abundant will not last forever. The process of star formation which began around the 500,000-year mark will begin to subside at about the 65-billion-year mark. The stars in the Milky Way and other galaxies will begin to go out, one after the other, without new stars being born.

Now what we have been saying up to this point has assumed that we live in an open universe. There are other possibilities. Our universe may be flat or closed. Instead of expanding indefinitely, it just may collapse again. What happens depends on the density of the matter in the universe. The critical point is that quantity of mass necesary to slow and stop the process of expansion. Should we have just that amount, then our universe would be called flat. If the density is greater than that necessary for a flat universe, then gravitational pull will draw everything back again. This we call a closed universe. If the density is less, then the universe will be considered open and it will go on expanding forever. Or, almost forever.

How much mass do we need to slow down and reverse the expansion? At least one hydrogen atom in a volume of 10 cubic feet. Do we have it? We are not certain. If we simply add up all the mass we can see with our telescopes and compare it with the current volume of the universe, we fall short by a factor of 10 or perhaps 100. This clearly means we have an open universe, but it is not open by a wide margin.

However, there may be mass that we cannot see. It could take the form of dead stars, interstellar dust, nonluminous gas, galactic holes, black holes, neutrinos, or ambient hydrogen atoms. Should this be the case, and should, say, 95 percent of the existing mass be unseen by us, then 40 or 50 billion years from now expansion will cease and contraction begin. At 80 to 100 billion years the universe will be its present size again, but shrinking. The contraction process will continue until everything is reunited again in the Big Crunch. And if the eternal oscillationists have their way, the Big Crunch will become a Big Bounce, and everything will expand again just as it has before and will do again and again.

Such an oscillation theory, however, is contingent upon so many ifs as to render it peripheral to our consideration. Not only does it depend on as yet undetected mass, but barring some unforeseen change in the laws of nature everything would still walk the one-way path toward dissolution due to the second law of thermodynamics. Entropy would remain in effect. The work of Ilya Prigogine and others on the thermodynamics of non-equilibrium systems has shown quite convincingly that on the macroscale time moves in only one direction, from the past toward the future; and it is irreversible.[5] Things simply will not go on as they are forever. Therefore, even if the oscillation theory were to hold, each oscillation would bring more equilibrium into the universe so it too would eventually run down.

Therefore, let us assume there is less than the critical mass, making the universe either flat or open. Now the future will be basically unidirectional, moving from a state of hot density toward one of cool dispersion. The farther it expands the lower will be its temperature and the more extensive its decay. The protons and neutrons that make up all matter will destabilize and disintegrate at about 10^{32} years. Solid objects will disappear. Only some extra radiation and widely separated electrons and positrons along with X-ray-producing black holes would persist until 10^{65} years had passed. As the temperature continues to decrease, the black holes would give off their thermal radiation, brightening the sky temporarily until finally going out like dying embers. This process would go on until all the black holes were gone. Then there would be nothing left in the universe to produce any change.

James Trefil, who spoke glowingly about the bright beginning of the cosmos, spreads a nihilistic shadow over its dark conclusion.

> At some distant time in the future, the universe will be a cold, thin, expanding sea of radiation, with a few forlorn particles to break the monotony. Perhaps it was this gloomy prospect that caused Steven Weinberg to remark, "The more the universe seems comprehensible, the more it also seems pointless."[6]

Hence, according to the above theory—the standard Big Bang model—there is no everlasting future to intelligent living beings or even to the laws of nature as we know them. In the case of the closed universe everything will be destroyed in the reheating of the Big Crunch. In the case of the open universe everything will dissipate into cold inertness. Whether fried or frozen, all life will end.

God at the Edge?

Thinking about the beginning and in this case the end of all things one cannot help raising questions regarding God. This is true for both scientists as well as theologians. This is also true whether you want to believe in God or not.

Take Stephen Hawking, for example. He fully recognizes that the concept of the absolute beginning implied in the standard Big Bang model implies the existence of God. The notion of a beginning means that there is an edge to the cosmos, and the acknowledgment of an edge requires us to ask what lies beyond the edge. "If there is an edge," he once told Renée Weber in an interview, ". . . you would really have to invoke God." Yet Hawking does not want this, so he fishes for a theory that will eliminate the edge. He does this by challenging the hypothesis that there once was a singularity prior to the bang.

Said by some to be the most brilliant theoretical physicist since Einstein, the Cambridge University professor argues that the Big Bang theory has readied us to lay the groundwork for a unified theory of the physical universe. He argues that relativity theory is not enough to solve the problem of the nature of the originating singularity, because relativity theory applies only to the macro-universe. If the alleged original singularity was in fact very small and very dense, then we need to resort to another theory that applies more appropriately, namely, quantum mechanics. The central thesis of Hawking's work has to do with GUT (Grand Unified Theory) and is this: the theories of relativity and quantum mechanics combine into a single uniting *quantum theory of gravity*. This means ultimately that we may be able to describe the universe by a single mathematical model that would be determined by the laws of physics alone. Incorporated into the uniting theory is Heisenberg's uncertainty principle which implies, among other things, that the subsequent course that the developing universe would follow is not fixed by original boundary conditions. In fact, there is no boundary condition for either time or space. There is only a curved space-time dimension, which is finite; but it does not take us back to a point of absolute zero, before which there was no time.

Hawking does not shrink from drawing out what he believes to be the theological implications of his proposal. The universe needs no transcendent creator to bring it into existence at $t = 0$, nor does it need God to tune the laws of nature to carry out a divinely appointed evolutionary purpose.

> The quantum theory of gravity has opened up a new possibility, in which there would be no boundary to space-time and so there would be no need to specify the behavior at the boundary. There would be no singularity at which the laws of science broke down and no edge of space-time at which one would have to appeal to God or some new law to set the boundary conditions for space-time. One could say: "The boundary condition of the universe is that it has no boundary." The universe would be completely self-contained and not affected by anything outside itself. It would neither be created nor destroyed. It would just BE.[7]

Hawking belongs to that club of natural scientists who, on the one hand, drive as big a wedge as possible between rational science and allegedly irrational religion; while, on the other hand, invoking scientific discoveries to buttress their belief that belief in God is atavistic. Writing in the introduction to Hawking's book, *A Brief History of Time*, Carl Sagan somewhat smugly advertises Hawking's argument for "the absence of God" on the grounds that there is "nothing for a Creator to do." We will take this up later when we discuss the work of Fred Hoyle. In the meantime, with Shakespeare, "Me thinks thou dost protest too much!"

What should theologians think about the theology of Hawking? The first observation is that the belief in God he is rejecting belongs in the "God-of-the-gaps" category. He is rejecting the God affirmed by the kind of physico-theology that once sought to find a divine explanation wherever scientists failed to give us a natural explanation. In the case of the Big Bang in particular, many of us are tempted to think of God as the one who set the original boundary conditions, who brought time and space out of a prior nothingness. If the Hawking proposal makes headway—and he freely admits at this point that he is talking about a proposal for a theory and by no means an established fact—then there is no scientific reason to look for a creator transcendent to the creation.

To be more precise, the God who is being rejected by Hawking is the God of deism. The deistic position is that God brought the world into existence at the beginning and then left the universe to run according to its built-in natural laws. God has only one job to do, namely, create at the beginning. Thus, if the Hawking proposal holds, God is not needed for this. God should now go stand in the unemployment line.

Christians and Jews, on the other hand, are theists, not deists. The theistic belief is that, regardless of what God did at the beginning, God is still active in world events today. Another British physical cosmologist, C. J. Isham, has taken the Hawking proposal into account and argued that the Christian doctrine of creation out of nothing still makes good sense. Rather than view it simply as crossing the boundary from pre-temporal existence into temporal existence at $t = 0$, God's divine work of creation should be seen as ongoing. At a Vatican conference on theology and natural science in September 1987, Isham argued that the initial event does not have a different status. Rather, all "times" are co-present to God and the ongoing indeterminacy of quantum processes represents the continuing activity of God's bringing something out of nothing. What is at stake for the theist is to understand God as a contemporary factor in world events. This means that God's creative work is not limited to a one-time event in the ancient past; but it continues now and we can expect more things yet in the future. Today's research in physics challenges us to think through what this means.[8]

What is significant about Hawking's challenge is that he has seen that physical cosmology cannot avoid entering into theological discussion. He has seen that the question of the beginning of all things—the edge to reality—leads ineluctably to the question of God. He is right on this point. And this is the case whether one gives a positive or a negative answer to the question of God's existence or relevance to the Big Bang.

Despite the accuracy of his intuition, however, Hawking has posed the issue in too primitive a fashion. His question is oblique in that it does not open the gate to more fruitful discussion. It presupposes deism, so it fails to open up the discussion of theism. If we are to be able to ask just how we might conceive of our cosmos as a creation, then we need a more sophisticated way of identifying issues and pursuing research. What we need to do in our era is search for avenues of consonance that will open out into orchards of fruitful conversation. This is the path we hope to take in the following pages, but first we need to clear the way by setting aside some oblique questions that might be posed by theologians.

Some Interesting but Misleading Theological Questions

As we have already mentioned, thinking about the beginning and the end of all things cannot avoid raising questions regarding God. But formulating these questions is important. As we saw with Stephen Hawking, it is easy to fall into the trap of formulating them wrongly so that the pursuance of the answers leads us down paths irrelevant to the Christian doctrine of creation. Wrongly formulated questions may not produce wrong answers, but they may produce oblique answers, i.e., answers that do not help make intelligible what Christian faith has to say about God's relation to the world.

If we assume the credibility of the standard Big Bang model for the creation of the cosmos, then one tempting oblique question would be, How can we correlate the sequence of Big Bang events with the creation account in the first chapter of Genesis? Although this question looks exciting at first glance, in fact it is quite misleading for three reasons. First and least of which, the question may assume that with the discovery of a temporal beginning the remaining sequence of events in Genesis are similarly confirmable. Just a quick overview will dispel this hope, however. Whereas Genesis describes the creation of the earth on the third day, prior to that of the sun and stars on the fourth day, astronomers hold that our sun and solar system were formed together about 5 billion years ago, meaning that the sky was filled with stars and galaxies for perhaps 10 billion years previous to the creation of the earth. And, whereas Genesis pictures God on the sixth day resting, his creative work now completed, astronomers contend that new stars perhaps with accompanying planets are being formed now and will continue to be formed for some time yet, i.e., creation is continuing. What this means is that the biblical chronology cannot be pressed easily into the scientific chronology. Yet we may be tempted to gerrymander one or the other to make them fit. We might yield to this temptation unless we understand the other two problems with this question.

The second reason for the obliqueness of trying to correlate Genesis 1 with Big Bang cosmology is that we might fail to apprehend the hermeneutical problem. The Priestly writer who edited if not authored Genesis 1:1–2:4a obviously did not have the Big Bang theory in mind during the sixth century B.C. He or she most probably was thinking about *Enuma Elish* or some similar Mesopotamian creation myth, and the sequence of events purposely reflects this context. It is only to be expected that the biblical writers would reflect the cultural milieu and world view of their respective context and not that of a scientific age some 2,500 years into their future. Our own situation is parallel. Our cosmological thinking today cannot help reflecting the world view of modern science, which provides the framework within which we do our thinking.

Third, and most important, the Christian doctrine of creation expounded in New Testament and patristic times was not originally constructed on the basis of knowledge scientific or otherwise regarding the chronology of primeval events. It was rather a response to hearing the gospel and the growing realization that the God who redeemed Israel from slavery in Egypt and who raised Jesus from the dead is also Lord of the universe. Unless we apprehend the basic motive behind the Christian notion of creation, the technical comparison of biblical passages with scientific scenarios will only lead us into an intellectual quicksand.

Let us turn to another potentially misleading but very interesting question, Did God start the Big Bang in the first place and, if so, how did he do it? Was it God who lit the fuse on the cosmic dynamite? This is an interesting question because many of the factors important to the Christian notion of creation are present in the Big Bang theory, e.g., one-directional time, a temporal beginning, contingency, the historical advent of natural forces, and a de-divinized cosmos. It looks like Big Bang cosmology complements well our theological commitments. It looks like we might have found a point of contact at which we can integrate scientific insight with theological understanding.

This is a much better question than the first one, but there are pitfalls here too. First, even if we could ascertain through either empirical science or intuitive insight just how God as prime mover set everything else moving in the first place, then what have we got? If we stop here then we end up with deism: a God who acted once, at the beginning, but since then the four forces and other laws of nature have been sovereign. This is not yet the Lord, the combination of carer and creator whom we have come to know through his saving acts within the historical process.

A second pitfall in a prematurely theologized Big Bang cosmology is that what we gain on the front end we lose on the back end. Yes, we may gain a God who creates from a point of temporal beginning. But what about the future? An eschaton wherein the entire universe becomes totally dissipated into an energyless and matterless plenitude is hardly the salvation proclaimed by scripture. We will return to this problem later.

What makes these questions misleading is their common assumption that we can start to develop a doctrine of creation from reflection upon strictly intracosmic experience. Scientists are very aware of the limits—often stringently self-imposed limits—which their method places on the kind of knowledge produced by their research. It is knowledge about the cosmos gained from the cosmos. For example, they do not allow themselves to speak to the question, What happened before the beginning? To do so, of course, would be to press the beginning back a farther step and simply enlarge the temporal

span of the cosmos of which we are a part. Then a new
beginning would appear, i.e., a new frontier—what physicist
Stephen Hawking calls "the edge"—that marks the end of finite
knowing. The point is that all scientific knowing is admittedly
intracosmic knowing. It does not deal with the Beyond, with
God.

Modern astrophysicists are not the only ones to impose such
limits on inquiry. Ancient theologians did too. Irenaeus, in
affirming that God holds supremacy over all the creation, adds:
"But whence or in what way He produced it, neither has
Scripture anywhere declared; nor does it become us, . . . in
accordance with our own opinions, to form endless conjec-
tures." Augustine agrees. To the question, What did God do
before he made heaven and earth? Augustine refuses to joke
and hurt someone's feelings by answering with the insulting
remark: "He was preparing hell for those prying into such deep
subjects." Nevertheless, Augustine acknowledges that this
subject lies beyond the possibility of human knowing. "I do not
know," is all he can say.[9] Because our speculations all take place
within the train of temporal events, our questions about what
lay before or outside the temporal train only bounce back upon
us like reflections in a mirror. No matter how intensely we
inquire, what is beyond remains beyond. God remains God. So
the problem with a direct inquiry into the mechanics of how
God started everything off at the beginning may divert us from
inquiring into just why Christians hold the commitments they
do regarding why nature should be considered creation.

The point of departure for Christian thinking about the
creation—in fact the point of departure for even conceiving of
the term "creation" as describing something created by a
creator in the first place—is an experience with that which is
beyond the creation. It begins with a revelation from a source
outside the cosmos. It begins with the gospel of salvation.

I wish to emphasize that it begins here. It does not end here.
What Christians have to say about creation does not spring
full-blown from the head of Zeus or any other divine
spokesperson such as Moses. It is not the report of an inspired
intuition. It is rather a construction, an explication, a drawing

out of cosmological implications inherent in the experience of the gospel and the salvation that it proclaims. It has grown and continues to grow in a circuitous and not quite predictable way.

Retrieving the pattern of this growth toward the Christian understanding of creation is not easy, but we are trying to do so here. It will be our argument that the primary human experience with the world leads to the mythological articulation of a closed cosmos, wherein the power and form of being are determined by the past and wherein the divine is thought to be contained within the cosmos as one factor among others. As human consciousness begins to differentiate and historical thinking begins to take root, the notion of a temporal beginning to things makes its appearance and the result is historiogenesis, i.e., a historical account of the origin of the cosmos. The experience of transcendence, what we will here call "the Beyond," precipitates further reflection on the beginning which leads eventually to the notion of creation out of nothing. The decisive factor producing the Christian notion of creation is the experience of salvation due to the power of the Beyond proclaimed by the prophets and confirmed in the Easter resurrection of Jesus. The power of eschatological newness means that the creation was originally something new too. It also means that the God who raised Jesus is the Lord of the universe.

Such affirmations cannot be considered as simply the result of intracosmic reflection, whether mythological or scientific. They represent a complex pattern of inferences based upon a revelation from the beyond and a commitment that can only be described as faith.

The Archonic Experience of the Cosmos: Myth

There are two basic ways of conceiving the origin and nature of the universe, the *archonic* and the *epigenetic*. According to the archonic view everything is, in one way or another, given at the beginning. So named because of the Greek root ἀρχή, which means both beginning as well as governance, this view assumes that the nature of things is defined and fixed by its origin. If we can find the origin of something, we will have found its essence. According to the epigenetic view, in contrast, a certain minimum is assumed as given in the beginning, but over time new things occur. Theories of evolutionary development and continuous creation are epigenetic in character.

The primary experience of the cosmos as articulated in myth and the first stage of historical consciousness is clearly archonic. Let us define cosmogonic myth as a story telling how the gods created the world in the beginning, *in illo tempore,* which explains why things are the way they are today. Such thinking seems to presuppose that reality and power are inextricably linked to the past, to the origin, to the beginning. Thus, to be able to return to the beginning would be to recapture the ruling or governing power of things and thereby to ward off the insecurity caused by the threats of chaos, violence, and death. Myth helps us do just this. Through its telling and ritual reenactment the myth collapses time by drawing together past and present, creation and providence.

What myth brings to articulation is a more primary human experience with the world which is wholistic. This is meant both psychologically as well as historically. Psychologists of human development have long chronicled the breaking of the symbiotic relationship, the primitive consciousness of the infant who cannot initially distinguish his or her own life from that of the mother. In the modern West we have defined such things as maturity and human fulfillment in terms of integrity, independence, self-reliance, self-actualization, and personal achievement. We are not born independent. We must strive for and declare our independence, thereby breaking our initial sense of naïve oneness with others and with the whole. Therefore, it will take some effort on our part to retrieve this more primitive experience.

The beginnings of religious consciousness in archaic societies seem to follow a pattern of movement from wholism toward differentiation. The symbolic systems of ancient peoples indicate that they experience the complex of self-world-whole as belonging to a single piece, as a homogeneous reality. This is not the modern world view of Cartesian dualism with its split between subject and object. Nor is it the world shocked by the revelation of a transcendent God with its split between creator and creation. It is a single whole with divinity built right in. Philosopher Eric Voegelin puts it this way:

> The cosmos of the primary experience is neither the external world of objects given to a subject of cognition, nor is it the world that has been created by a world-transcendent God. Rather, it is the whole, τὸ πᾶν, of an earth below and a heaven above—of celestial bodies and their movements; of seasonal changes; of fertility rhythms in plant and animal life; of human life, birth, and death; and above all, as Thales still knew, it is a cosmos full of gods. This last point, that the gods are intracosmic, cannot be stressed strongly enough, because it is almost eclipsed today by such facile categorizations as polytheism and monotheism. The numbers are not important, but rather the consciousness of divine reality as intracosmic or transmundane.[10]

The first break in consciousness is the distinction between the sacred and the profane, between cosmos and chaos. The sacred is the principle of order that establishes cosmos and distinguishes it from the surrounding and ever-threatening chaos. This distinction does not break the naïve wholism described above, because it is part of it. It constitutes a tension within it. It brings to symbolic articulation a constant in human experience, namely, the feeling of insecurity or anxiety created by the relentless threat of destruction and death. We are provoked by a sense of contingency, awareness of our dependence upon others, the environment, and perhaps on the gods.

What the sacred does is locate that upon which we are dependent. It establishes the center of reality, the source of our being. It orders things and in so doing creates our world, our cosmos. In biblical times there existed a common Near Eastern world view including a creation-theology (shall we call it "generic genesis"?) with local variants in which the sacred could be located in space, at the sacred mountain which constituted the center of the universe, or located in time, at the point of cosmic origin depicted in the myth of a divine champion slaying the monster of chaos. The religious inclination toward fuller being—what Mircea Eliade calls "ontological thirst"—draws us toward this sacred. In the sacred we find security, protection against the threat of nonbeing.

This basic experience of wholeness of the cosmos with its intracosmic split between sacred and profane comes to articulation first in myth, in a cosmogony that tells us the origin of all things and that distinguishes two kinds of time. Archaic peoples did not live strictly in the historical present as we moderns do. They also lived in a retrievable past, in the moment of creation. The new year's festivals of so many agricultural societies include rites and myths that reflect the notion of rebirth. Through the cycle of death and rebirth we can abolish the period of historical time wherein corruption and evil crept into the cosmos; we can return ritually to the pristine order of things as it left the creative hands of the gods. The cosmos is born again each year: the spring seeds sprout and the creative work of the gods—originary yet concurrent with the religious festival—yields a harvest that sustains the livelihood of the people. Similarly, the recitation of the cosmogonic myth is important to healing and is part of the shaman's therapeutic procedures. It is assumed that life cannot be repaired; it can only be recreated through symbolic repetition of the cosmogony. Thus, the power of life and healing which sustains us in the face of insecurity is gained by returning via myth to the source of reality, to the origin of all things. Eliade expresses this quality of the cosmogonic myth.

> *In illo tempore* the gods had displayed their greatest powers. *The cosmogony is the supreme divine manifestation*, the paradigmatic act of strength, superabundance, and creativity. Religious man thirsts for the real. By every means at his disposal, he seeks to reside at the very source of primordial reality, when the world was in *statu nascendi*.[11]

In short, the power of being is located in the past, *in illo tempore*, and the myth has the capacity to reconnect us with that power.

Now we may ask, Is Big Bang cosmology in any sense mythical? Mary Hesse believes so. She makes the ironic point that "for the general public in educated Western society, scientific accounts of the origin and destiny of the world, and of the status of human beings in it, have replaced the traditional mythical accounts given in various forms in all religions." She says evidence that science functions as a myth "can be seen in the way 'origins' are taught in schools."[12] Now no doubt the question of origins is central, but there are at least two significant elements in the mode of scientific thinking that distinguishes it from myth. First, the Big Bang theory is not archonic. It is epigenetic. The theory contends that the original simplicity at $t=0$ differentiated into four forces and atomic units in contingent and unpredictable fashion. The archetype was not fixed at the beginning. Second, astrophysics today has incorporated a sense of history and the assumption of unidirectional temporality. Contemporary science is so imbued with historical consciousness that it does not seek to collapse the originary time and present time as ancient myth once did. It is to the rise of this historical sense of origin that we now turn.

Historiogenesis: The Beyond and the Beginning

With the term "historiogenesis" we will refer to the form of cosmological thinking that proffers a unilinear construction of history which begins with a divine origin and leads up to the historian's present. Historical thinking differs from mythical thinking in that it places events on a line of irreversible time where the past is singular and irrecoverable. It remains past forever. Furthermore, it eventually gives rise to future consciousness so that the cosmos is opened up to possibilities for new realities beyond its past inventory, for epigenesis. In its initial stages of differentiation, however, the historical understanding of the cosmos overlaps considerably with the mythical, and even today it is still struggling to free itself from the closed cosmos of the primary experience.

There are two substages in the development of historiogenesis. The first substage we will call "historiomachy," wherein the notion of unilinear history differentiates itself from the time-collapsing concepts of myth but wherein the experience of the Beyond is not yet clearly articulated. Here divinity is still intracosmic. In the second stage, prophetic history, the impact of divine revelation and the opening up of the cosmos is more clearly discerned.

Historiogenesis Substage One: Historiomachy

It appears that historical consciousness first arises as a form of legitimation for kingship, as historiomachy. One of the earliest examples of historiogenesis is the Sumerian king list, dating about 2050 B.C. What is thought to be the Sumerian Empire had for the most part consisted of an agglomeration of separate city-states ruled by local dynasties with their own local histories. Occasionally one or another city-state would rise to hegemony and impose its imperial reign on the others. After the establishment of such an empire under Utuhegal of Uruk, the authors of the king list constructed a unilinear history by placing the stories of the parallel city-dynasties in a single chronology. They constructed a temporal line of successive rulers stretching back beyond the great flood to the creation of the world. The preamble opens by asserting that kingship originally belonged to the god Eridu and was lowered from heaven. After the dynasties of five cities the flood swept everything away. The royal reign was then lowered again from heaven and established at Kish. History begins when the order ordained by the gods is bequeathed to the course of temporal events and embodied in the king who presently sites on the throne. We use Voegelin's term "historiomachy" here, because it refers to the empowerment granted the emperor by this form of cosmological revisionism. The parallel histories of other kings are co-opted and, along with the creative power of the gods, made to serve the authority of the present terrestrial rule.

The Sumerian kings were not the only ones to cultivate historical consciousness. It happened in Egypt too. One variant begins the succession of earthly rulers with Ptah, patron god of Memphis, while another variant begins with Re of Heliopolis. The earliest dates for the supporting documents are from the time of Dynasty XIX (circa 1345–1200 B.C.), making them rather late in Egyptian history. The Palermo stone of Dynasty V (2500–2350 B.C.) reveals that the Egyptians had already recorded facts regarding the parallel histories of various pre–Egyptian peoples and city-dynasties. Voegelin concludes from this that historiogenetic speculation appears late in the history of Egypt and that it derives from some new interest in legitimizing kingship.

What about Israel? The primeval histories of the Jahwist and Priestly writers including the *toledoth* genealogies of the Old Testament reflect this historiogenetic if not the historiomachic view of the cosmos. Almost embarrassingly, Gerhard von Rad comments, "presumptuous as it may sound, Creation is part of the aetiology of Israel."[13] And in the genealogy of Luke 3, the king whose power and authority is legitimated is the babe in the Bethlehem manger. The genealogy traces his ancestry back through King David to Adam, the son of God.

When historiogenesis becomes historiomachy, the power and authority of the origin becomes transferred to the present. Although the modern West has rid itself of most of its kings and queens, historiomachy lives on in disguised form in religion through such things as the apostolic succession of the clergy. In secular life it lives on through adherence to constitutions, charters, and founding documents.

Historiomachy is not fully differentiated from myth. It is distinguished of course by its sense of linear time and the once-and-for-allness of events. But like myth it places great reliance upon the archonic past. Power and authority belong to the point of origin. And the power and authority that once belonged to the gods in the past is made manifest in the present through the rule of the king. In an oblique sense, then, the divine—or at least the divine authority—remains intracosmic.

Historiogenesis Substage Two:
Prophetic History

What interests us here in this study, however, is a later development, namely, prophetic history. This is the more profound form of historical consciousness and it is prompted by an experience with what Eric Voegelin calls "the Beyond," i.e., with a radically transcendent reality. A translation of the Greek ἐπέκεινα, the Beyond is the ultimate and in itself indefinable reality that surpasses all categories of intracosmic understanding. Though indefinable and transcendent, it is not absent. It calls, and something within the human soul mumbles an answer. We know about the Beyond only through revelation. This revelation comes not through the objects of the world around us but through a secret restlessness within the psyche. Such restlessness follows upon an experience of pneumatic ecstasy, prophetic oracle, or inspired insight.

In the tension of human existence the Beyond is the pole of perfection for which the human soul longs. It is that which, in Mircea Eliade's terms, can ultimately quench our thirst for ultimate being. In seeking to quench our thirst with a reality beyond our world, our naïve bond with the world is broken. The self becomes more individuated and distinguishable as it orients itself to extracosmic reality.

What is significant for our discussion of cosmology is that the revelatory experience of the Beyond raises questions regarding the beginning. The awareness of transcendent reality prompts new questioning regarding the meaning of life, the structure of the cosmos, the dependent or contingent nature of our world. And it raises the big question, What is the source of all that is? A historical cosmology is the result of this experience and these questions coming to symbolic articulation. Voegelin describes the movement:

Though the divine reality is one, its presence is experienced in the two modes of the Beyond and the Beginning. The Beyond is present in the immediate experience of movements in the psyche; while the presence of the divine Beginning is mediated through the experience of the existence and intelligible structure of things in the cosmos. The two models require two different types of language for their adequate expression. The immediate presence in the movements of the soul requires the revelatory language of consciousness. This is the language of seeking, searching, and questioning, of ignorance and knowledge concerning the divine ground, of futility, absurdity, anxiety, and alienation of existence, of being moved to seek and question, of being drawn toward the ground, of turning around, of return, illumination, and rebirth. The presence mediated by the existence and order of things in the cosmos requires the mythical language of a creator-god or Demiurge, of a divine force that creates, sustains, and preserves the order of things.[14]

Thus, stories of creator gods who establish a reality separate from themselves—the reality we presently experience as history—describe the beginning in response to an experience with the Beyond. For Plato writing in the *Timaeus* the creator god was the Demiurge; but, contra Voegelin's interpretation, most scholars, including Mircea Eliade, understand the *Timaeus* as prototypical of mythical thinking, not history.[15] In the case of Israel, however, we have a better example of genuine historical consciousness. The Beyond in Israel was understood as the author of a salvation history. Voegelin is correct in pointing out how this experience of salvation raised questions regarding the very beginning of things. Eventually in Israel the beginning of salvation history and the beginning of the world came to be thought of as the same. This conjecture became the first step leading ineluctably down the road toward what would later become the Christian concept of *creatio ex nihilo*.

It was in the burning bush that the Beyond made its presence known in the soul of Moses. The Beyond was responding to the cry of anguish rising up to heaven from the muffled voices of oppressed slaves in Egypt, the land in which allegedly the gods had ordained the Pharaoh to rule. It was through an act of salvation, the Exodus from Egypt, that the Beyond made itself known to the Hebrew people. What we have in the Hexateuch is the recitation of a salvation history, the remembering of events within time—not remembering the origination of the world—whereby Israel was created and established as a nation in Canaan. The core of historical consciousness is found in the credos, the brief summaries of the divine actions and events that brought Israel into existence.

> A wandering Aramean was my father; and he went down into Egypt and sojourned there, a few in number; and there he became a nation, great, mighty, and populous. And the Egyptians treated us harshly, and afflicted us, and laid upon us hard bondage. Then we cried to the Lord the God of our fathers, and the Lord heard our voice, and saw our affliction, our toil, and our oppression; and the Lord brought us out of Egypt with a mighty hand and an outstretched arm, with great terror, with signs and wonders; and he brought us into this place and gave us this land, a land flowing with milk and honey (Deut. 26:5-9).

Gerhard von Rad argues that this confessional statement represents the earliest form of Hebrew self-understanding and identity. The rest of the Hexateuch is built up around this.

Note how the credo depicts the creation of Israel but not the creation of the world. Thinking about cosmic creation comes later, probably first with the Jahwist and the dawn of kingship in Israel about the eleventh century B.C., followed by deutero-Isaiah and the Priestly writer in later periods. No doubt for many of those centuries the picture of the cosmos in the minds of the Hebrews was basically the same as that of their non-Hebrew myth-oriented neighbors. They shared the generic genesis common to the Near East. Only as the significance of God's saving acts began to sink in and implications drawn out did the Hebrews begin to develop their own particular creation theology. And what they had to say about creation would be an extension of their experience of redemption. Gerhard von Rad observes:

Probably the sole reason for the lateness of the emergence of a doctrine of creation was that it took Israel a fairly long time to bring the older beliefs which she actually already possessed about it into proper theological relationship with the tradition which was her very own, that is with what she believed about the saving acts done by Jahweh in history. In the old cultic Credo there was nothing about creation. And Israel only discovered the correct theological relationship of the two when she learned to see Creation too as connected theologically with the saving history.[16]

In Isaiah 44:24 we find a clear parallel between God the redeemer and God the creator. Psalm 136 opens by offering praise to the Creator who "made the heavens" and who "spread out the earth upon the waters" before making "the sun to rule over the day" and "the moon and stars to rule over the night." It then follows with the story of the Exodus and God who "with a strong hand and an outstretched arm . . . divided the Red Sea" and "overthrew Pharaoh" to "rescue us from our foes." Thus, creation, though added later, became the first chapter in God's story of salvation.

This move from salvation to creation is a key to understanding the prophets, especially when they introduce a new and dynamic element into historical consciousness, namely, eschatology. With the prophets the future begins to take precedence over the past. The sins of Israel, the violation of the covenant and the refusal to repent, bring the previous history of Jahweh with his people to an end. Jahweh is about to start something new: a new Exodus, a new covenant, a new Moses. Jahweh is about to act in a fashion that will be understandable in light of the old history, but his future saving acts will be even more splendid.

Von Rad calls this "eschatology." It is not eschatology in the more recent sense of positing a final end to all things. At this early stage of differentiation in Hebrew consciousness it represents a shift from past-dependence to future-dependence, even though the future is thought to be an open future. In the prophetic message we are drawn toward a "break which goes so deep that the new state beyond it cannot be understood as the continuation of what went before."[17] The significance of this is that reality is not dependent upon its past. It is cut free from the principles established at the point of origin. All ties with the mythically conceived cosmos are finally severed. The God of our future salvation—the God beyond the present state of reality—is not dependent upon what already exists. Therefore, salvation is itself an act of creation.

This thinking does not fit neatly into either archonic or epigenetic categories. When we extrapolate from eschatology backward toward the point of origin, then we begin to think of the beginning as the advent of something absolutely new, as creation from nothing. It is not just the making of order out of a preexisting chaos. Certainly this was the assumption of the author of II Maccabees 7:28, who emphasizes that God did not create heaven and earth out of anything that already existed, and of Paul, who describes God as calling "into existence the things that do not exist" (Rom. 4:17b).

The Gospel and Creation

The movement from salvation to creation as the form in which the Hebrews move from the Beyond to the beginning repeats itself in the Christian understanding of the gospel. Here it is the experienced power of new life in the Easter resurrection that provides the foundation for our faith and trust in God to fulfill his promise to establish a new creation in the future. What does it take to raise the dead? What does it take to consummate history into a new and everlasting kingdom? It takes mastery over the created order. It takes a loving Father who cares but who is also a creator whose power is undisputed and unrivaled.

The gospel begins with the story of Jesus told with its significance. Its significance is that in this historical person, Jesus Christ, the eternal God who is the creator of all things has acted in the course of temporal events to bring salvation to all the things he has created. Salvation consists here in the forgiveness of sins and the promise of a final redemption from evil to be attained through the eschatological resurrection of the dead. The logic here is: the God who saves must be the God who creates. Nothing less will do.

The promise of Paul in Romans 8 that nothing can separate us from the love of God depends upon the belief that all powers in nature and history are subject to the saving will. Only the creator of all can make such a promise. Martin Luther says it dramatically:

> Since He is able out of a droplet of water to create sun and moon, could He not also defend my body against enemies and Satan or, after it has been placed in the grave, revive it for a new life? Therefore we must take note of God's power that we may be completely without doubt about the things which God promises in His Word. Here full assurance is given concerning all His promises; nothing is either so difficult or so impossible that He could not bring it about by his Word. [18]

The primary experience is with the good news of the gospel and with the assurance that it brings. Evangelical explication leads to commitments about the creation that are implied in the gospel. The heart of the Apostles' and Nicene Creeds is the gospel, the second article wherein the account of Jesus Christ is given. But in each case it is preceded by a preamble, the first article about the Creator: "I believe in God the Father Almighty, maker of heaven and earth." That the Creator is both a loving parent and almighty is implied by the gospel.

Langdon Gilkey, who has examined the doctrine of creation over the last three decades, contends that the identity of God the creator and God the redeemer, of the almighty power of existence with the love of Christ, is the theological axis of the gospel of good news.

> The idea of creation provides, therefore, the only framework in which the Christian Gospel can be preached effectively and believed intelligibly. The knowledge of God that we have in historical revelation is, it is true, the sole basis for our understanding of the purpose and meaning of creation. But

the God revealed there as our Lord and Savior is inescapably
He who infinitely transcends His creation in power and
glory, and so who must be understood, not only as a
personal Father, but also as the self-existent ground of all
being.[19]

Creatio Ex Nihilo and Christian Apologetics

If we put together what we have so far—one way unilinear
time, the move from the Beyond to the Beginning, the
historical character of divine activity, the eschatological power
of creating new things, and the gospel of salvation—we have
the latent ingredients for the idea of an absolute beginning and
the doctrine of *creatio ex nihilo* (creation from nothing). What
actualizes this latent doctrine is the challenge of an alternative
viewpoint, especially the belief that the material of the
universe has always existed. This challenge came from two
competitors to the Christian view in the early centuries of the
church, namely, dualism and pantheism.

The essence of dualism is the belief that God or the gods
create the cosmos by ordering preexisting matter—the word
"cosmos" means order. This is dualistic because it posits two or
more equally fundamental or eternal principles, the world as
well as the divine. The essence of pantheism (or monism) is that
everything is fundamentally identical with the divine. But by
identifying God and the world, pantheism collapses all the
plurality and multiplicity of the cosmos into a unity and this
finally denies the independent reality of the world and its
history.

In response to dualism and pantheism the early Christian
thinkers proffer the concept of *creatio ex nihilo*. Against the
dualists, this means that God is the sole source of all finite
existence, of matter as well as form. There is no preexisting
matter coeternal with and separate from the divine. If the God
of salvation is truly the Lord of all, then he must also be the
source of all. Theophilus of Antioch in the middle of the second
century, for example, praises Plato for acknowledging that God

is uncreated. But then he criticizes Plato for averring that matter is coeval with God, because that would make matter equal to God. "But the power of God is manifested in this, that out of things that are not He makes whatever He pleases."[20]

Against the pantheists, Christians hold that the world is not divine. It is a creation, brought into existence by God but something separate from and over against God. The world is not coeternal with God, because it has a temporal beginning and is distinct from God. Irenaeus puts it this way:

> But the things established are distinct from Him who has established them, and what have been made from Him who has made them. For He is Himself uncreated, both without beginning and end, and lacking nothing. He is Himself sufficient for this very thing, existence; but the things which have been made by Him have received a beginning. . . . He indeed who made all things can alone, together with His Word, properly be termed God and Lord; but the things which have been made cannot have this term applied to them, neither should they justly assume that appellation which belongs to the Creator.[21]

This led to the distinction between generation and creation. "Generation," coming from the root meaning to give birth, suggests that the begetter produces out of its own essence an offspring that shares that same essence. But terms such as "creating" or "making" mean that the creator produces something that is external, a creature of dissimilar nature. The patristic apologists applied the term "generation" to the perichoresis *within* the divine life of the Trinity, not to the creation *without*. Hence, John of Damascus could state emphatically that the creation is not derived from the essence of God, but it is rather brought into existence out of nothing.[22]

In sum, creator and created are not the same thing. Nor can we have only one thing, God, and make everything else a misinterpreted illusion. Finite reality is not an illusory course of events to be penetrated by depth analysis to a mystical core of timeless divine unity. History is the real arena of give and take between God and those whom God loves.

What Is the Logic of Creation Out of Nothing?

What is the basic thrust of the Christian doctrine of *creatio ex nihilo?* Most theologians agree: the creature is entirely dependent upon the creator. The point is that God's power is unrivaled, even when it comes to the brute existence of things. God is responsible for existence. We look to the past, to the coming into existence of the first creation, to see that God has the power to create out of nothing. We do so on the basis of the promise of Easter, namely, that in the future God will raise the dead and establish a new creation. Only a God who can create something from nothing will be able to create life out of death. This is the religious force of the doctrine.

The doctrine also defines God as creator. The creative act begins with nothing, and then something is produced. What is produced is not merely the creation per se, but also a relationship between the creation and its creator. It is an asymmetrical relation, of course, according to which the creature is totally dependent upon the creator in the act of creating. One could say that prior to the act of creating, God is not yet a creator. God becomes a creator only through creating. This opens up the question as to whether the creation can have a determining effect upon God. Exactly *how* it is we should understand God as creator will depend upon the history of creation, i.e., on what actually happens. Just because God is the creator we dare not preclude prematurely that God in Godself may not be affected by what happens in temporal affairs.

We also need to consider the nature of nothing. It has become customary in theological circles to distinguish two forms of nothing, the nondialectical and dialectical forms. Following an ancient Platonic distinction, nothing understood as oὐκ ὄv or *nihil negativum* is nonbeing in the absolute or nondialectical sense; it has no relation to being. In contrast, μὴ ὄv or *nihil privativum* is nonbeing in dialectical relation to being; it is the relative negation of what is. This dialectical nothing does not yet have being but has the potential for giving rise to new being. It represents the quality of temporal passage that erodes what is now and makes way for what is yet to come. It is the power of not-yet-being. Ordinarily, the Christian doctrine of *creatio ex nihilo* presumes we begin with οὔκ ὄν with an absolute abyss of nothingness out of which God brings a creation due solely to his free will. It is this sense of nothingness that presses Christian thinking toward a temporal beginning, prior to which there was only nothing. Yet, this by no means dismisses μὴ ὄν as unimportant to Christian theology. The God of Israel can do new things. Dialectical nonbeing is necessary to think of divine creativity as continuing.[23]

It is frequently said that the essence of *creatio ex nihilo* is that all existing things are dependent for their existence upon the creator God. This is true. But it is also abstract. We from time to time need to ask, Just *how* are we dependent upon our creator? To say that at the point of temporal origin God brought forth a space-time reality out of a primeval nothingness is to attempt to say concretely what it means. In the era of the early Christian apologists as well as in our own era of Big Bang cosmology, such attempts at concrete explanation have some consonance with the world view that surrounds us.

One can see here that the arguments in behalf of the Christian doctrine of *creatio ex nihilo* do not originate or depend strictly upon an exegesis of Genesis 1:1–2:4a or a word study on P's use of the term *bara*. Even if one were to acknowledge the exegetical ambiguity of phrases such as "In the beginning God created" (RSV) vs. "When God began to form" (Moffatt), or God's Spirit moving "over the face of the waters" (are these preexistent waters?), the weight of the argument for a creation with a temporal beginning rests upon more wide-ranging theological concerns. Specifically, it rests upon the processes of *evangelical explication*, i.e., of drawing out implications based on our apprehension of the saving message of the gospel. Eschatology and the promise of new things—such as a new creation—seem to warrant worship of a Lord against which there is no rival yet over against which stands a created order.

Absolute Beginnings and Continuing Creation

We have seen how the doctrine of *creatio ex nihilo* developed through a process of explicating implications inherent in the compact experience of God's saving acts in history. But times have changed. We in our modern and now emerging post-modern culture are similarly engaged in evangelical explication, therefore we must ask, Does *creatio ex nihilo* help make the gospel intelligible today? It is my own position that it does. However, we must note that some contemporary thinkers believe the doctrine is outdated due to the change in world view. On the grounds that we moderns have a more dynamic understanding of reality than did the ancients, many are recommending that *creatio ex nihilo* be replaced by one or another version of *creatio continua*. It will be my judgment here that these two concepts are complementary and that we need not substitute one for the other. Christian theology needs both.

This debate is not strictly an intramural sport among theologians. It occurs among scientists too. Fred Hoyle among others has expounded a theory of continuous creation under the banner of the "steady state theory." His position is that matter is always coming into being uniformly throughout finite time and infinite space. Hydrogen atoms are appearing *de novo* at a constant rate throughout space, condensing, combining, and giving birth to new stars.

Hoyle is playing against the much larger Big Bang team, contending that the very notion of an absolute beginning is irrational and unscientific. He seeks to score by arguing that the theory of a unidirectional expanding universe rests on a time-singularity beyond which the history of the universe could not be traced. Hoyle's opponents counter by showing how his alleged spontaneous creation of hydrogen atoms violates the laws of local conservation and, further, that this alleged phenomenon of continuing creation is as yet unobserved. For most players the game was decisively won in 1965 with the 3 degree Kelvin radiation discovery by Nobel Prize winners Robert W. Wilson and Arno A. Penzias, confirming earlier hypotheses that such a universal radiation would be a relic of an early stage in cosmic expansion. The victory, quite decisive, went to the Big Bang team. Hoyle has since sought to make a comeback by modifying his theory, but most science fans have eventually begun to root for the Big Bang side.

One might ask just why Fred Hoyle is so adamant, especially when the preponderance of scientific evidence favors the Big Bang cosmology. The answer is that Hoyle is doing battle against religion and believes that the Big Bang idea aids and abets the enemy. Ernan McMullin's analysis is that Hoyle has an unashamedly anti-Christian bias and is quite willing even to gerrymander the scientific evidence so as to avoid giving even the slightest quarter to religious forces. What is significant for us here is that this debate among scientists seems to press against the borders of their own disciplines and, further, it seems there is tacit agreement that the notion of a temporal beginning has the greater religious relevance.[24]

Although Hoyle and other scientists have automatically assumed the relevance of a temporal beginning to Christian theology, Ian Barbour is one theologian who has denied such relevance. In one of his earlier books, he says there are no strictly theological grounds for favoring either Big Bang or steady state theories. Both theories are capable of either a naturalistic or a theistic interpretation. Both theories push explanation back to an unexplained situation which is necessarily treated as a given—the primeval nucleus that exploded in the case of the Big Bang or the constant creation of matter in the case of Hoyle's steady state. Neither theory asks about the pre-temporal or supratemporal source or framework for the natural events that occur within the stream of finite time. Finite time is simply assumed. Therefore, Barbour concludes:

> We will suggest that the Christian need not favor either theory, for the doctrine of creation is not really about temporal

beginnings but about the basic relationship between the world and God. The religious content of the idea of creation is compatible with either theory, and the debate between them can be settled only on scientific grounds, when further data are available.[25]

Does he mean, in other words, science is science and religion is religion, and never the twain shall meet? Barbour's position here comes close to holding that theologians have no investment in the winner of the match between a point of origin and continuous creation. We will see, however, that while the science fans have increased their rooting for the temporal beginning, most theologians are now cheering for continuing creation.

It is not clear just what continuing creation could mean for a theologian. Is it likely to mean what it does for Fred Hoyle? We should note that the early church doctors did not operate with the distinction between creation from nothing and continuing creation in quite the same way we do today. What they did operate with was the distinction between creation and change.

For Thomas Aquinas it was important to nurse the distinction between absolute creation and changing things already created. In fact, the term "creation" for him refers solely to what appears *ab initio*, to God's bringing things into being from nothing. "Creation is not change," he writes, because "change means that the same something should be different now from what it was previously."[26] God's role in creation, then, was that of the first cause. If we were to translate Thomas directly into the present medium, then we might say that God lit the fuse on the cosmic dynamite . . . after creating the dynamite itself, of course.

What Thomas has done here is make the move from the Beyond to the beginning. Thomas makes this move based on what he reads in the Bible. In principle one could mount a doctrine of creation from nothing without positing an absolute beginning. One could simply assert that the world—even an eternal world—is totally dependent upon God for its existence. Aristotle did something like this. But this is a metaphysical argument. The view Thomas develops requires more than metaphysical logic. It requires revelation, and this is what he gets when he reads scripture. For Thomas, God creates all things out of nothing at the beginning of time. This is what "creation" refers to.

Thus, God transcends the cosmos. As the uncaused cause, the cosmos is originally dependent upon him yet God is not just one factor among others within the world system. The world process is itself a dynamic process in that it involves change, but in itself it does not create new things out of nothing. No created thing can create absolutely. Only God can, and God did it already back at the beginning.

Langdon Gilkey is quite critical of Thomas on this score, especially his use of the causal analogy in making the move from the Beyond to the beginning. The causal analogy for describing God's relation to the world, in Gilkey's judgment, is misleading on two counts. First, it eliminates God from the world. Causality implies external relations. If God is the first cause and the world is his dependent effect, then God and world are set over against each other. God's immanence is denied. Second, Thomas compromises the transcendence of God by drawing him into the world system. It makes God one more factor in the endless chain of cause and effect. Once we have placed God in the causal chain, there is no escape from the inevitable question, What caused God? Thus, the analogy drawn from the human experience of cause and effect, when applied to the divine, is misleading.[27]

Gilkey appears to be most unfair here. He tries to get Thomas both coming and going. On the one hand, if God for Thomas transcends the world, then he is faulted for loss of immanence. On the other hand, if God for Thomas is a factor in the intracosmic process, then he is faulted for loss of transcendence. Why is Gilkey so harsh? The answer is that Gilkey's own agenda is another version of Barbour's mentioned above, namely, to avoid too close a mixture of science and religion. Gilkey says it is the task of science to answer the How? questions, such as How did the cosmos begin? It is the task of theology to answer the Why? questions, such as Why did God create? Gilkey's beef with

Thomas is that he sought to answer the How? question by saying that God had caused the world to come into being.

Thus, if we were to follow people such as Gilkey scrupulously, we would end up making no theological commitments whatsoever regarding whether or not the cosmos ever had a beginning or, if it did, just how God was involved in its beginning. We would have to carry on our theological discussion in a field of discourse that would be fenced off from scientific speculations on origin and change in nature. Yet, as we shall see, few theologians in our time, including Barbour and Gilkey, in practice hold to keeping the fence very high. The major case in point is the widely accepted theological postulate that God's relationship to the world is best described in terms of *creatio continua*.

From *Creatio Ex Nihilo* to *Creatio Continua*

We need to ask, Just what can *creatio continua* mean? Even though their positions are quite different, both Fred Hoyle and Thomas Aquinas would agree that the term refers to the constant process of bringing *de novo* into existence things that hitherto had not existed, i.e., ongoing *creatio ex nihilo*. It does not mean changing things that already exist. Hoyle and Thomas would simply disagree as to when this occurs. Hoyle would say that there never was a beginning, that the cosmos is now and always has been a steady state of creative activity. Although there are new beginnings every day, there never was an absolute beginning to all these absolute beginnings. Thomas, in contrast, would say that creation happened once at the beginning of all things, and that what is happening today is due to a chain of intracosmic causes that are constantly forming and reforming the already created stuff of the universe. For Hoyle there is no creator and creation is contemporary. For Thomas there is a creator and creation is past. If we were to avoid the strictures of Barbour and Gilkey and mix science and religion, then we would observe how clear it is that the Thomistic view would be more consonant with the Big Bang theory than it would with Hoyle's.

Thomas is a medieval theologian. Contemporary theologians, in contrast, shrink back from *creatio ex nihilo*, especially if it is associated with an absolute beginning. Instead they prefer *creatio continua*. Why? There are two reasons. First, they say continuing creation is the biblical view. Quoting Old Testament scholar Edmund Jacob, who wrote that the meager "distinction between the creation and the conservation of the world make it possible for us to speak of *creatio continua*." In his book of 1966, *Issues in Science and Religion*, Ian Barbour argues that creation out of nothing is not a biblical concept.[28] But I believe this is an overstatement. It is certainly the case that what we know as *creatio ex nihilo* came to flower only in post-biblical times, but this should not lead us to deny that it has biblical roots. *Ex nihilo* is the result of evangelical explication, according to which the implications inherent in the compact experience of salvation witnessed to in scripture were drawn out by the theologians of the earlier church. Even if there are only a few references to *ex nihilo* in the Bible itself—and there are the references we pointed out above— evangelical explication ought to count for something. To say that *ex nihilo* is not a biblical concept is overkill.

Oddly enough, the second reason for advocating continuing creation has to do with mixing science and religion. Theologians are saying that modern understandings of nature reveal a basically dynamic rather than a static world view. Because it is assumed that the ancients who formulated *creatio ex nihilo* had lived in a static cosmos, and that we moderns now live in a dynamic cosmos, therefore it follows that we need a modern understanding of creation that is more dynamic. *Creatio continua* seems to fit the bill. Ian Barbour supports continuing creation by arguing that:

> Today the world as known to science is dynamic and incomplete. Ours is an unfinished universe which is still in the process of appearing. Surely the coming-to-be of life from matter can represent divine creativity as suitably as any postulated primeval production of matter "out of nothing." Creation occurs throughout time.[29]

Now let us note two things Barbour is saying. First, despite his earlier mentioned rejoinders to the contrary, Barbour here asserts that our modern scientifically produced picture of a dynamic world is in fact relevant to the theological doctrine of creation. He is assuming that some sort of dynamism in theology should parallel the dynamism found in science. Having committed himself now to following the scientific lead, one would expect him to affirm an absolute beginning over against continuing creation. After all, that is where the preponderance of scientific evidence lies, but instead we get continuing creation.

Perhaps we should ask what Barbour means by continuing creation. This brings us to the second item we note in this citation. It is not *creatio de novo* as proffered by Hoyle. It is, following the model of biological evolution, the process of bringing life out of already existing matter. It is what Thomas would call change. Barbour wants the doctrine of creation to refer to God's continuing activity within the world, not the creation of the world at the beginning per se. He wishes to merge creation with providence. Gilkey uses the term "continuing creation" similarly to combine creation and preservation. "Creation is seen now to take place throughout the unfolding temporal process. . . . thus, creation and providential rule seem to melt into one another. . . . The symbol of God's creation of the world points not to an event at the beginning."[30]

It seems that the shells have been slid all around the table, but once we lift them up we find the same old pea. What we have arrived at is simply a change in vocabulary. Whereas Thomas used the term "creation" to refer to the absolute beginning of things and to distinguish this from ongoing change, theologians such as Barbour and Gilkey use creation to refer to the process of change within the already existing creation. The alleged motive for the switch is to merge creation together with preservation or providence, but the result is the total elimination of any theological commitment to a temporal beginning. In fact, such a beginning cannot even be discussed theologically because we have lost the word for it. For temporal beginnings these days we need to go to the scientists.

The scrupulous analysis given these questions by Barbour and Gilkey reveal just where we are as theologians today. On the one hand, we must acknowledge that our fundamental commitment to understanding nature as God's creation is based on an experience with the Beyond that is peculiar to Christian faith. This means that in some sense what we say theologically is independent of what we say scientifically. On the other hand, when we find areas of common conceptuality between our theological commitments and scientific theorizing, we cannot help greeting this with some enthusiasm. The as-yet-unanswered question is just how we can consider theological knowledge and scientific knowledge as consonant or, perhaps even further, as belonging to the same domain of knowledge.

An Ontology of the Future

The doctrine of continuing creation is well worth theological development, but its development should not be at the expense of creation out of nothing. We need both. My reasons here are quite different from those already given by Barbour and Gilkey. The main reason for developing the concept of *creatio continua* in concert with *creatio ex nihilo* is that evangelical explication, based upon the compact experience of God doing something new, leads us in this direction. It derives from the eschatological realities promised through the prophets. It infers from this that the future is not determined solely by past actualities. This leads to the thought that creation is not over and done with.

If creation refers to the coming-to-be of things, then our modern understanding of reality as concrete and dynamic would imply that coming-to-be is a process that will not be completed until the whole of reality is actualized, i.e., until the end of history. What we call the essence of things or the being of things ought not to refer simply to the way things are at the present moment. The concept of a present time is an abstraction from a more concrete reality, the durative flow of what is real toward its eschatological definition. To avoid misleading abstractions, we should think of essence or being in reference to the final outcome of all things. It is destiny that is determinative.

It is of course our intention here to uphold both *creatio ex nihilo* and *creatio continua*, but to do so by understanding them in terms of the ontological priority of the future and determination by the whole. Let us look a bit more at each of these.

The Power of Creation from the Future, Not the Past

Let us enunciate a principle: God creates from the future, not the past. Now this may seem to contradict the commonly accepted Christian view as well as common sense understandings of causality. But I believe this principle provides a rich explication of the scriptural understanding of God and actually makes more sense than the common sense view of efficient causality because it better accounts for the realities of indeterminacy and freedom.

Our common sense view of time and causality—at least in Western culture with its historical consciousness—is that time consists of a linear one-way passage from the past, through the present, toward the future. The power of being in this scheme is thought of as coming from the past, i.e., a past cause and a present effect. Within this framework the initiating creative activity, whether the *ex nihilo* of the church fathers or the Big Bang of the astrophysicists, is assumed to be a single event that happened once upon a time—at the beginning of time—long ago. God is said to have created all things once and for all at the onset of time. That is, out of abject nothingness God built a lovely machine complete with parts and principles of operation, then wound it up, and it has been operating ever since.

According to this scheme, the power of being is presumed to be a push from the past. The state of affairs today is the result of yesterday's causes, which in turn are the result of the previous day's causes, on back to the divine first cause on the first day. I call this the "bowling ball" theory of creation. The image is that of a divine bowler providing the power of being by hurling the creation down the alley of time. We at present are somewhere on the alley, having left the divine hand behind but not yet colliding with the eschatological strike still ahead of us. As for human decision and responsibility, because we can contribute a modest influence on the course and direction of the roll, we strive to keep ourselves in line with God's original aim so as to avoid a gutter ball.

But does this image adequately describe how we experience time and the power of being? No. Although we certainly do experience some current effects due to past causes, this applies only to some things within what-is rather than what-is itself. What-is itself is future-dependent; it is yet to come. We experience anxiety regarding what is to come, wondering whether or not we will be here to share the future or even if there will be a future for anybody. The power of being is preconsciously apprehended as that which can overcome anxiety by assuring the future. To be is to have a future. To lose one's future and to have only a past is to die; and deep down we know it. The dynamic perdurance of the present moment is contingent on the power of the future to draw us into it.

The first thing God did for the cosmos was to give it a future. Without a future it would be nothing. When referring to the temporal beginning with the phrase *creatio ex nihilo* we are referring to God's first gracious gift of futurity. This gift of a future is the condition for the coming into existence and the sustaining of any present reality. From our perspective today, of course, we have the sense that we are looking back upon this first divine act. It seems to be part of our dead past. But God continues to bestow upon us a future, and this continuity of future-giving is the source of our life and being.

The power of the future is also the source of freedom. When in the present moment we feel overwhelmed by trends set in motion by past causes, we feel cramped and contained and constrained. To look at a future we believe to be predetermined is to feel that life has been lost. The bowling ball theory of time places all power in the past, which cannot help resulting in a determinism regarding the present. The power of God, however, comes to us not as a brute determination from the past but as that which counters such determinations. Each moment God exerts divine power to relieve us from past constraints so as to open up a field for contingency, for free action, for responsible living.

Instead of a push from the past, I suggest we think of God's creative power as a pull from the future. Instead of a bowling ball thrown from behind, I suggest the perhaps less-than-adequate image of a motorcycle with sidecar. The motorcyclist sits a few inches in front of the rider in the sidecar. Although there is a sense in which the divine is the leader and the riding creation the follower, both are being carried along at the same speed due to the power under the driver's control. All of what-is is moving at the speed of the cylcers, so that what is left behind is the nonbeing of what is now past, and what is ahead is the yet-to-be of the future.

The concept of time we are presupposing here may appear to be anthropocentric, but it is cosmic as well. We must acknowledge that it is because of memory in human consciousness that we think in terms of past-present-future. But what about nonhuman nature? Doesn't it have a past-present-future structure? We know at least from special relativity theory that all subsystems within the universe do not share the same temporal frame of reference, i.e., there is no absolute notion of the present. Nevertheless, the Big Bang concept of a singular beginning in conjunction with the second law of thermodynamics makes it intelligible to speak of a universal arrow of time, an arrow aimed in the direction of the future. Cosmic futurity is not dependent upon human consciousness. If we think of God as creating the whole of the cosmos—the space-time whole—then we, who live amidst the cosmos, will experience the power of God as the draw of the future toward completion.

According to the idea that God creates from the future, creation is not a single event that happened just once in the past. Rather, it is a single event incorporating the whole history of the cosmos. We, living within this history experience it as a constant durative process, wherein the past is being constantly left behind while what is actual continually moves on. God is every moment drawing reality out of the nonbeing of the past into the actual existence of the present moment while maintaining a trajectory toward his own as-yet-unrealized purposes for the consummate future. God is constantly providing all of nature and all of history with a call forward, with a divine lure toward greater reality. *To be is to have a future, God's future.* If we do not have a future, we drop into the nonbeing of the dead past and may or may not be remembered by those who care to look from time to time at history's wake. God—the power of the future—is the continuing source of life and being.

To return to our motorcycle analogy, one could conceive of the unlikely possibility that the rider might seek to uncouple the sidecar and steer it in a direction independent of that taken by the motorcyclist. The very attempt to do this might so destabilize the tandem movement as to cause a collision between the two that results in damage to both. Should the rider succeed in uncoupling the sidecar from its source of power and direction, it would wander aimlessly for a period, and then as its inertia wanes it would eventually slow to a stop. The power of being would move on without it, leaving it to the oblivion of the dead past. There is an outside chance that the motorcyclist might deviate from the previously mapped out direction and return to offer recoupling and renewed power. This would be tantamount to bringing the power of the future back into the past, bringing direction into aimlessness, bringing life into death. The motorcyclist would not be required to do this, of course. It would be an act of grace.

At this point we need to abandon our motorcycle analogy to pursue a little more directly the idea that continuing creation is something that God does, that it is an act of God. But before going on we should briefly note an area of consonance, i.e., that theology shares with the standard Big Bang theory the idea of an arrow of time. The eschatological promise, however, comes from uniquely theological sources.

The Determining Power of the As-yet-uncompleted Whole

In attempting to grasp what it means to say, "God acts," let us employ for a moment the concept of wholism. The chief doctrine of wholism is that the whole is greater than the sum of its parts. It is this "greater than" that distinguishes a whole from a simple totality or agglomeration of otherwise individual things. A corollary of this principle is that the parts are defined by their relationship to one another and by the whole that frames that relationship. I think these insights help illuminate the Christian understanding of creation. Let us formulate a second principle: *God's creative activity within nature and history is derivative from his act of creating and redeeming the whole of the cosmos*.

This principle is anti-reductionistic. We seek to avoid the fallacy of reduction to origin, the archonic fallacy committed by myth and historiomachy wherein all reality is thought to be determined by what happened at the point of past origination. The problem with this archonic view is that it precludes the coming into being of anything fundamentally new. If incorporated into theology it would produce only deism, not theism. We also seek to avoid the fallacy of atomic reduction, the fallacy afoot in modern academe that assumes that the macrocosm is simply a composite of much more fundamental building blocks at the microcosmic level. The problem with this assumption is that it fails to recognize as ontologically fundamental patterns of interaction that exist only at more complex and comprehensive levels of reality. If incorporated into theology it would produce only naturalism.

One of the problems the wholistic vision helps us solve is the question of how God acts *vis-à-vis* nature and history. The reductionism of the modern mind had painted us into a corner. The mechanistic world view emerging from eighteenth-century science saw all events as inextricably linked together on a single chain of cause and effect. Since all events have finite causes, adequate explanations consisted in identifying these finite causes. But there is no way here to understand how God, an infinite being, could be understood as one finite factor among others in the causal nexus. Miracles, understood as supranatural interventions of the Beyond into the causal chain, would be precluded because they would make the otherwise natural universe unintelligible. The laws of nature are thought to be inviolate.

Once on this track, however, modern science was led ineluctably toward determinism. Once the machine is running and we understand its principles of operation, then everything becomes predictable. But such determinism found itself constantly at odds with another firm commitment of modernity, namely, human freedom. Free human acts cannot be accounted for by the mechanistic model, because they cannot be explained exhaustively by their antecedent causes. As long as the tendency toward reductionism remains, the rivalry between mechanical determinism and freedom—whether divine freedom or human freedom—will remain.

Wholism helps extricate us from this painted-in corner because it attributes equal reality to complex forms of interrelationship where freedom is exercised while still affirming efficient causation at relatively more simple levels. Let us offer an example. Suppose I am confronted with the option of going either to the refrigerator to eat some leftover apple pie or to the athletic field for jogging. If I devour the apple pie, my body will start processing its sugars and I will begin to feel sleepy. My breathing rate and skin reaction to the environment within the house will remain the same, but my metabolism will shoot up and my heart will beat faster for a brief period. Then everything will slow down and I'll feel like taking a nap. Eventually this will result in my loosening my belt to one notch larger. On the other hand, if I decide to jog around the athletic field, my breathing will become rapid and my skin will react to the cold outside air. My heart and metabolism rates will increase as they process the fats already present in my body. This activity will be sustained for a long period of time and I will feel energetic and ready for hard work. Eventually I may be able to tighten my belt one notch.

What is going on here is that the decision I make becomes itself an ordering factor in the causal nexus constituting my bodily activity. There are generally operative principles governing breathing cycles, skin reaction, heart and metabolism rates, and so forth. However, my decision introduces an independent factor into the causal chain and reorders the actual pattern of interaction. A decision of the whole has reordered the parts. But we need not say the causal chain has been broken. We need only say that the lower-level causal nexus is less than completely deterministic and that human freedom is not reducible to the level of biophysical causes.

If we could imagine this situation from the point of view of the heart within my body, it would be impossible for the heart to comprehend the whole person of which it is a vital part. The heart is an organism—it is not a machine even though the machine model helps us understand the heart—that responds to stimuli by serving the various life needs of the body as a whole. It will respond somewhat differently if stimulated by the digestion of apple pie than it would if stimulated by jogging. But in itself it cannot comprehend the deliberative processes of the person whose decision will determine which stimulus will come its way. The heart does not know if I am making a decision in behalf of good health or in behalf of culinary pleasure. Certainly there is reciprocity between the life-giving work of the heart and the health decisions made by the person, but the whole-part dialectic gives a certain prerogative to the whole personality that the heart cannot govern or understand.

By taking seriously the determining power and influence of more comprehensive wholes such as persons, wholism can account for human freedom without breaking the nexus of finite relations at the physiological, biochemical, or physical levels. Having observed this, we may now ask the theological question, Can we by analogy see ourselves as part of a still larger whole, the whole of reality? Can we like the heart accept the fact that this more comprehensive whole enjoys a more comprehensive freedom and governing power than we can understand? Can we affirm that through the macro-whole God acts to alter the course of historical events but does not break the nexus?

Such a view of God's activity would have to be produced by analogy, because its content could not be experienced directly. If the whole person is somehow more than the sum of his or her constitutive parts, heart included, then we can understand how the larger whole of which we are a part is not reducible to the human level of reality. As human beings we retain our integrity and a degree of freedom, to be sure. But as part of a larger whole, which in itself is greater than the sum of its parts and enjoys still greater freedom, we must realize that there is a level of reality that is beyond our grasp. It follows that we cannot fully comprehend that whole itself. It must remain mysterious. Our knowledge of its existence is a formal construction of the human imagination, and its material content must remain elusive. Nevertheless, it is quite understandable how this whole can be determinative of who and what we are.

What this line of thinking does for us is to provide a model that can account for the appearance of genuinely new things without breaking the continuity of history. Jahweh's redemptive action foretold by the Hebrew prophets could not be reduced to principles established by the divine ἀρχή *in illo tempore*. They were new acts. They were eschatological acts. Yet their effects were intra-historical. Novelty and continuity belong together. When looking at such activity strictly in terms of historical continuity, the hand of the divine is invisible. When looking at the quality of redeeming newness, however, the intervention of the Beyond may be surmised.

Being Versus Acting

There is some risk in pressing too far the analogy between the person-heart relationship and the God-world relationship. There is a vital reciprocity between the person and his or her heart that just may not apply fully to God's relationship with the creation. In describing the whole of reality that is determinative of who and what we are, are we describing the being of God himself? Is God equivalent to this macro-whole or transcendent to it? This is difficult to answer. The logic of wholism seems to lead to an identification of God with the world. If we are successful at accounting for divine activity in history and nature using the whole-part model,then it is a small step to the equation of God and the cosmos as a whole. There is little or no room for a supra-cosmic Beyond. It is no accident that post-modern theorists who have pressed their premises into the religious sphere have repeatedly arrived at a form of pantheism or panentheism.

Recall that the early church apologists were reluctant to follow the path of pantheism available at that time. Why? Because there is a significant element in the compact experience of the gospel for which a strictly pantheistic explication is unable to account, namely, the experience of the redemption of an unholy world by a holy God. When the being of the world becomes identified with the being of God, then any serious notion of redemption is eviscerated. For to identify God and the world would imply that God himself is in need of redemption, but that is not part of the compact gospel experience or its primary symbolization.

Another and related factor that mitigates wholistic logic and that tends to reaffirm the transcendence of God over against the created world is the present incompleteness of the world. The cosmos at present simply is not a whole. It is dynamic. It is on the move. It has an open future. What we know as the cosmos is a collection of contemporary events that are interrelated to their past and open to future unity, but at present they are contiguous with one another. Wholeness is still something awaited. The world will not become a unified whole until it is redeemed, until God's will is finally done, until the kingdom of God is fully established.

Rather than conceiving of the macro-whole that transcends and includes the realm of human freedom in terms of divine being, I suggest we conceive of it as divine acting. Creation is not a thing; it is an act. Redemption similarly is not a thing; it is an act. We as creatures are products of the creative activity of God's redemptive love.

What conceiving the creation-process as an action does for us is relieve the pressures toward pantheism, where the being of the world and the being of God are drawn together in a more inclusive whole. To understand creation as an act is simultaneously to understand God as the actor, and his independence over against the whole of creation is maintained.

Here we might find helpful the distinction offered by Gordon Kaufman between an act proper, called a "master act," and a sub-act. Kaufman develops his doctrine of creation on the analogy of human action. He defines an act as an event in which something is done or performed. It is a deliberate ordering of behavior toward the realization of a previously posited end. By analogy, God is one who has purposes and acts to realize them. But how does God do this?

God's primary action is his master act with which he creates the whole cosmos. En route to the completion of this creative work, God engages in sub-acts. A carpenter, for example, may build a house. The house is the master act. But en route to completion the carpenter must perform certain sub-acts such as: examine the blueprints, deliver materials to the site, measure, saw, hammer, and clean up. There is one act, but it incorporates numerous sub-acts, all of which can be identified by their contribution to the purpose of completing the house.

There is no house—no whole—until the creative work is completed. So also, God's act consists in a purposive event of creation that will not become an event until its completion, until the eschaton. Kaufman puts it this way: "It is the whole course of history, from its initiation in God's creative activity to its consummation when God ultimately achieves his purposes that should be conceived as God's act in the primary sense."[31]

The Kaufman proposal has the merit of engaging seriously the implications of the whole-part dialectic in light of the difficulty of identifying God's sub-acts within the intra-historical nexus. He makes clear that knowledge of God's sub-acts depends upon prior knowledge of God's master act. To understand the escape of the Hebrew slaves from the hand of Pharaoh's army at the bank of the Red Sea as a divine rescue would require advance knowledge of God's overall plan for cosmic redemption. The parts, i.e., the individual events that make up our daily experience, do not in themselves communicate the purpose of the whole. For us to be able to discern an event to be a sub-act within the divine master act would require having the eschatological completion in sight. Is it possible to have the end revealed ahead of time? Kaufman answers affirmatively, saying that the divine cosmic agent has revealed to his creatures that he has a purpose, and this purpose can be discerned in the ministry and death of Jesus Christ. In Jesus Christ we see God's purpose for the whole, the single purpose that runs from creation through providence to eschatology.

Hence we may think of the whole of cosmic history as a single divine act, a whole of which our own personal histories are minute but indispensable parts. And because that history has not yet come to its completion, it is not yet whole. The future is still open. Reality is on the way to being determined and defined in mutual reciprocity between the actual course of finite events and the overall divine design. What permits us to think wholistically is the promise of the future completion of God's master act. In the meantime, we find ourselves within the creative work of God, a work yet to be completed, and hence appropriately called from our point of view "continuing creation."

The Creative Word in Genesis 1:1–2:4a

How do we reconcile my proposal of durative creation with the Genesis account wherein God creates the cosmos out of nothing by speaking his word? Genesis 1 is traditionally interpreted as referring to a single week's activities which occurred only once a long time ago. God labored for six days and on the seventh he took a vacation. Is he still on vacation? If creation happened only once, then he might as well be.

But if we conceive of creation as a presently continuing process, then it might be helpful to think of Genesis as describing the present, not just the past. God is not yet resting, nor will he rest until his creative work is done. We today are still somewhere within the first six days and looking forward to the seventh. The first book of Moses, then, might be speaking not about what happened once upon a time but rather about what is happening now and what will yet be.

How about the concept of the Word of God? Let us first observe something about spoken words in general. Human words are transient, ephemeral. Once spoken, they are heard for an instant. Then they disappear. They are immediately replaced by silence or by other words. They may be forgotten or they may be remembered and repeated, but they themselves do not endure.

When we speak of God's Word, however, we think of an eternal word. It is not ephemeral or evanescent. It has a future. It is not subject to the perpetual perishing of temporal passage. Could we on this basis indulge in a bit of anthropomorphic imagination and think of God as having opened his mouth and as still speaking? Perhaps he has not yet finished the primal performative utterance: "Let there be . . . a cosmos!" The sentence is not yet finished. We today stand in the midst of his holy and creative speaking, somewhere between the first syllable and the final period. And God will not close his mouth until all things are fulfilled, until all reality is consummated into his everlasting Kingdom.

Scientific Creationism

Now we might pause to ask what implications this has for the debate over scientific creationism. As the reader can quickly see, the theory of creation being developed here is quite different from that employed by scientific creationists. But just what is the difference? In answering this I wish to set aside for the time being misleading distinctions such as literal versus non-literal interpretation of Holy Scripture. The difference lies in the basic cosmological vision. The scientific creationists are fundamentally archonic and derive their conceptual framework from historiomachy, whereas the notion of continuing creation being put forth here is much more epigenetic and derives from prophetic eschatology.

What is scientific creationism? It is a theological and political movement which seeks to loosen the intellectual grip held by the theory of evolution upon the public school systems of North America. As a theological movement it affirms the following thesis: the biblical record in Genesis, accepted in its natural and literal sense, provides the best scientific account of the origin of all things. Note the conflation of scripture and science here. The creationist argument no longer relies strictly on an appeal to biblical authority as it did during the fundamentalist-modernist controversy of the 1920s. It has now entered the scientific arena itself by arguing that the accumulated geological data are better accounted for by a theory of absolute creation than by a theory of progressive evolution.

As a political movement, creationists complain that the theory of evolution leads to an unnamed religion that is naturalistic, materialistic, atheistic, amoral, and may even be the root source of the present degeneration of Western society. Therefore they seek parity in public education, which means—as illustrated by the case of a 1981 bill passed in the Arkansas legislature—that if either evolution or scientific creationism is taught in a public school, a balanced treatment must be given to the other viewpoint.

Such activities on the part of the creationists have made enemies. The American Civil Liberties Union takes them to court for violating the First Amendment. Harvard paleontologist Stephen Jay Gould criticizes them for misusing the theory-fact relationship and says the term "scientific creationism" is "meaningless and self-contradictory, a superb example of what Orwell called 'newspeak.' "[32] Theologian Langdon Gilkey says the creationists are quite right about attacking the predominantly secularistic and even atheistic character of most of contemporary intellectual life, but he sharply criticizes them for a confusion of categories. Science deals with finite causes. Its province is the temporal world, the created order. Religion, on the other hand, deals with the infinite ground of reality, with God. Its province is the transcendent. What the creationists do—and what makes them so undeniably modern—is to confine knowledge to a single level of truth, i.e., to the level of factual knowledge regarding finite cause and effect. Gilkey advocates a sensitivity to multiple layers of truth that eliminates the conflict between a scientific apprehension of finite facts and a religious vision of the comprehensive meaning of life.[33]

My own criticism is of a different nature. It is the assumption that creation must be understood archonically, which effectively eliminates any insights gained from eschatological experience. That this position is archonic is unmistakably demonstrated by Duane T. Gish of the Institute for Creation Reasearch in San Diego:

> By creation we mean the bringing into being of the basic kinds of plants and animals by the process of sudden, or fiat, creation described in the first two chapters of Genesis. . . . During the creation week God created all of these basic animal and plant kinds, for the Bible speaks of a finished creation (Gen. 2:2). The variation that has occurred since the end of the creative work of God has been limited to changes within kinds.[34]

In other words, God's creative work stopped when he began to rest on the seventh day of the first week. In contrast to Gish, I believe the word "creation" applies to God's continuing relationship to the cosmos and is yet to be completed. That it will be completed in the future is something we have learned from the prophets interpreted in light of the gospel. It is something we hold as an article of faith.

Law: Continuity and Divine Faithfulness

As we have already said, the notion of continuous creation is intelligible because we have recognized the contingency of the future. The future activity of God cannot be deduced from the previous course of events. The future activity of finite beings within the cosmos similarly cannot be so deduced either. Creativity is built right into the ongoing process of things.

This raises the question of continuity. If we have only creativity, then what would there be to connect future events with past events? If everything has the quality of newness, then the old can no longer exist. It must fall away into the nonbeing of the past. It would be as if the whole cosmos were created brand-new every day or even every moment, so that its actuality was totally independent of everything that had preceded it. There would be no such thing as constancy, normativity, sameness, or even order. Creativity without continuity would make temporality and historicity vacuous.

Or, to put the question another way, What effect does the past have on the present and the future? The cause-effect nexus is fundamental to common human experience, though it is certainly not all-determinative. We experience freedom and openness as well. But if we had no confidence that the future at least in part would consist in effects of present causes, then we would have no motive for making any plans or taking any action. There must exist some form of continuity through time that incorporates an influence of the past upon its future while not obviating contingency, freedom, and creativity.

The continuity seems to be provided by law and memory, which are due to God's faithfulness. The term "law" describes the regularities and causal connectedness between otherwise contingent events. The actual stream of unique events through time, where no single happening repeats a previous one, is the concrete reality in which we live. But it seems to have an ordered structure. Scientists seek continually to discover the laws that apparently govern this structure. Such laws are formulated inductively after observing a single pattern frequently repeated. To know that a pattern has been repeated, however, depends upon memory. The laws of regularity in nature are formulated on the basis of cumulative and remembered experience. What we know as the laws of nature constitute a conceptual framework abstracted from the more fundamental experience with the durative flow of actuality.

It does not follow, then, that these laws are themselves eternal or everlasting. Although they cover the scope of our own experience and reflection, it does not mean they must have always existed in the past nor must they continue to exist into the indefinite future. As we saw in our review of the Big Bang cosmogony, the very forces along with the material makeup of the cosmos themselves came into being at a specified time in the past. They are contingent. The universe could be otherwise. Things do not have to be the way they are. The validity of natural laws is also time-dependent. What we know as the regularities of nature are here for a season, but then they too are subject to subsumption into future contingent and perhaps more comprehensive events.

Therefore, we must acknowledge that the whole of reality cannot be explained by laws, because the concept of law requires repeatability. But the concrete reality of which we are a part consists in an irreversible and unrepeatable series of events, and whatever repeatability we apprehend is an abstraction which describes only one unrepeateable chapter in the larger history that is the cosmos. In other words, our experience of law and the continuity of events that accompanies it constitutes a meso-experience between individual finite events and the more comprehensive history of reality. It is a truth-disclosure, but as with all experiences of truth it is provisional and subject to further subsumption into a more comprehensive reality.

Is law then simply a figment of our abstract imagination? Or does it in some way reflect contemporary actuality? What is the ontology of law? Law is one form of divine activity within the cosmos. Laws are the result of the interaction of God's faithfulness with the course of otherwise contingent events. God in the Godself is *a se*, not bound to the cosmic order. What we experience as governing principles are ordinances freely invoked by God to keep the world in being—to keep it organized as a cosmos—for a given duration. Because we always look at such law from the side of the governed, it is difficult if not impossible for us to imagine what things were like before there was a law or before there was a Big Bang. Because we always look at things from within our cosmos, we cannot imagine how things could operate in any other cosmos not subject to the form of governance by natural law to which we have become accustomed. Much less can we imagine the freedom of the governor, the Beyond.

But it is out of freedom that God acts. One form of this free divine activity is the provision for continuity. The ancient

Hebrews understood this as an aspect of God's faithfulness.[35]
Nature is ordered not because of eternal or immutable laws but
because God can be trusted to keep his promises. We learn that
someone is faithful only after an experience with his or her
loyalty. Although ancient Israel's Near Eastern neighbors
conceived of nature as governed by eternal archetypes fixed by
the gods *in illo tempore*, Israel was given promises that new
things would happen. These promises were fulfilled. Israel
experienced this curious combination of newness and faithfulness, both freedom and law. Our understanding of continuous
creation is an extrapolation based upon this experience of Israel
with God.

We today find ourselves between promise and fulfillment, a
metaxic tension that is calling us to relate to God's faithfulness
through our own faith. Faith is here understood as trust in the
God of the future. The final evidence of God's trustworthiness
will be available only at the end of history. In the meantime this
can be made intelligible by noting the temporality if not
ephemerality of natural law, the constant contingency of the
cosmos as we know it. Hence the call to faith is not a call to place
our trust in the ordered cosmos but rather in the faithfulness of
the Beyond which has committed itself to determine a future
that is redemptive. In short, trust God, not nature!

The Orders of Creation

This has implications for the Reformation doctrine of the
Schöpfungsordnungen, the so-called orders of creation. If we
wish to know the orders of creation, we will have to await the
completion of the whole. We need to see what perdures and
what does not. What we experience as the orders of creation
now represent only one chapter in the long story of God's
faithfulness.

Although having some roots in the Reformers themselves,
the doctrine of the orders of creation grew out of the desire of
later Protestant orthodoxy to establish an evangelical equivalent to the Roman Catholic natural law ethic. According to the
doctrine, God has built into the creation certain principles that

order human social life. General categories of social organization—such as nation, race, ethnicity, marriage, family, and productive work—represent divinely established patterns intended to govern human affairs. These patterns become laws, so that we are exhorted to conform to them. To live according to the orders of creation is to live according to God's will and to obtain his blessing; whereas to attempt to live outside the orders is to court judgment and ruin. Thus, the orders-of-creation concept follows an is-ought movement: the way things are is the way things should be.

Theologians who proffer the orders of creation doctrine are generally quick to deny that their position describes a static or inflexible reality, but their denials are not always convincing. Emil Brunner, for example, insists that the actual forms of the social life we experience are historically variable, but their underlying structure is invariable. This invariability is ultimately rooted in the nature of God because, according to Brunner, "God is a God of order."[36] Now we must grant that order is part of our experience with God, but Brunner's way of putting it almost makes God look like an eternal neurotic who is so constrained by his ordered personality that he cannot relate to the world in a free and responsive fashion.

This doctrine of the orders of creation has been criticized for supporting conservative tendencies in ethical thinking, because it seems ill equipped to deal with rapid or widespread social change. Our concern here is slightly different, however. Our concern has to do with the issue of contingency and continuity in creation. We need to ask, How are these patterns of order fixed? There seem to be three options.

First, we can say the orders are eternal, that they belong to the mind of God and are imparted into history from beyond. When we live faithfully in our family or are loyal to our nation, then we are participating in an eternal form.

The second option is the archonic position, which holds that the orders came into being at the moment of creation. They are temporal orders, but as archonic they remain fixed throughout the course of history. Edmund Schlink is an example of a systematic theologian who embraces this second option as an attempt to repudiate the first position. The orders do not emerge from an eternal source, he says; rather they belong strictly to the historical process and represent God's manner of organizing temporal things. Schlink then places God's organizing activity at the foundation of the world, which he locates at the beginning. He seems to assume that they will remain as they are until the eschaton. He proceeds in this fashion because he recognizes that contemporary science is contingency-conscious. But his solution is still archonic, and the orders of creation have the same effect they would have had they been copied from eternal forms. Schlink says he wants to think of the orders in a dynamic rather than a static fashion, but one wonders what dynamic could possibly mean in this context if nothing changes from beginning to end.[37] In the final analysis, Schlink's historically fixed orders are indistinguishable from eternally fixed ones.

The third option, which is the position I am trying to develop here, deems the idea of the orders of creation helpful for comprehending the continuity of otherwise contingent events. However, their nature and value is much qualified. What order we experience is neither eternal nor archonic. Rather, it is something that developed over time and will subsequently dissolve over time. Order is itself contingent. What is not contingent is God's faithfulness. Whatever order we experience in either nature or society is a temporary blessing that emerges from God's constancy. Order is neither an eternal form within the divine mind nor an archonic form established at a deterministic beginning of temporal history. It is rather a responsive act of God in relation to the ongoingness of events.

What we mean by God's faithfulness and the sense of order that it bestows amidst our metaxy has been called the doctrine of preservation (*conservatio*) in traditional dogmatics. So also here the concept of preservation is offered as a complement to that of creation. With the notion of continuing creation we are developing here, however, preservation takes on the meaning of preparation.

God is constantly in the process of creating the world in light of its forthcoming end. Just as the present redefines the meaning of the now past past, so also will the ultimate future redefine the totality of what has come before. It is only the whole at the end that will determine the meaning and the being of each of its parts, and the constitutive parts include the whole passage of historical time. Hence the all-determining reality must be understood as the consummate reality, the fulfilling whole that takes past and present up into itself, and redefines and redetermines it according to God's loving will.

The position being advocated here is not one of teleological evolution. It is not a doctrine of development or progress toward a goal. There is no immanent *telos* buried in the heart of the natural processes that is driving everything like a seed toward its eventual flowering. The continuity of events can be discovered only in retrospection, only in memory. The connection between events and what appears to be purpose is the result of interpreting the past in light of the present and interpreting the present in light of its destiny. It is not simply a question as to whether hindsight is better than foresight, because hindsight is all we have. It is all we have because that is the way reality is.

The future is genuinely open. Creation is genuinely continuing. What we experience as continuity can at any moment undergo radical and total change at the behest of God's will. What draws the course of events together into a whole so that a sense of continuity can be maintained is the faithfulness of the Beyond. That there is an integrating coherence to reality is something we can affirm only through faith, only through trust in God to bring all things into a consummate whole.

Conclusion:
Creatio Ex Nihilo, The Big Bang, and Gospel Explication

Our basic question in this essay has been, How can we think of the cosmos as God's creation? This question has taken on new excitement as scientists ponder the implications of the emerging Big Bang theory of the origin of the universe. Conceptual doors seem to be opening toward the Beyond, or at least toward a reality that might lie beyond the recognized limits of scientific conceptuality. It is time for us to take up again the important question of the relationship between scientific knowledge and theological thinking.

What is clearly attractive to a theologian about Big Bang cosmology is the prospect of identifying a datable beginning to all things followed by a temporally irreversible (perhaps even historical) sequence of events and, most importantly, a sense of contingency. There is no archonic principle of necessity built in at the beginning. The world does not have to be the way it is. It could have been otherwise. It may even be different in the future. Thus with our commitment to *creatio ex nihilo* there will be a great temptation to embrace Big Bang thinking wholeheartedly, perhaps even to baptize it theologically. Our analysis of the rise of the Christian concept of creation, however, ought to help us in locating three cautions.

First, although Big Bangism may be the dominant theory at the moment, it is not the only one. Eternal oscillationists among others employ the same data yet deny the notion of an absolute beginning. Oscillationism has potential theological significance because it tends toward a position comparable to Greco-Roman dualism, wherein the material substance of the cosmos is eternal. Even if the form—in our case the form would correspond roughly to the laws of nature, the fundamental forces, etc.—were to change after each Big Bounce, the stuff of the universe has no absolute arrival nor does it ever go away. Although Big Bang is currently out in front, eternal oscillation is still in the race and we do not even know if we are in the home stretch yet. We do not even know what would count as the finish line, because science is in principle a never-ending mode of inquiry. To place our bets on the current leader in the scientific field seems like a risky way to pursue theology.

Second, the apparent absoluteness of Big Bang's absolute beginning may be less absolute than it looks. It appears to be an ontological absoluteness. It, in fact, may be only a methodological absoluteness. What we have confronted with Planck time is the frontier of our knowledge, the current limit beyond which we cannot go with present theory. To press beyond Planck time would require a superunification conceptuality that would include among other things a quantum mechanical theory of gravitation. No such theory exists at the present time. But, as one might assume, an intense effort is well under way to find one. Should such a theory be found we would move the frontier of knowledge further back.

Another way to look at this is to suggest that the question regarding the origin of the universe simply cannot be answered within the scientific method. Scientific laws are based on observation and experiment, yet we have no experience whatsoever with a universe that does not contain mass. Time began when mass was created. To ask what happened before the beginning or what precipitated the beginning is meaningless. Science is admittedly an intracosmic inquiry. And any further advance in scientific knowledge will simply advance our intracosmic knowledge.

Our religious commitment, however, is of a different order. It begins with an experience with the Beyond, with that which transcends the cosmos. What is relevant about the Beyond is that it is the source and Lord of all that is. But because it transcends the cosmos it must remain shrouded in mystery, not subject to intracosmic modes of comprehension. This is an ontological commitment of great import, because we are affirming the divine ground for all reality. The scientific method cannot deny the relevance of the Beyond; but it cannot affirm it either. The Beyond is just what the word implies, namely, something beyond the domain of inquiry. The Beyond lies outside the perimeter of scientific knowing, and always will. Consequently, no matter how much the Big Bang theory complements *creatio ex nihilo,* it represents a methodological frontier and not the full ontological affirmation made by Christian theology. This should lead us to observe the caution expressed by Notre Dame philosopher of science, Ernan McMullin.

> What one could say . . . is that if the universe began in time through the act of a Creator, from our vantage point it would look something like the Big Bang that cosmologists are talking about. What one cannot say is, first, that the Christian

doctrine of creation "supports" the Big Bang model, or,
second, that the Big Bang model "supports" the Christian
doctrine of creation.[38]

This is just a caution, however; it is not a hands-off policy.
Theology may begin with an experience with the Beyond, but it
does not end there. It seeks to explicate this experience in
terms of the scientific knowledge available. Wherever possible,
it seeks consonance between science and theology.

Third, the significance of the power of God as it is ascertained
in Christian faith is associated with the future and not with the
past. The ground for asserting the radical newness of the
beginning in *creatio ex nihilo* is the promise of the new reality
that is yet to come. Jesus' resurrection from the dead is a foretaste
of the eschatological reign of God which will be resurrected from
the death of the present aeon. God's future action is not just one
more expression of natural laws first formed during the Big Bang
of the past. God acts independently, and it is this independence
that is the ground of our hope.

Here the Big Bang cosmology with its open universe does not
directly complement the Christian apperception. If we bring
existential questions to its forecast about a long process of
winding down toward a cold dark nothingness, the whole
cosmic reality begins to appear pointless and we drop into the
deep funk of nihilism. "However far ahead may be the demise
of life in the cosmos, the fact of its inevitability undermines any
intelligible grounds for hope being generated from within the
purely scientific prospect itself," writes A. R. Peacocke. "The
Revelation of John is but a pale document compared with these
modern scientific apocalypses!"[39]

We must admit that the intracosmic discoveries of science
may not buttress our hope for a transformed reality and the
bright new eternal day of the Lord. This is because our hope is a
response to a revelation from the Beyond, from that *a se* God
whose plans for the future are not fully governed by principles
or processes produced in the past. Our hope, in short, is the
result of our faith.

And we should not by any means underestimate the severity

of this faith commitment. It flies in the face of widely accepted intracosmic knowledge and its corresponding nihilism. Bertrand Russell threw down the gauntlet some decades ago in his "A Free Man's Worship."

> All the labor of the ages, all the devotion, all the inspiration, all the noonday brightness of human genius is destined to extinction in the vast death of the solar system, and that the whole temple of Man's achievement must inevitably be buried beneath the debris of a universe in ruins—all these things, if not quite beyond dispute, are yet so nearly certain, that no philosophy which rejects them can hope to stand.[40]

Yet Christians proffer just the philosophy that rejects this conclusion. Will it stand? If it stands it will do so not necessarily because of complementary theories in science. If it stands it will have to stand on faith.

We have been insisting here that what makes the Christian doctrine of creation Christian is that it consists in explicating truths inherent in the more compact experience of the gospel. In the distant and more recent past some theologians have sought to say something like this by affirming that our knowledge of creation derives solely from faith (cf. Heb. 11:3). It was Clement of Alexandria who said, "Faith is the ear of the soul." Bultmann modifies the metaphor a bit when saying, "To every other eye than the eye of faith the action of God is hidden."[41] What can the soul hear or the eye see? It can hear things that natural reason is deaf to and see things invisible to mundane research. It can hear the call of the Beyond. It can spot the shadow of the ultimate.

Luther, as one might expect, acknowledged that the philosophers could stumble upon general knowledge about the beginning of the world, but the exalted truth that everything was created by God requires our hearing the divine Word.[42] But one with no less confidence in natural reason than Thomas Aquinas states flatly that faith is required to ascertain *creatio ex nihilo*. "We hold by faith alone," writes Thomas, "and it cannot be proved by demonstration, that the world did not always exist." So insistent is Thomas that he warns us not to erect our cosmologies on the shifting sands of science lest we "give occasion to unbelievers to laugh" at us for less than cogent reasoning.[43] Karl Barth follows suit by saying, "The doctrine of the creation no less than the whole remaining content of Christian confession is an article of faith, i.e., the rendering of a knowledge that no man has procured for himself or ever will; which is neither native to him nor accessible by way of observation and logical thinking."[44]

The position I am advocating here modifies yet affirms this apparently exclusivistic claim that knowledge regarding the nature of creation comes *sola fide*. I would not want to set aside completely the powers of natural reason or knowledge gained through observation and logical thinking. Not only does empirically based research yield a grand accumulation of intracosmic facts, it even provokes our curiosity and stimulates our imaginations to ask about what lies beyond. Nevertheless, what Christians want to say about the cosmos is not simply the result of our powers of observation and natural reasoning. The Christian notion of creation is prompted by a provocation from the Beyond, from the extracosmic reality we call "God." An event has taken place at which time the infinite entered the finite and made itself known through saving activity. Our intellectual response to this event consists in a process of thinking whereby we employ our natural capacity for reason to reflect upon the saving activity of the Beyond. We ponder the significance of our intracosmic observations in light of our awareness of the extracosmic reality.

The awareness of the Beyond is a matter of faith. Thinking about the Beyond is an intellectual activity, the structure of which we share with all other thinking activities. The Christian doctrine of creation as we have it, then, is a product of both revelation and reason, of both faith and science. It is the result of evangelical explication.

NOTES

1. Robert Jastrow, *God and the Astronomers* (New York: W. W. Norton, 1978), p. 116; cf. p. 14. Isaac Asimov is one of those with such faith in science that Jastrow himself comes as a bad dream. For Asimov there

should be a high wall of separation between church and laboratory, because religious intuition, which produced the dark ages, is no match for empirical science and its triumph in our modern and enlightened age. So when the astronomers climb Jastrow's mountain, Asimov claims, it is irrelevant that the theologians are already sitting there. "Science and the Mountain Peak," *Skeptical Inquirer*, 2, Winter 1980–81, pp. 42-50. A quite different, third approach is that of philosopher Stephen Toulmin, who would advocate that theologians and scientists set out together to scale the as-yet-unclaimed mountain. They may climb together now in our post-modern age due to increasing acceptance of the participant-observer factor in scientific research. *The Return to Cosmology* (Berkeley: University of California Press, 1982).

2. *Bulletin of Atomic Scientists*, 8 (1952), pp. 13 ff. The view of Pope Pius XII has not been universally endorsed. Some have criticized him for advocating a God-of-the-gaps position, according to which the role of God is relegated to filling in the gaps in an otherwise complete scientific theory. Cf. S. L. Jaki, *Cosmos and Creator* (Edinburgh: Scottish Academic Press, 1980). We cite the Pope here to show the inherent attraction of Big Bang cosmology to theologians. It might be worth noting that Pope John Paul II has a sustained interest in the relationship between science and faith, and in September 1987 he himself convened a panel of scientists and theologians to probe the interactions between physical cosmology and the doctrine of creation. See, "Message of His Holiness Pope John Paul II" in *Physics, Philosophy, and Theology*, eds. Robert John Russell, William R. Stoeger, S. J., and George V. Coyne, S.J. (Notre Dame: University of Notre Dame Press, 1988).

3. *Time* (Feb. 5, 1979) p. 149.

4. James S. Trefil, *The Moment of Creation* (New York: Scribner's, 1983), pp. 156-57.

5. Ilya Prigogine and Isabelle Stengers, *Order Out of Chaos* (New York: Bantam, 1984).

6. Trefil, *The Moment of Creation*, p. 217.

7. Stephen Hawking, *A Brief History of Time: From the Big Bang to Black Holes* (New York: Bantam, 1988), p. 136; cf. "If There's an Edge to the Universe, There Must Be a God," in *Dialogues with Scientists and Sages: The Search for Unity*, ed. Renée Weber (London & New York: Routledge & Kegan Paul, 1986), p. 209.

8. C. J. Isham, "Creation of the Universe as a Quantum Process," in *Physics, Philosophy, and Theology*, pp. 375-408.

9. Irenaeus, *Against the Heresies*, II, 28, 7; Augustine, *Confessions*, Book 11, chap. 12.

10. Eric Voegelin, *The Ecumenic Age*, vol. 4 of *Order and History* (Baton Rouge: Louisiana State University Press, 1956–74), p. 68.

11. Mircea Eliade, *The Sacred and the Profane* (New York: Harcourt, Brace, & World, 1959), p. 79. Eliade's italics.

12. Mary Hesse, "Cosmology as Myth," in *Cosmology and Theology*, ed. David Tracy and Nicholas Lash (New York: Seabury; Edinburgh: T. & T. Clark, 1983), p. 51.

13. Gerhard von Rad, *Old Testament Theology*, 2 volumes (New York: Harper & Row, 1957–65), 1:138; cf. Voegelin, 1:179f.

14. Voegelin, *The Ecumenic Age*, 4: 17-18.

15. Mircea Eliade, *Cosmos and History: The Myth of the Eternal Return* (New York: Harper & Row, 1959), pp. 9, 34, 120 ff.

16. Von Rad, *Old Testament Theology*, I:136.

17. Ibid., II:115.

18. Martin Luther, *Lectures on Genesis*, vol. I of *Luther's Works* (St. Louis: Concordia, 1958), p. 49.

19. Langdon Gilkey, *Maker of Heaven and Earth* (Garden City, N.Y.: Doubleday, 1959), p. 285.

20. Theophilus, *Autolycus*, II: 4; cf. *Shepherd of Hermes*, II:1; Tatian, *Address to the Greeks*, V; Irenaeus, *Against the Heresies*, II:10:4; Justin Martyr, *First Apology*, I:59; Origen, *On First Principles*, I:iii:3; II:i:4.

21. Irenaeus, *Against Heresies*, III:X:3; cf. Gilkey, *Maker of Heaven and Earth*, pp. 44-66.

22. John of Damascus, *Exposition of the Orthodox Faith*, I:vii.

23. Cf. Paul Tillich, *Systematic Theology*, 3 vol. (Chicago: University of Chicago Press, 1951–63), I:188f; and Jürgen Moltmann, *God in Creation* (San Francisco: Harper & Row, 1985), pp. 74 ff.

24. Fred Hoyle believes the Jewish and Christian religions have been outdated by modern science. He explains contemporary religious behavior as escapist, as pursued by people who seek an illusory security from the mysteries of the cosmos. *The Nature of the Universe* (New York: Mentor, 1950), p. 125. Cf. Ernan McMullin, "How Should Cosmology Relate to Theology?" in *The Sciences and Theology in the Twentieth Century*, ed. A. R. Peacocke (Notre Dame, Ind.: University of Notre Dame Press, 1981), pp. 32 ff.

25. Ian Barbour, *Issues in Science and Religion* (San Francisco: Harper & Row, 1966), p. 368. Barbour's line here separating science and religion looks quite like the one drawn by neoorthodoxy earlier this century, and he owns up to it, p. 414. More recently, however, Barbour has noted that increased evidence supporting Big Bang makes it—and *creatio ex nihilo* as well—increasingly attractive to the theologian. It is attractive because it draws out the theological meaning of contingency. Nevertheless, Barbour still does not want to associate *ex nihilo* with a beginning. See his essay elsewhere in this volume.

26. Thomas Aquinas, *Summa Theologica*, Pt. I: Q. 45: Art. 2. Thomas is concerned about the tension between the ideas of an eternal universe and a temporal universe. Eternity belongs to God, says Thomas, not to the creation. He argues that Aristotle could go either way, i.e., although the philosopher held that the world is eternal, it would not be contrary to Aristotle to accept a beginning to the world of finite time. Thomas accepts that we cannot prove rationally either that the world always existed or its opposite; so he contends that the Christian belief in a temporal beginning to creation must be based upon special revelation and faith.

27. Gilkey, *Maker of Heaven and Earth*, p. 70.

28. Barbour, *Issues in Science and Religion*, p. 384.

29. Ibid., p. 385.

30. Langdon Gilkey, *Message and Existence* (New York: Seabury, Crossroad, 1980), p. 90; cf. *Maker of Heaven and Earth*, p. 312; and Barbour, *Issues in Science and Religion*, p. 458.

31. Gordon Kaufman, *God the Problem* (Cambridge: Harvard University

Press, 1972), p. 137. For a similar position see Wolfhart Pannenberg, "Gott und die Natur," *Theologie und Philosophie* 58:4 (1983), pp. 481-500.

32. Stephen J. Gould, "Evolution as Fact and Theory," in *Discover* 2:5 (May 1982), p. 34; reprinted in *Hen's Teeth and Horses' Toes: Reflections in Natural History* (New York: W. W. Norton, 1983), p. 254.

33. Langdon Gilkey, "The Creationist Issue: A Theologian's View," in *Cosmology and Theology*, pp. 55-69. Cf. also Gilkey *Creationism on Trial: Evolution and God at Little Rock* (San Francisco: Harper & Row, 1985) and Conrad Hyers, *The Meaning of Creation* (Atlanta: John Knox Press, 1984), p. 12.

34. Duane T. Gish, *Evolution: The Fossils Say No!* (San Diego: Creation-Life Publishers, 1973), pp. 24 ff. Cf. Henry M. Morris, *The Remarkable Birth of Planet Earth* (Minneapolis: Bethany Fellowship, 1978), pp. vi ff.

35. Cf. Wolfhart Pannenberg, "On the Theology of Law," in his *Ethics*, trans. Keith Crim (Philadelphia: Westminster, 1981), p. 31.

36. Emil Brunner, *The Christian Doctrine of Creation and Redemption, Dogmatics II* (Philadelphia: Westminster, 1952), p. 25.

37. Edmund Schlink, *Ökumenische Dogmatik* (Göttingen: Vandenhoeck & Ruprecht, 1983), pp. 91-94.

38. McMullin, "How Should Cosmology Relate to Theology?" p. 39.

39. A. R. Peacocke, *Creation and the World of Science* (Oxford: Clarendon Press, 1979), p. 329. Not everyone is so pessimistic. Princeton physicist Freeman J. Dyson posits an open universe eschatology according to which life evolves from its present fleshly embodiment into an interstellar black cloud, and as the universe cools it slows its metabolism and adopts patterns of hibernation, thereby making it possible to gain an infinitely long subjective lifetime. "Time Without End: Physics and Biology in an Open Universe," *Review of Modern Physics* 51:3 (July 1979), pp. 447-60. Robert Russell would contend that theology and science do not speak separate languages and, therefore, Dyson's partial corroboration of the Christian vision is theologically significant.

40. Bertrand Russell, *Why I Am Not a Christian* (New York: Simon & Schuster, 1957), p. 107.

41. Clement, *Stromata*, V:1. Rudolf Bultman, *Kerygma and Myth* (New York: Harper & Row, 1961), p. 197.

42. Martin Luther, *Lectures on Genesis*, I:3-7.

43. Thomas Aquinas, *Summa Theologica*, Part I: Q:46: Art. 2.

44. Karl Barth, *Church Dogmatics* (Edinburgh: T. & T. Clark, 1958), III:i, p.3.

THREE

Creation and Cosmology

IAN G. BARBOUR

On Christmas Eve, 1968, the first astronauts in orbit around the moon appeared live on TV in millions of American homes. Frank Borman read the opening verses of Genesis:

> In the beginning God created the heavens and the earth. The earth was without form and void, and darkness was upon the face of the deep; and the Spirit of God was moving over the face of the waters.
>
> And God said, "Let there be light"; and there was light. (Gen. 1:1-3)

Borman's message concluded: "Greetings from the crew of Apollo 8. God bless all of you on the good earth." Those astronauts were the first people to see the beauty of the earth as a blue and white gem spinning in the vastness of space, and the reading from Genesis seemed an appropriate response. But how can the Genesis story be reconciled with the findings

---

This chapter was originally an address delivered to the Isthmus Institute in Dallas in 1985.

Ian G. Barbour, now retired, is professor emeritus at Carlton College. He is author of the landmark book which, for all practical purposes, has defined the discipline of theology and natural science, *Issues in Science and Religion* (San Francisco: Harper & Row, 1966).

of twentieth-century astronomy? What are the theological implications of recent cosmological theories?

The Big Bang

Theories in Astrophysics

Let us look first at the evidence from physical cosmology, the study of the physical structure of the cosmos as a whole.[1] In 1917, Wiliem de Sitter, working with Einstein's general relativity equations, found a solution that predicted *an expanding universe*. In 1929, Edwin Hubble, examining the "red shift" of light from distant nebulae, formulated Hubble's Law: the velocity of recession of a nebula is proportional to its distance from us. Space itself, not just objects in space, is everywhere expanding. Extrapolating backward in time, the universe seems to be expanding from a common origin about 15 billion years ago. In 1965, Arno Penzias and Robert Wilson discovered a faint background of microwaves coming from all directions in space. The spectrum of those waves corresponded very closely to the 3°K residual radiation which had been predicted from relativity theory. The radiation is the cosmic fireball's afterglow, cooled by its subsequent expansion.

Indirect evidence concerning the early moments of the Big Bang have come from both theoretical and experimental work in high-energy physics. Einstein himself spent his later years in an unsuccessful search for a unified theory that would integrate gravity with other physical forces. More recent research has moved closer to this goal.

There are *four basic physical forces:* (1) the electromagnetic force responsible for light and the behavior of charged particles, (2) the weak nuclear force responsible for radioactive decay, (3) the strong nuclear force which binds quarks together in protons and neutrons, and (4) the gravitational force evident in the long-distance attraction between masses. There have been several stages in the recent unification of these forces.

In 1967, Stephen Weinberg and Abdus Salam showed that the electromagnetic and weak forces could be unified within an *Electroweak Theory*. The theory predicted the existence of two massive particles, the W and Z bosons, which mediate between the two kinds of force. In 1983, Carlo Rubbia and co-workers found particles with the predicted properties of W bosons among the products of high-energy collisions in the CERN accelerator in Geneva.

There has been some progress in attempts to unite the electro-weak and strong forces in a *Grand Unified Theory* (GUT). The unification would be mediated by massive X-particles that could only exist at energies higher than those in any existing accelerator. However, the GUT theory implies that protons decay spontaneously, very slowly, rather than being stable as previously supposed. Physicists are trying to detect this extremely low level of proton decay with experiments in deep mines, designed to screen out other stray particles.

The final unification of gravity with the other three forces within one *Supersymmetry Theory* has appeared more difficult because there has been no successful quantum theory of gravity. But there has been recent excitement concerning *Superstring Theory*, which escapes the anomalies of previous attempts. The basic constituents would be incredibly massive tiny one-dimensional strings which can split or loop. With differing patterns of vibration and rotation, they can represent all known particles from quarks to electrons. The theory requires ten dimensions; six of these would somehow have to disappear to leave the four dimensions of space-time. There is no experimental evidence for strings; the energy required for their existence would be far beyond those in the laboratory, but it would have been present at the very earliest instants of the Big Bang.[2] Physicists have a strong commitment to simplicity, unity, and symmetry, which motivates the search for a unified theory even when direct experimentation is impossible.

Putting together the evidence from astronomy and high-

Figure 2

Time	Temp.	Transition	Era
15 billion years		(today)	
12 '' ''		Microscopic life	Life
10 '' ''		Planets formed	Planets
1 '' ''		Galaxies formed (also heavier elements)	Stars
5,000,000 years	2000	Atoms formed	Atoms
3 mins.	10^9	Nuclei formed (hydrogen, helium)	Nuclei (plasma)
10^{-4} sec.	10^{12}	Quarks to protons and neutrons	Protons, neutrons
10^{-10} '' ''	10^{15}	Weak and electro-magnetic forces separate	Quarks
10^{-35} '' ''	10^{28}	Strong nuclear forces separates	Electro-weak
10^{-43} '' ''	10^{32}	Gravitational force separates	Grand Unified Theory
(0	Infinite	Singularity)	Supersymmetry

energy physics, a plausible reconstruction of cosmic history can be made. Imagine a trip backward in time. Twelve billion years after the Big Bang, microscopic forms of life were beginning to appear on our planet. Ten billion years after the bang, the planet itself was formed. One billion years from the beginning, the galaxies and stars were coming into being. At $t = 500,000$ years, the constituent atoms appeared. A mere three minutes from the beginning, the nuclei were starting to form out of protons and neutrons. Plausible theories concerning these events can account for the relative abundance of hydrogen and helium, and for the formation of heavier chemical elements in the interior of stars (see Figure 2).[3]

The farther back we go before three minutes, the more tentative are the theories, because they deal with states of matter and energy further from anything we can duplicate in the laboratory. Protons and neutrons were probably forming from their constituent quarks at 10^{-4} seconds (a ten-thousandth of a second from the beginning), when the temperature had cooled to 10^{12} (a thousand billion) degrees. This fantastically dense sea of hot quarks had been formed at around 10^{-10} seconds from an even smaller and hotter fireball—which had expanded and cooled enough for the electro-weak forces to be distinguishable from the strong and gravitational forces.[4]

Before 10^{-35} seconds, the temperature was so high that all the forces except gravity were of comparable strength. This is the period to which a *Grand Unified Theory* would apply. We have almost no idea of events before 10^{-43} seconds, when the temperature was 10^{32} degrees. The whole universe was the size of an atom today, and the density was an incredible 10^{96} times that of water. At these very small dimensions, the Heisenberg uncertainties of quantum theory would have been significant, and all four forces were united. This would have been the era of Supersymmetry. I will return to examine some remarkable features of these early stages.

But what happened before that? At the time $t = 0$, was there a dimensionless point of pure radiation of infinite density? And how is that point to be accounted for? To the scientist, $t = 0$ is inaccessible. It appears as a "singularity" to which the laws of physics do not apply. It represents a kind of ultimate limit to scientific inquiry, something which can only be treated as a given, though one can speculate about it.

Theological Responses

How might theologians respond to these new theories in astrophysics? Should they rejoice that, after centuries of conflict between theologians and astronomers, there now seems to be a common ground in the idea that the universe had a beginning—a beginning that science cannot explain? Would it be appropriate to identify that point of radiation of infinite density with those words in Genesis, "Let there be light," since light, after all, is pure radiation?

Pope Pius XII welcomed the Big Bang theory as support for the idea of creation in time.[5] More recently, the astrophysicist Robert Jastrow has argued that "the astronomical evidence leads to a biblical view of the origin of the world." He ends his book, *God and the Astronomers,* with this striking passage:

> At this moment it seems as though science will never be able to raise the curtain on the mystery of creation. For the scientist who has lived by his faith in the power of reason, the story ends like a bad dream. He has scaled the mountains of ignorance; he is about to conquer the highest peak; as he pulls himself over the final rock, he is greeted by a band of theologians who have been sitting there for centuries.[6]

On the other hand, some contemporary theologians claim that theology has no stake in the debates among astronomers. Arthur Peacocke, for example, writes: "Theology is agnostic about the how of creation. . . . Whether the big bang wins out or not is irrelevant theologically."[7]

I want to start with a word of caution about identifying the religious idea of creation too closely with scientific ideas of cosmology. Later I will indicate some points at which I think contemporary cosmology is relevant to theology. One reason for caution is that in the past God has often been invoked to explain gaps in the prevailing scientific account. This has been a losing enterprise as one gap after another has been filled by the advance of science—first in the seventeenth-century astronomy and physics, then in the nineteenth-century geology and biology. The present case appears different because events at the time $t = 0$ seem to be in principle inaccessible to science. Yet this situation might conceivably change, for much of contemporary cosmology is tentative and speculative.

Thirty years ago, some astronomers thought they had avoided the problem of a beginning by postulating an infinite span of time. The *Steady State Theory* proposed that hydrogen atoms come into being, slowly and continuously, throughout an infinite time and space. Frederick Hoyle, in particular, defended the theory long after most of his colleagues had abandoned it. Hoyle's writings make clear that he favored the *Steady State Theory*, not just on scientific grounds, but partly because he thought infinite time was more compatible with his own atheistic beliefs.[8] But today Big Bang theories have clearly won the day.

However, it is possible to combine the Big Bang and infinite time if one assumes *an oscillating cosmos*. Before the present era of expansion there could have been an era of contraction—a Big Crunch before the Big Bang. Any evidence of past cycles would have to be indirect, since their structure would have been totally wiped out in the fireball. One would expect from the law of entropy that there could only have been a finite rather than an infinite number of oscillations, though under such conditions the applicability of the law is uncertain. Concerning the future of the cosmos, observations suggest that the velocity of expansion is very close to the critical threshold between expanding forever (an *open* universe) and expanding a long time before contracting again (a *closed* universe). There does not seem to be enough mass in the universe to reverse the expansion, but there may be additional mass not yet detected (in black holes, neutrinos, and interstellar matter, for instance).

There are some atheistic or agnostic astronomers who feel more comfortable with the idea of an infinite series of oscillations, just as there are some theists who welcome a beginning of time. But I would say it is equally impossible to imagine a beginning of time or an infinite span of time. Both are unlike anything we have experienced. Both start with an unexplained universe. I will argue that the choice of theories should be made on scientific grounds alone, and that the difference between them is only of secondary importance religiously. If a single, unique Big Bang continues to be the most convincing scientific theory, the theist can indeed see it as an instant of divine origination. But we must be clear that this is not the main concern expressed in the religious notion of creation.

Creation in Judaism and Christianity

Historical Ideas of Creation

Look again at the opening verses of Genesis:

In the beginning God created the heavens and the earth. The earth was without form and void; and darkness was upon the face of the deep; and the Spirit of God was moving over the face of the waters.

The relation between those first two sentences is not clear in the Hebrew, and the RSV Bible gives the alternative translation: "When God began to create the heavens and the earth, the earth was without form and void." Instead of creation from nothing, *ex nihilo*, there is the creation of *order from chaos*. Scholars see here an echo of the Babylonian creation story which also starts with a primeval watery chaos. There are several references elsewhere in the Bible to taming the waters and conquering the sea monster Rahab, which are also features of the Babylonian story (Isa. 51:9; Ps. 74:14; 89:10).

But clearly the biblical story differs from other ancient creation stories in its assertion of the sovereignty and transcendence of God and the dignity of humanity. Creation is orderly and deliberate, following a comprehensive plan and resulting in a harmonious and interdependent whole. God is portrayed as purposive and powerful, creating by Word alone.

In the Babylonian story, humanity was created to provide slaves for the gods; in Genesis, humanity was given a special status in God's plan, superior to the rest of creation.[9] The biblical narrative asserts the essential goodness and harmony of the created order. After each day, God saw that it was good; and after the sixth day, "God saw everything that he had made, and behold, it was very good" (Gen. 1:31a).

Most historical scholars hold that within the Hebrew scriptures the first chapter of Genesis is a relatively late writing, probably from the fifth century B.C. It appears that God was worshiped as the redeemer of Israel before being worshiped as the creator of the world. The Exodus and the covenant at Sinai were the formative events for Israel as a people. Early Israelite religion centered on God's act of liberation and revelation in history—that is, the creation of Israel. Von Rad argues that the Genesis story was of secondary importance, a kind of cosmic prologue to Israel's history, written to give the covenant faith a more universal context.[10]

Other writers, such as Westerman and Anderson, hold that creation was of considerable importance throughout the Hebrew Scriptures.[11] Challenged by the nature gods of surrounding cultures, the people of Israel asserted that Yahweh was both redeemer and creator. Several early Psalms celebrate Yahweh's enthronement as Creator and King (Pss. 47; 93; 99). Again, Psalm 19 expresses gratitude for *both* creation and revelation: "The heavens are telling the glory of God," but also, "The law of the Lord is perfect." Our "help comes from the Lord, who made heaven and earth" (Ps. 121:2). In Job, the voice from the whirlwind asks: "Where were you when I laid the foundations of the earth?" and goes on to portray with poetic power the wonders of the created order (Job 38–41). In the book of Proverbs, Wisdom is personified as God's agent in creation.

Many biblical phrases do refer to a primordial creation "in the beginning" (though not *ex nihilo*); they seem to imply that creation has been completed. But, as Jacob points out, "Other texts, generally more ancient, draw much less distinction between the creation and conservation of the world, and make it possible for us to speak of a *creatio continua*."[12] There is a recurring witness to God's continuing sovereignty over both history and nature. God is still creating through natural processes. "Thou dost cause the grass to grow for the cattle, and plants for man to cultivate. . . . When thou sendest forth thy Spirit, they are created" (Ps. 104:14, 30). Again, "Thou didst form my inward parts, thou didst knit me together in my mother's womb" (Ps. 139:13).

Isaiah gives the most powerful synthesis of creation and redemption, and he ties past, present, and future together. God is indeed the creator of Israel, but also of all humanity and all nature. Moreover, says Isaiah, God will in the future re-create a people out of the chaos of bondage and exile (Isa. 40; 45; 49). Here is the theme of a new creation, including a new harmony in nature, which is picked up in the later apocalyptic literature. The idea of creation thus pervades the Hebrew Scriptures; we do not have to rely on Genesis alone.

In the New Testament, too, creation is closely linked to redemption. The opening verses of John's Gospel recalls Genesis: "In the beginning was the Word, and the Word was with God. . . . all things were made through him." Here the term "Word" merges the *Logos*, the Greek principle of rationality, with the Hebrew image of God's Word active in the world. But John then links creation to revelation: "And the Word became flesh" (v. 14). In Christ's life and death, according to the early church, God had made known the purpose of creation. Paul, in his devotion to Christ, gives him a kind of cosmic role in several passages: "In him all things were created, in heaven and on earth. . . . He is before all things, and in him all things hold together" (Col. 1:16-17; cf. I Cor. 8:6; Heb. 1:2). The Spirit was understood as God's continuing presence in nature, in individual life, and in the gathered community.

The Nicene Creed (A.D. 381) refers to God as "maker of heaven and earth." The creed was important in the liturgical life of the church in affirming its identity and its commitment to God and Christ. The doctrine of creation was formulated more explicitly as part of the self-definition of the Christian community in relation to rival philosophies, especially in response to the challenge of Hellenistic dualism. The idea of *creatio ex nihilo*, creation out of nothing, was elaborated to exclude the gnostic teachings that matter is evil, the work of a lesser being, not the work of the God who redeems.

Against claims that preexisting matter limited God's creativity, *ex nihilo* asserted that God is the source of matter as well as of form. Against the gnostic disparagement of the material world, it asserted the goodness of the created order. Against pantheism, it asserted that the world is not divine or part of God, but is distinct from God. Against the idea that the world was an emanation of God, made of the divine substance and sharing its characteristics, it asserted that God is transcendent and essentially different from the world. All of these theological assertions are still important today, but I will argue that they can be made without specific reference to an absolute beginning.

By the fourth century, Augustine was willing to accept metaphorical or figurative interpretations of Genesis and said that it was not the intent of scripture to instruct us about such things as the form and shape of the heavens. "God did not wish to teach men things not relevant to their salvation." He held that creation is not an event in time; time was created along with the world. Creation is the timeless act through which time comes to be and the continuous act by which God preserves the world. When asked what God was doing before creating the world, Augustine replied that it is meaningless to ask what God was doing before creating the world, for there was no time prior to the creation.[13]

Thomas Aquinas accepted a beginning in time as part of scripture and tradition and said that creation in time helps make God's power evident. But he argued that a universe which had always existed would equally require God as creator and sustainer. All that is essential theologically could be stated without reference to a beginning or a singular event. To be sure, one of the versions of his cosmological argument did assume a beginning in time: every effect has a cause, which in turn is the effect of a previous cause, back to a First Cause that initiated the causal chain. But in another version, he asks, Why is there anything at all? He replies that the whole causal chain, whether finite or infinite, is dependent on God. God's priority is ontological rather than temporal.

Jaroslav Pelikan traces the subordination of continuing to instantaneous creation through the Middle Ages, the Reformation, and the Enlightenment. "Deism carried to its conclusion the definition of creation as the original establishment of the universe *ex nihilo*." God's priority in status had been equated with temporal priority. But Pelikan says the *continua* theme was always present, even when not prominent, from biblical to modern times, and he holds that it assumes great importance in considering evolution and contemporary science.[14] I will later suggest that astrophysics, along with geology and evolutionary biology, shows us a dynamic world with a long history of change and development and the appearance of novel forms. Coming-to-be is a continuing process throughout time, and it continues today. We can see the emergence of new forms as signs of God's creativity.

The Interpretation of Genesis Today

How then are we to understand the opening chapter of Genesis? A literal interpretation of the seven days would conflict with many fields of science. I believe that the attempt to find scientific information in Genesis is dubious theology as well as dubious science. By treating it as if it were a book of science ahead of its times, we tend to neglect both the human experiences that lie behind it and the theological affirmations it makes.

I would list the *human experiences* that lie behind the idea of creation as follows: (1) a sense of dependence, finitude, and contingency; (2) a response of wonder, trust, gratitude for life, and affirmation of the world; and (3) a recognition of interdependence, order, and beauty in the world. These were all part of the experience of the astronauts as they looked at the earth from the moon, and their reading of Genesis seems an appropriate expression of their response. The religious idea of creation starts from wonder and gratitude for life as a gift.

What are the basic *theological affirmations* in that chapter of Genesis? I would list the following: (1) the world is essentially good, orderly, coherent, and intelligible; (2) the world is dependent on God; and (3) God is sovereign, free, transcendent, and characterized by purpose and will. Note that these are all assertions about characteristics of God and the world in every moment of time, not statements about an event in the past. They express ontological rather than temporal relationships.[15]

The intent of the story was not to exclude any scientific account, but to exclude, in the first instance, the nature gods of the ancient world. In later history it stood against alternative philosophical schemes, such as pantheism, dualism, and the belief that the world and matter are either illusory or evil or ultimate. Against these alternatives it asserted that the created order is good, an interdependent whole, a community of being, but not the object of our worship. These theological affirmations were expressed in Genesis in terms of a pre-scientific cosmology that included a three-decker universe and creation in seven days. But the affirmations are not dependent on that cosmology or on any other cosmology. Reform and Conservative Judaism, the Roman Catholic Church, and most of the mainline Protestant denominations today maintain that we do not have to choose between theism and astronomy or evolutionary biology. We can look on the Big Bang and subsequent evolution as God's way of creating.[16]

But should we take a *beginning of time* literally, even if we do not interpret the seven days in Genesis literally? Here theologians are divided. For one thing, the biblical concept of finite linear time has contributed to the Western view of history. The West has differed from the ancient cultures and the Eastern religions which assumed an infinite succession of cycles; these cultures have generally evidenced less interest in historical development. But other theologians suggest that even a beginning of time is not crucial to the theological notion of creation. David Kelsey, for instance, says that the basic experience of gratitude for life as a gift has no essential connection with speculations about unique events at the beginning. Science and religion, he maintains, address different questions which should not be confused.[17]

Without denying the distinctive features of Genesis, we can note that creation stories in various cultures fulfill similar functions. They locate human life within a cosmic order. The interest in origins may be partly speculative or explanatory, but the main concern is to understand who we are in a framework of larger significance. Anthropologists and scholars of the world's religions have looked at a variety of creation stories and studied their function in the ordering of human experience in relation to a meaningful world. These stories provide patterns for human behavior, archetypes of authentic human life in accord with a universal order. They portray basic relationships between human life and the world of nature. Often they express structures of integration and creativity over against powers of disintegration and chaos.

There are various ways in which a religious community appropriates and participates in its sacred stories. Often the stories are symbolized or enacted in rituals. Frederick Streng speaks of the passing on from one generation to another of stories that "manifest the essential structure of reality." Mircea Eliade says that exemplary patterns in primordial time are made present in ritual and liturgy.[18] Consider an example from the traditional Jewish morning prayer that uses the present tense:

> Praised are You, O Lord our God, King of the universe.
> You fix the cycles of light and darkness;
> You ordain the order of all creation. . . .
> In Your goodness the work of creation
> Is continually renewed day by day.[19]

The prayer goes on to express gratitude for the world and the gift of life, continuing into the present. The Statement of Faith of the United Church of Christ also uses the present tense: "We believe in God. . . . You call the worlds into being, create persons in your own image, and set before each one the ways of life and death."

Or consider the prayer in one of the communion services in the Episcopal prayer book. These lines could not have been written before the space age, yet they express traditional themes. The celebrant (C) is at the altar and the people (P) respond:

C: God of all power, Ruler of the Universe, you are worthy of glory and praise.
P: *Glory to you for ever and ever.*
C: At your command all things came to be: the vast expanse of interstellar space, galaxies, suns, the planets in their courses, and this fragile earth, our island home.
P: *By your will they were created and have their being.*
C: From the primal elements you brought forth the human race, and blessed us with memory, reason, and skill. You made us the rulers of creation. But we turned against you, and betrayed your trust; and we turned against one another.
P: *Have mercy, Lord, for we are sinners in your sight.*[20]

Here again the focus is on the significance of human life in relation to God and the world. That is what is important religiously.

The New Cosmology

So far I have been emphasizing that the religious idea of creation is not dependent on particular physical cosmologies, ancient or modern. I turn now to examine several features of recent astrophysics that raise some interesting questions concerning design, chance, and necessity. The general character of the argument can be followed, even if the details are somewhat technical. The final section will then consider the theological implications of these ideas.

Design: The Anthropic Principle

In the traditional argument from design, it was claimed that both biological forms and the physical conditions favorable for life must be the product of an intelligent designer because it is inconceivably improbable that they could have occurred by chance. Even before Darwin, Hume and other critics replied that when we have only one case (one universe) from which to judge, we cannot make judgments of probability. But the argument from design has been revived by recent cosmologists who compare our universe with the set of *possible* universes allowed by the laws of physics.

A striking feature of the new cosmological theories is that even a small change in the physical constants would have resulted in an uninhabitable universe. Among the many possible universes consistent with Einstein's equations, ours is one of the few in which the arbitrary parameters are right for the existence of anything resembling organic life. Thus Carr and Rees conclude that the possibility of life as we know it "depends on the value of a few basic constants" and is "remarkably sensitive to them."[21] Among these fine-tuned phenomena are the following:

1. The expansion rate. If the early rate of expansion had been less by even one part in a thousand billion, the universe would have collapsed again before temperatures had fallen below 10,000 degrees. On the other hand, if the rate had been greater by a part in a million, the universe would have expanded too rapidly for stars and planets to form. The expansion rate itself depends on many factors, such as the initial explosive energy, the mass of the universe, and the strength of gravitational forces.[22] The cosmos seems to be balanced on a knife-edge.

2. The formation of the elements. If the strong nuclear force were even slightly weaker we would have only hydrogen in the universe. If the force were even slightly stronger, all the hydrogen would have been converted to helium. In either case, stable stars and compounds such as water could not have been formed. Again, the nuclear force is only barely sufficient for carbon to form; yet if it had been slightly stronger, the carbon would all have been converted into oxygen. There are of course many other special properties of particular elements, such as carbon, which are crucial to the later development of organic life as we know it.[23]

3. *The particle/antiparticle ratio*. For every billion antiprotons in the early universe, there were one-billion-and-one protons. The billion pairs annihilated one another to produce radiation, with just one proton left over. A greater or smaller number of survivors—or no survivors at all if they had been evenly matched—would have made our kind of material world impossible. The laws of physics seem to be symmetrical between particles and antiparticles; why was there a tiny asymmetry?[24]

One could list other unexplained "remarkable coincidences," such as the fact that the universe is homogeneous and isotropic. The simultaneous occurrence of many independent improbable features appears wildly improbable. Reflection on the way the universe seems to be fine-tuned for intelligent life led the cosmologists Dicke and Carter to formulate the Anthropic Principle: "What we can expect to observe must be restricted by the conditions necessary for our presence as observers."[25] The principle does underscore the importance of the observer, to which quantum theory also testifies. But it does not in itself provide any causal explanation of those conditions. However, this fine-tuning could be taken as an argument for the existence of a designer, perhaps a God with an interest in conscious life.

Some physicists see evidence of design in the early universe. Stephen Hawking, for example, writes: "The odds against a universe like ours emerging out of something like the Big Bang are enormous. I think there are clearly religious implications."[26] And Freeman Dyson, in a chapter entitled "The Argument from Design," gives a number of examples of "numerical accidents that seem to conspire to make the universe habitable." He concludes: "The more I examine the universe and the details of its architecture, the more evidence I find that the universe in some sense must have known we were coming."[27]

Chance: Many-Worlds Theories

One way of explaining the apparent design in these "remarkable coincidences" is to suggest that there were many worlds existing either successively or simultaneously. If there were billions of worlds with differing constants, it would not be surprising if by chance one of them happened to have constants just right for our forms of life. That which is highly improbable in one world might be probable among a large enough set of worlds. There are several ways in which many worlds could occur:

1. *Successive cycles of an oscillating universe.* Wheeler and others suggest that the universe is reprocessed in each Big Crunch before the next Big Bang. The universe and all its structures are completely melted down and make a new start as it expands and cools again. In the quantum uncertainties entailed by those very small dimensions there are indeterminate possibilities. If the constants vary at random in successive cycles, our particular combination will eventually come up by chance, like the winning combination on a Las Vegas slot machine. As indicated earlier, present evidence does not favor cyclic theories, but they cannot be ruled out.

2. *Multiple isolated domains.* Instead of multiple bangs in successive cycles, a single Big Bang might have produced multiple domains existing simultaneously. The domains would be like separately expanding bubbles isolated from one another because their velocity of separation prevents communication even at the speed of light. The universe might have frozen into many domains with different constants or even laws.[28] Some of the new inflationary models of the universe involve infinite time and regions very different from ours, beyond our horizon of possible observation. Perhaps this just happens to be one of the few regions in which life could be present.

3. *Many-worlds quantum theory.* If one has a particular atomic or subatomic system in the laboratory, quantum theory cannot predict exactly what will happen. One can only calculate the probability of various possible outcomes. Everett and others proposed that every time there are such alternative quantum potentialities, the universe splits into several branches.[29] This interpretation of quantum theory involves a mind-boggling multiplicity of worlds, since each world would have to split again into many branches during each of the

myriad atomic and subatomic events throughout time and space. But being mind-boggling is not enough to disqualify an idea, though this proposal violates Occam's Razor with a vengeance. More to the point, it seems to be inherently unverifiable, since there could be no communication between the various branching worlds.

4. Quantum vacuum fluctuations. A strange feature of quantum theory is that it permits brief violations of the law of conservation of energy. It is permissible for a system's energy to go into debt, if the debt is rapidly paid back—so rapidly that it could never be detected within the limits of the uncertainty principle. This means that empty space, a vacuum, is really a sea of activity in which pairs of virtual particles are produced and almost immediately annihilate one another again. Since the magnitude of the allowable energy debt is inversely proportional to the repayment time, the energy needed to create a universe could be borrowed only for a fantastically brief instant, but conceivably this could get things going. Moreover, the energy needed might be small or even zero if the negative gravitational energy is taken into account.

All four of these theories—many cycles, many domains, many quantum worlds, or many quantum fluctuations—would allow us to explain the combination of constants favorable to life as a chance occurrence among a set of worlds most of which would be lifeless. John Leslie has argued that the God-hypothesis is simpler and more plausible as an explanation of the fine-tuning than these many-worlds hypotheses.[30] These theories, he says, are all ad hoc and unsupported by any independent evidence, whereas there are other kinds of evidence to which one can appeal in support of belief in God. Note that Leslie assumes here that God and chance are mutually exclusive hypotheses.

I suggest, however, that one could interpret many-worlds hypotheses *theistically*. It is common for theologians to understand evolution as God's way of creating and to accept chance and the wastefulness of extinct species as part of this long process. One might similarly hold that God created many universes in order that life and thought would occur in this one. Admittedly, this gives chance an inordinately large role, and it involves a colossal waste and inefficiency if there are many lifeless universes. But then again, one might reply that for God neither space nor time is in short supply, so "efficiency" is a dubious criterion. In any case, the first three of these theories are highly speculative and have no experimental support. It is simpler, from the viewpoint of both science and theology, to assume that there has been only one world.

The *vacuum fluctuation theory* is also speculative, but it is consistent with the fact that the creation of virtual particles occurs in the laboratory. It has sometimes been viewed as a secular version of creation *ex nihilo*, because it starts with a vacuum, which is literally "nothing." Space and time would have come into existence along with the appearance of matter-energy in a random quantum fluctuation. However, this hypothesis is at the limits of our concepts and our imagination, since all our experiments with a vacuum are within an already existing space-time framework. How do we account for the situation in which a gigantic quantum fluctuation could have occurred?

Necessity: A Theory of Everything

We have tried to account for the value of parameters favorable to the emergence of life, first on the basis of design, and then on the basis of chance. But there is a third possibility: necessity. Perhaps the values of the constants, which appear arbitrary, are in fact dictated by a more basic structure of relationships. Perhaps there is a more fundamental theory that will show that the constants can only have the values that they have. In the history of science there have been many apparent coincidences or apparently arbitrary numbers which later received theoretical explanation.

We have seen that a *Grand Unified Theory* (GUT) offers the prospect of bringing the two nuclear forces and the electromagnetic force into a single theory. Such a theory would help us understand that momentary era, prior to the hot quark era, when these three forces were merged. The theory already suggests that the slight imbalance between particles and antiparticles may have arisen from a slight asymmetry in the decay processes of the X and the anti-X bosons (the heavy particles that mediate the unified force of the GUT theory).

There are also promising new *inflationary theories* that may explain why the present expansion rate is so close to the critical balance between an open and a closed universe (the so-called flatness problem). Inflationary theories could also explain why the microwave radiation is isotropic (arriving equally from all directions). These theories entail a rapid expansion at around 10^{-35} seconds, due to the tremendous energy released in the breaking of symmetry when the strong force separated out. Before inflation, the universe would have been so small that its parts could have been in communication and thus could have achieved thermal equilibrium, which would account for its later homogeneity over vast distances.[31]

Current theories are quite inadequate to deal with the even earlier period before 10^{-43} seconds when the temperature would have been so high that the fourth force, gravity, would have been united with the other three. The hope is to develop theories of *Supersymmetry* or *Supergravity* that would provide a quantum theory of gravity. We saw that String Theory, in particular, may bring these diverse phenomena together. Because it would unite all the basic physical forces, it has been referred to as a Theory of Everything (TOE). Perhaps the whole cosmos can be derived from one simple and all-inclusive equation. Such a theory has been called the Holy Grail of the current quest in physics.

Successful GUT and TOE theories would seem to undermine the argument from design in the early universe. Perhaps self-consistency and fundamental laws will show that there is only one possible universe, i.e., that it is *necessary* and not contingent. I would reply that such theories would only push the argument back a stage. For it is all the more remarkable if a highly abstract physical theory, which itself has absolutely nothing to say about life, turns out to describe structures that have the potential for developing into life. The theist could welcome this as part of God's design. Such an orderly universe seems to display a grander design than a universe of chance. A theory that starts with a superlaw and a singularity would leave unanswered the question, Why that superlaw and that singularity? And why the laws of logic that end with such amazing consequences? Can a TOE ever explain itself, or how it comes to be instantiated in the real world?

In physics, moreover, predictions can be made only from a combination of *universal laws* and *contingent boundary conditions* (particular initial conditions). From universal premises alone one cannot derive conclusions about particulars. To be sure, there are some situations in which an outcome is indifferent to the boundary conditions; paths from diverse initial states may converge to the same unique final state (e.g., thermodynamic equilibrium). But there are other situations where paths diverge because chance enters at a variety of levels. Evolution must be described by a historical account of events and not by predictive laws alone. There would be contingent boundary conditions even if it turned out that time is infinite and there was no "beginning." At any point, however far back, there was a particular given situation which, along with laws and chance, affected the subsequent course of history.

Finally, it would be the ultimate in *reductionism* to expect that all events could be predicted from one basic principle. It would deny the emergence of new kinds of phenomena at higher levels of organization and activity in life, mind, and culture. The price of the simplicity and abstractness of an equation of physics is that it ignores the multiplicity and diversity of things in the world, from galaxies, apples, and robins, to human love. Perhaps *Hamlet* and Beethoven's Ninth could not exist without Supersymmetry, but they could hardly be predicted from it. Neither necessity nor chance can provide a total explanation of the world.

Theological Implications

Let us consider the theological implications of these cosmological considerations under four headings: (1) Intelligibility and Contingency, (2) *Ex nihilo* and Continuing Creation, (3) Models of Creation, and (4) The Significance of Humanity.

Intelligibility and Contingency

We have seen that the search for a unified theory is partly motivated by the conviction that the cosmos is rationally intelligible. Physicists must of course check their theories against experimental evidence, but they are convinced that a valid general theory will be conceptually simple and aesthetically beautiful. To the critical realist, simplicity in our theories reflects a simplicity in the world and not just in our minds. Einstein said that the only thing that is incomprehensible about the world is that it is comprehensible.

Historically, the conviction that the cosmos is unified and intelligible has both Greek and biblical roots. The Greeks, and the Stoics in the Roman world, saw the universe as a single system; this unitary assumption was also implied by the biblical belief in one God. The Greek philosophers had great confidence in the power of reason, and it is not surprising that they made significant progress in mathematics and geometry. But historians have claimed that the biblical doctrine of creation made a distinctive contribution to the rise of experimental science because it combined the ideas of *rationality* and *contingency*. If God is rational, the world is orderly; but if God is also free, the world did not have to have the particular order that it has. The world can then only be understood by observing it—rather than by deducing its order from necessary first principles, as the Greeks tried to do.[32] The church fathers said that God voluntarily created form as well as matter *ex nihilo*, rather than imposing preexisting eternal forms on matter.

Thomas Torrance has written extensively on the theme of *"contingent order."* He stresses God's freedom in creating as an act of voluntary choice. God alone is necessary, and both the existence and the structure of the world are contingent in the sense that they might not have been. The world might have been differently ordered. We can discover its order only by observation. Moreover, the world can be studied on its own because in being created it has its own independent reality, distinct from the transcendent God. Science can legitimately assume a "methodological secularism" in its work, while the theologian can still assert that the world is ultimately dependent on God.[33]

Einstein, on the other hand, saw any contingency as a threat to belief in the *rationality* of the world, which he said is central in science. "A conviction, akin to religious feeling, of the rationality or intelligibility of the world lies behind all scientific work of a high order."[34] He spoke of a "cosmic religious sense" and "a deep faith in the rationality of the world." He rejected the idea of a personal God who arbitrarily interferes in the course of events. He subscribed to a form of pantheism, identifying God with the orderly structure itself. When asked if he believed in God, he replied: "I believe in Spinoza's God, who reveals himself in the orderly harmony of what exists."[35] Einstein equated rationality with orderliness and determinism; he never abandoned his conviction that the uncertainties of quantum theory only reflect temporary human ignorance which will be left behind when the deterministic underlying mechanisms are discovered. He was mainly concerned about the necessity of events, but he also thought that the laws of physics are necessary. In a similar vein, Geoffrey Chew holds that all the laws of physics will be uniquely derivable from the requirement of self-consistency alone.[36]

The physicist James Trefil describes the search for unified laws in cosmology, and in an Epilogue writes:

> But who created those laws? . . . Who made the laws of logic? . . . No matter how far the boundaries are pushed back, there will always be room both for religious faith and a religious interpretation of the physical world. For myself, I

feel much more comfortable with the concept of a God who is clever enough to devise the laws of physics that make the existence of our marvelous universe inevitable than I do with the old-fashioned God who had to make it all, laboriously, piece by piece.[37]

Here the assumption seems to be that of deism rather than pantheism: the laws of physics are contingent but events governed by those laws are "inevitable."

John Polkinghorne, physicist and theologian, discusses the intelligibility of the world in a theistic framework. The key to understanding the physical world is mathematics, an invention of the human mind. The fit between reason in our minds and in the world would be expected if the world is the creation of mind. God, in short, is the common ground of rationality in our minds and in the world. Orderliness can also be understood as God's faithfulness, but it does not exclude an important role for chance. Polkinghorne invokes the early Christian concept of *Logos* which combines the Greek idea of a rational ordering principle and the Hebrew idea of the active Word of God. He maintains that the theist can account for the intelligibility that the scientist assumes.[38]

Robert Russell makes a helpful distinction between global, nomological, and local contingency.[39] In the light of my earlier discussion of cosmology, I suggest a fourfold distinction:

1. Contingent existence. Why is there anything at all? This is the question of greatest interest to theologians. The existence of the cosmos as a whole is not self-explanatory, regardless of whether it is finite or infinite in time. The details of particular scientific cosmologies are irrelevant to the contingency of the existence of the world.

2. Contingent boundary conditions. If there was a beginning, it was a singularity to which the laws of physics do not apply, and as such it cannot be scientifically explained. If time is infinite, there would be no beginning, but at any point in time, no matter how far back, one would have to postulate a particular state of affairs, treating it as a given. Later events are always explained in terms of general laws and some particular set of earlier conditions, not in terms of laws alone.

3. Contingent laws. Many of the laws of cosmology appear to be arbitrary. The particular fine-tuned constants that made life and thought possible seem to be inexplicable coincidences. But many of them may turn out to be necessary implications of more fundamental theories. If a Theory of Everything is found, however, it will itself be contingent. Insofar as it is required by laws of logic (e.g., two-valued logic), those laws reflect axioms that are not necessary in any absolute sense. Moreover, there are laws applicable to higher emergent levels of life and mind that are not derivable from the laws of physics. Such higher laws would only be instantiated with the novel occurrence of the phenomena that they describe.

4. Contingent events. To the critical realist, uncertainty in quantum physics reflects indeterminacy in the world and not simply the limitations of our knowledge. (Similar contingency is present in random bifurcations in non-equilibrium thermodynamics, random mutations in evolution, and freedom in human life.) We have seen that quantum phenomena were crucial in the very early history of the Big Bang. The cosmos is a unique and irreversible sequence of events. Our account of it must take an historical form, rather than consisting of general laws alone. In many-worlds theories the scope of chance is much wider, but none of these theories at the moment seems plausible. But cosmology is a young science, and it is too early to know what balance between chance and law its new theories will reflect.

Of course, many scientists today are atheists or agnostics and confine themselves to strictly scientific questions. Yet wider reflection on cosmology seems to be an important way of raising what David Tracy calls "limit questions."[40] At the personal level, cosmologists often express a sense of mystery and awe at the power unleashed in the Big Bang, and the occurrence of phenomena at the limits of our experience, language, and thought. If there was an initial singularity, it appears to be inaccessible to science. At the philosophical level, cosmology encourages the examination of our presuppositions about time and space, law and chance, necessity and contingency. Above all, the intelligibility of the cosmos suggests questions that arise in science but cannot be answered within science itself.

Ex Nihilo and Continuing Creation

The Anthropic Principle does not provide a conclusive argument from design. Nor is the Big Bang direct evidence for the doctrine of creation. In the Christian community, belief in God rests primarily on the historical witness to redemption in the covenant with Israel and the person of Christ, and on the personal experience of healing and renewal. The doctrine of creation represents the extension of these ideas of redemption to the world of nature. It also expresses the experience of wonder, dependence on God, gratitude for life as a gift, and recognition of interdependence, order and novelty in the world.

But if the theological doctrine of creation is not derived from scientific cosmology, are the two sets of ideas in any way related? Ernan McMullin holds that between creation and cosmology there is no direct implication, but the Christian must seek "coherence" and "consonance":

> He has to aim for some sort of coherence to which science and theology, and indeed many other sorts of human construction, like history, politics and literature, must contribute. He may, indeed *must*, strive to make his theology and his cosmology consonant in the contributions they make to this world-view. But this consonance (as history shows) is a tentative relation, constantly under scrutiny, in constant slight shift.[41]

As possible examples of consonance, I suggest parallels with the four kinds of contingency mentioned earlier. The first two are related to *ex nihilo*, the third and fourth to continuing creation.

1. The contingency of existence corresponds to the central religious meaning of creation *ex nihilo*. On both sides the basic assertions can be detached from the assumption of an absolute beginning. On the scientific side, it now appears likely that the Big Bang was indeed an absolute beginning, a singular event, but we cannot rule out the possibility of a cyclic universe or infinite time. On the theological side, we have seen that

Genesis portrays the creation of order from chaos, and that the *ex nihilo* doctrine was formulated later by the church fathers to defend theism against an ultimate dualism or a monistic pantheism. We still need to defend theism against alternative philosophies, but we can do so without reference to an absolute beginning.

With respect to the central meaning of creation *ex nihilo* (though not with respect to continuing creation) I agree with the neo-orthodox and existentialist authors who say that it is the sheer *existence* of the universe that is the datum of theology and that the details of scientific cosmology are irrelevant here. The message of creation *ex nihilo* applies to the whole of the cosmos at every moment, regardless of questions about its beginning or its detailed structure and history. It is an ontological and not a historical assertion.

In terms of human experience, *ex nihilo* expresses the sense of wonder and mystery typical of numinous experience—and sometimes experienced by astronomers in reflecting on the cosmos. In its theological articulation, *ex nihilo* has served to assert the transcendence, power, freedom, and purposefulness of God and to express our dependence on God. It also expresses the eternal aspect of God as beyond time and related equally to every point in time. I believe these attributes must be expressed theologically. However, I think classical theism overemphasized transcendence and power; God was understood as the omnipotent sovereign who predestined all events, and other biblical themes were neglected.[42]

2. The contingency of boundary conditions also expresses the message of *ex nihilo* without requiring an absolute beginning. If it turns out that past time was finite, there was indeed a singularity at the beginning, inaccessible to science. Such a beginning was assumed by the church fathers in the classical *ex nihilo* doctrine, even though it was not their chief concern. As Aquinas said, such a beginning would provide an impressive example of dependence on God. On the other hand, if time was infinite, we would still have contingent boundary conditions; scientists could not avoid dealing with situations or states that they would have to treat as givens. In neither case could it be said that our particular universe was necessary.

3. *The contingency of laws* can be identified with the orderly aspect of *continuing creation*. Traditionally, creation has been identified with the provision of *order*. Such order, it was assumed, was introduced at the beginning, though it had to be continually sustained by God. By the eighteenth century, the order of nature seemed to be all-embracing, mechanical, and self-sustaining. In deism, God's role was simply to design and start the mechanism. But now we know that the history of the cosmos involves both law and chance, both structure and novelty. Here the findings of science are indeed relevant, though I suggest we should consider only the broadest and most well-established features of the world disclosed by science, not its narrower or more speculative theories.

The laws applicable to emergent higher levels of reality are not reducible to laws governing lower levels. New and more complex forms of order have emerged in successive eras. Life and mind would not be possible without these underlying structures which go back to the early cosmos, but they cannot be explained by the laws of physics. But cosmology adds its own grounds for wonder at the order, intelligibility, and aesthetic simplicity of the universe. We can still say that this order is not necessary and can only be understood by observing it.

4. *The contingency of events* corresponds to the novel aspect of *continuing creation*. We can no longer assume the static universe of the Middle Ages, in which the basic forms of all beings were thought to be unchanging. Coming-to-be is a continuing process throughout time, and it continues today. Nature in all its forms must be viewed historically. Here astrophysics adds its testimony to that of evolutionary biology and other fields of science. Time is irreversible and genuine novelty appears in cosmic history. It is a dynamic world with a long story of change and development.

On the theological side, continuing creation expresses the theme of God's *immanence* and *participation* in the ongoing world. God builds on what is already there, and each successive level of reality requires the structures of lower levels. Here I find the insights of process theology particularly helpful. For

Alfred North Whitehead and his followers, God is the source of both order and novelty. This is one of the few schools of thought that takes seriously the contingency of events, from indeterminacy in physics to the freedom of human beings. In this "dipolar" view, God is both eternal and temporal: eternal in character and purpose, but temporal in being affected by interaction with the world. God's knowledge of the world changes as unpredictable events occur.[43]

The God of process thought is neither omnipotent nor powerless. Creation occurs throughout time and in the midst of other entities. God does not predetermine or control the world, but participates in it at all levels to orchestrate the spontaneity of all beings, in order to achieve a richer coherence. God does not act directly, and nothing that happens is God's act alone; instead, God acts along with other causes and influences the creatures to act. God does not intervene sporadically from outside, but rather is present in the unfolding of every event. Creative potentialities are actualized by each being in the world, in response both to God and to other beings. The process view emphasizes divine immanence, but it by no means leaves out transcendence. If it is carefully articulated, I believe that it can express the ideas that in the past have been represented by both the *ex nihilo* and the continuing creation themes. It is along such lines that I am exploring a theology of creation that can be related to various fields of science in addition to cosmology.[44]

Models of Creation

Compared to abstract theological doctrines, models are less conceptually precise, but are more powerful in personal religious life and communal liturgy.[45] In the Bible itself there is a variety of models of God as creator. Sometimes God is imaged as a potter or a craftsman making an artifact, or an architect laying out the foundations of a building. In other passages God is referred to as father, and in a few instances in a maternal role. The analogy is usually drawn from a parent nurturing a growing child, but occasionally it is drawn from a parent's role in procreation or birth. Again, the world is breathed forth by God's life-giving Spirit. It is also a manifestation of God's Word, or an expression of divine Wisdom which communicates meaning. Here is a rich diversity of models, each a partial and limited analogy, highlighting imaginatively a particular way of looking at God's relation to the world.

The potter and craftsman analogies assume the production of a completed product; they are less helpful today in thinking of an ongoing process. But the analogies of sustaining spirit and communicative word can readily express the idea of continuing creation. The analogy of the nurturing parent and the growing child seems particularly appropriate; the wise parent allows for an increasing freedom and independence in the child, but also offers parental love, encouragement, and guidance. Such an image reflects a balance between what our culture thinks of as masculine and feminine qualities, in contrast to the heavily "masculine" monarchial model of omnipotence and sovereignty.[46]

Among contemporary theologians, Conrad Hyers has asked what models of creation are compatible with a world of order and chance. He suggests that the combination of intention and unpredictability in an artist's interaction with a medium provides an apt analogy. Again, God is like a poet or dramatist in whose work there is both plan and surprise, or like the writer of a novel whose plot shows both coherent unity and the novelty of the unexpected.[47]

Peacocke speaks of God as the choreographer of a dance or the composer of a still unfinished symphony, experimenting and improvising and expanding on a theme and variations. He also suggests that God is to world as mind is to body. If the world is God's body, we could look on its activity as the action of an agent expressing intentions. The nexus of events, says Peacocke, is itself God's creative action. God is creating in every moment in and through the creativity of the world.[48] This is indeed a promising model, but can it represent the pluralism and partial independence of individual beings in the world? Does the world have as much unity and coordination as the body of an organism? Perhaps the social model of process thought is better able to preserve the separate identity of both God and individual creatures along with a recognition of their interdependence and relatedness.

In another analogy, Peacocke says that chance is like God's radar beam sweeping through the diverse potentialities that are invisibly present in each configuration in the world. Chance is a way of exploring the range of potential forms of matter. God has endowed the stuff of the world with creative potentialities that are successively disclosed. The actualization of these potentialities can only occur when suitable conditions are present. Events occur not according to a predetermined plan but with unpredictable novelty; God is experimenting and improvising in an open-ended process of continuing creation. I find this a helpful model, though I believe that the essentially social model of process philosophy can more readily be developed in metaphysical categories that allow both for God's action and the action of beings in the world.

The Significance of Humanity

We noted earlier that the function of creation stories is not primarily to explain events in the distant past, but to locate present human experience in a framework of larger significance. Creation stories manifest the essential structure of reality and our place in it. They provide archetypes of authentic human life in accord with a universal order. They are recalled and celebrated in liturgy and ritual because they tell us who we are and how we can live in a meaningful world.

Much of the resistance to Copernicus and Galileo arose because in their cosmologies the earth was no longer the center, but only one of several planets going around the sun. Darwin carried further the demotion of humanity from its central place in the cosmic scheme and seemed to challenge the biblical understanding of the significance of human life. What are the implications of modern cosmology for our self-understanding? Can they be reconciled with the message of the biblical creation story?

1. The immensity of space and time. Humanity seems insignificant in the midst of such vast stretches of time and space. But today those immensities do not seem inappropriate. We now know that it takes around 15 billion years for heavy elements to be cooked in the interior of stars and then scattered to form a second generation of stars with planets, followed by the evolution of life and consciousness. A very old expanding universe has to be a huge universe—on the order of 15 billion light years. Moreover, as Teilhard de Chardin pointed out, we should not measure significance by size and duration, but by such criteria as complexity and consciousness.[49] The greatest complexity has apparently been achieved in the middle range of size, not at atomic or galactic dimensions. There are a thousand billion synapses in a human brain; the number of possible ways of connecting them is greater than the number of atoms in the universe. There is a higher level of organization and a greater richness of experience in a human being than in a thousand lifeless galaxies. It is human beings, after all, that reach out to understand that cosmic immensity.

2. Interdependence. Cosmology joins evolutionary biology, molecular biology, and ecology in showing the interdependence of all things. We are part of an ongoing community of being; we are kin to all creatures, past and present. From astrophysics we know about our indebtedness to a common legacy of physical events. The chemical elements in your hand and in your brain were forged in the furnaces of stars. The cosmos is all of a piece. It is multi-leveled; each new higher level was built on lower levels from the past. Humanity is the most advanced form of life of which we know, but it is fully a part of a wider process in space and time. The new view may undercut anthropocentric claims that set humanity completely apart from the rest of nature, but it by no means makes human life insignificant.

3. Life on other planets. Planets are so numerous that if even a small fraction of them are habitable, life could exist in many stellar systems. Most scientists are open to the possibility of intelligent life on relatively nearby galaxies, though biologists seem to consider it less likely than do astronomers or science fiction writers. But the possibility of beings superior to us, living in more advanced civilizations, is a further warning against anthropocentrism. It also calls into question exclusive claims concerning God's revelation in Christ. Here we can recall that even on our planet the work of the *Logos*, the Eternal Word, was not confined to its self-expression in Christ. If that Word is active in continuing creation throughout the cosmos, we can be confident that it will also have revealed itself as the power of redemption at other points in space and time, in ways appropriate to the forms of life existing there.

4. Chance and purpose. Traditionally, we said, God's purpose in creation was identified with order. An emphasis on God's sovereignty led to a determinism in which everything happens in accordance with a detailed divine plan. Any element of chance was viewed as a threat to God's total control. It is not surprising, then, that some scientists and philosophers who are impressed by the role of chance are led to reject theism. (Bertrand Russell, Jacques Monod, Stephen Jay Gould, and Stephen Weinberg, for example, view life as the accidental result of chance and assume that chance and theism are incompatible.) Whereas the appropriate response to design is gratitude and thanksgiving, the response to pure chance is despair and a sense of futility and cosmic alienation.

One possible answer is to say that God really controls all the events that appear to us to be chance—whether in quantum uncertainties, evolutionary mutations, or the accidents of human history. This would preserve divine determinism at a subtle level undetectable to science. But I would suggest that the presence of genuine chance is not incompatible with theism. We can see design in the whole process by which life came into being, with whatever combination of probabilistic and deterministic features the process had. Natural laws and chance may equally be instruments of God's intentions. There can be purpose without an exact predetermined plan.

There is also a contingency of events in personal life which each of us faces at the existential level. We are all vulnerable to unpredictable events: the actions of other people, natural catastrophes, illness, and, above all, death. Our freedom is always limited by events that we cannot control. We know the anxiety and insecurity of temporality and finitude. In the face of all such contingency, the gospel does not promise immunity from suffering or loss, but rather the courage to affirm life in spite of them and the confidence that God's love is with us in the midst of them.

We have been discussing cosmology only in relation to creation, past and present. The question of human meaning also involves the scientific understanding of the *future* of the cosmos and how it relates to religious ideas of *eschatology*. But this would take us into other issues beyond the scope of this essay.

To sum up, I think we can join the astronauts in celebrating the beauty of our amazing planet and in expressing gratitude for the gift of life. Standing under the stars at night, we can still experience wonder and awe. Now we know the cosmos has included stretches of space and time that we can hardly imagine. What sort of world is it in which those strange early states of matter and energy could be the forerunners of intelligent life? Within a theistic framework it is not surprising that there is intelligent life on earth; we can see here the work of a purposeful Creator. Theistic belief makes sense of this datum and a variety of other kinds of human experience, even if it offers no conclusive proof. We still ask, Why is there anything at all? Why are things the way they are? With the Psalmist of old we can say: "O Lord, how manifold are thy works! In wisdom hast thou made them all. . . . When thou sendest forth thy Spirit, they are created" (Ps. 104:24, 30).

NOTES

1. Readable general accounts of recent work in physical cosmology can be found in James Trefil, *The Moment of Creation* (New York: Charles Scribner's, 1983), and John Barrow and Joseph Silk, *The Left Hand of Creation* (New York: Basic Books, 1983).
2. Michael Green, "Superstrings," *Scientific American* 255 (September 1986), pp. 48-60; Mitchell Waldrop, "Strings as a Theory of Everything," *Science* 229 (1985), pp. 226-28.

3. For data in Table 1, see Trefil, *The Moment of Creation*, p. 34; Barrow and Silk, *The Left Hand of Creation*, pp. 86, 156.

4. Steven Weinberg, *The First Three Minutes* (New York: Basic Books, 1977).

5. Pope Pius XII, "Modern Science and the Existence of God," *The Catholic Mind*, March 1952, pp. 182-92.

6. Robert Jastrow, *God and the Astronomers* (New York: W. W. Norton, 1978), p. 116.

7. A. R. Peacocke, *Creation and the World of Science* (Oxford: Clarendon Press, 1979), chap. 2.

8. Fred Hoyle, *Ten Faces of the Universe* (San Francisco: W. H. Freeman, 1977).

9. Joan O'Brien and Wilfred Major, *In the Beginning: Creation Myths from Ancient Mesopotamia, Israel and Greece* (Chico, Calif.: Scholars Press, 1982).

10. Gerhard von Rad, *The Problem of the Hexateuch* (New York: McGraw-Hill, 1966), pp. 131-43.

11. Claus Westerman, *Creation* (Philadelphia: Fortress Press, 1974); *Creation in the Old Testament*, ed. Bernhard Anderson (Philadelphia: Fortress Press, 1984).

12. Edmund Jacob, *Theology of the Old Testament* (New York: Harper & Brothers, 1958), p. 139.

13. See Ernan McMullin, "How Should Cosmology Relate to Theology?" *The Sciences and Theology in the Twentieth Century*, ed. A. R. Peacocke (Notre Dame, Ind.: University of Notre Dame Press, 1981), pp. 19-21.

14. Jaroslav Pelikan, "Creation and Causality in the History of Christian Thought," *Journal of Religion* 40 (1960), p. 250. See also John Reumann, *Creation and New Creation* (Minneapolis: Augsburg, 1973), chap. 3.

15. Langdon Gilkey, *Maker of Heaven and Earth* (Garden City, N.Y.: Doubleday, 1959); also *Creationism on Trial* (Minneapolis: Winston Press, 1985), chap. 8.

16. See Ian G. Barbour, *Issues in Science and Religion* (Englewood Cliffs, N. J.: Prentice Hall, 1966), chap. 12.

17. David Kelsey, "Creatio Ex Nihilo," *Evolution and Creation*, ed. Ernan McMullin (Notre Dame, Ind.: University of Notre Dame Press, 1985).

18. Frederick Streng, *Understanding Religious Life*, 3rd ed. (Belmont, Calif.: Wadsworth, 1985); Mircea Eliade, *Myth and Reality* (New York: Harper & Row, 1963).

19. *Weekday Prayer Book* (New York: Rabbinical Assembly, 1962), p. 42.

20. *Book of Common Prayer* (New York: Seabury, 1977), p. 368.

21. B. J. Carr and M. J. Rees, "The Anthropic Principle and the Structure of the Physical World," *Nature* 278 (1979), pp. 605-12. See also John Barrow and Frank Tipler, *The Anthropic Cosmological Principle* (New York: Oxford University Press, 1986); George Gale, "The Anthropic Principle," *Scientific American* 245 (December 1981), pp. 154-71.

22. S. W. Hawking, "The Anisotropy of the Universe at Large Times," in *Confrontation of Cosmological Theories with Observational Data*, ed. M. S. Longair (Dordrecht, Holland: Reidel, 1974).

23. Carr and Rees, "The Anthropic Principle and the Structure of the Physical World."

24. Barrow and Silk, *The Left Hand of Creation*, p. 91; Paul Davies, *God and the New Physics* (New York: Simon & Schuster, 1983), p. 30.

25. B. Carter, "Large Number Coincidences and the Anthropic Principle in Cosmology," in Longair, ed., *Confrontation of Cosmological Theories with Observational Data*. See also Davies, *God and the New Physics*, chap. 12.

26. Stephen Hawking, quoted in John Boslough, *Stephen Hawking's Universe* (New York: William Morrow, 1985), p. 121.

27. Freeman Dyson, *Disturbing the Universe* (New York: Harper & Row, 1979), p. 250.

28. Weinberg, *The First Three Minutes*.

29. See P.C.W. Davies, *The Accidental Universe* (Cambridge: Cambridge University Press, 1982).

30. John Leslie, "Anthropic Principle, World Ensemble, Design," *American Philosophical Quarterly* 19 (1982), pp. 141-51; "Modern Cosmology and the Creation of Life," in McMullin, ed., *Evolution and Creation*.

31. Alan Guth and Paul Steinhardt, "The Inflationary Universe," *Scientific American* 250 (May 1984), pp. 116-28.

32. See Michael Foster, "The Christian Doctrine of Creation and the Rise of Modern Science," in Daniel O'Connor and Francis Oakley, *Creation: The Impact of an Idea* (New York: Charles Scribner's, 1969).

33. Thomas F. Torrance, *Divine and Contingent Order* (Oxford: Oxford University Press, 1981). See also Stanley L. Jaki, *The Road to Science and the Ways to God* (Chicago: University of Chicago Press, 1978).

34. Albert Einstein, *Ideas and Opinions* (London: Souvenir Press, 1973), p. 262.

35. Quoted in Robert Jastrow, *God and the Astronomers*, p. 28.

36. Geoffrey F. Chew, "Bootstrap: A Scientific Idea?" *Science* 161 (1968), pp. 762-65.

37. Trefil, *The Moment of Creation*, p. 223.

38. John Polkinghorne, *One World* (London: SPCK, 1986), pp. 45, 63, 98.

39. Robert John Russell, "Contingency in Physics and Cosmology: A Critique of the Theology of Wolfhart Pannenberg," *Zygon* 23 (1988), pp. 23-43.

40. David Tracy, *Blessed Rage to Order* (New York: Seabury, 1975), chap. 5.

41. Ernan McMullin, "How Should Cosmology Relate to Theology?" in Peacocke, ed., *The Sciences and Theology in the Twentieth Century*, p. 52.

42. See Ian G. Barbour, *Myths, Models and Paradigms* (New York: Harper & Row, 1974), chap. 8.

43. For an introduction to process thought, see John Cobb and David Griffin, *Process Theology: An Introductory Exposition* (Philadelphia: Westminster Press, 1976).

44. My first series of Gifford Lectures on "Religion in an Age of Science" is scheduled to be published in 1990 by Harper & Row, San Francisco.

45. See Barbour, *Myths, Models and Paradigms*, chap. 4.

46. Sallie McFague, *Models of God: Theology for an Ecological, Nuclear Age* (Philadelphia: Fortress Press, 1987).

47. Conrad Hyers, *The Meaning of Creation* (Atlanta: John Knox, 1984), chap. 8.

48. A. R. Peacocke, *Creation and the World of Science*, chaps. 2 and 3. Also his *Intimations of Reality* (Notre Dame, Ind.: University of Notre Dame Press, 1984), chap. 2.

49. Pierre Teilhard de Chardin, *The Phenomenon of Man* (New York: Harper & Brothers, 1959), pp. 226-28.

FOUR

The Doctrine of Creation and Modern Science

WOLFHART PANNENBERG

From the eighteenth century to the beginning of the twentieth century the relations between science and theology were marked by an increasing mutual alienation. In the course of this century, however, there has emerged a series of efforts to bridge the gulf that had developed. In England these efforts started as early as the second half of the last century, when there was an attempt to make a theologically positive evaluation of the doctrine of evolution in order to integrate it into a Christian vision of the world and of salvation-history. A considerable number of scientists, especially biologists, took part in these efforts, particularly in Britain and in America. Germany did not really participate in these efforts, although in the beginning of this century the remarkable Erlangen theologian Karl Beth did develop a similar approach in apologetics. Unfortunately, Beth has been largely forgotten. In Germany, the initiative to dialogue came from a number of

Wolfhart Pannenberg is a professor of systematic theology and director of the Ecumenical Institute at the University of Munich. He is author of numerous books and articles, including *Jesus—God and Man* (Westminster, 1968), *Theology and the Philosophy of Science* (Westminster, 1976), and *Anthropology in Theological Perspective* (Westminster, 1985).

A version of this essay appeared in *Zygon*, 23:1, March 1988, pp. 3-21.

leading physicists, beginning with Max Planck, but it did not take actual shape until the early postwar period. The dialogue was more difficult here because the concept of evolution was not used as a common denominator for both scientific and theological views.

Even to this day the history of the alienation between the natural sciences and theology has not been cleared up. Everywhere the systematic discussion of those substantial issues that resulted in the process of mutual alienation and that continued to be effective until the present day have rarely gotten off the ground. Part of the explanation of this failure may be the fact that not until the last decades has the discipline of the history of science provided results that make it possible to deal with these problems on the basis of sufficient information and a methodical procedure. I think here especially of the contributions of Max Jammer and Alexandre Koyre, of Mary Hesse and William Berkson as helpful examples.

Inertia as a Theological Problem

The reasons for the history of alienation between science and theology have to be looked for on both sides. In the beginning there was the fatal lack of appreciation by theology and church, not only on the Catholic, but also on the Protestant side, of the new doctrine of Copernicus. Both Martin Luther and Philip Melanchthon failed to realize the importance of Copernicus because of their reliance on the literal authority of the Bible. In one of his *Table Talks* in 1539 Luther said he would rather believe Holy Scripture that reports in the book of Joshua (10:12-13) that Joshua ordered the sun to stand still and not the earth.[1] This type of biblical fundamentalism and the resulting suspicion against the new astronomy continued in German Lutheran theology until the early eighteenth century. In the period of the Enlightenment, theologians tried to adapt the biblical seven-day scheme of creation to the new scientific picture of the natural world. But in the meantime other and even more fundamental problems had surfaced.

These problems emerged from drawing the consequences of

the new mechanical physics for understanding the basic relationship between God and world. Of special importance was the introduction of the principle of inertia. Already in the thought of Descartes this principle led to an emancipation of the natural processes from their dependence on God, although the general framework of Descartes' ideas on the creation of the world and on its need for continuous preservation by God was still quite traditional. Descartes' formulation of the principle of inertia stated that each part of natural matter tends to preserve its status as long as this is not changed by external factors. Such changes, however, can be initiated only by other parts of natural matter, i.e., by other bodies. The reason for this assumption was Descartes' concept of God. On the one hand he still considered it necessary to give a reason for the principle of inertia itself. Descartes did not yet take inertia simply as manifestation of a *vis insita*, a force of perseverance within the body itself, as Newton did later. Rather, Descartes took it to manifest the immutability of God, who—as far as he is concerned—preserves his creature in the same form in which he created it. The same principle of divine immutability, on the other hand, prevented Descartes from ascribing to God the changes that occur in the world of creation. All changes, therefore, had to be interpreted as resulting from the actions of other bodies, the presupposition of this being that bodies always are in some form of movement which they transfer upon one another by pressure and push. When the assumption that movement is intrinsic to the bodies themselves was combined with the principle of inertia, the need for the cooperation of God as first cause became superfluous in the explanation of natural processes.

Baruch Spinoza explicitly drew that consequence of the mechanical explanation of nature, and he protected it against theological suspicion by the argument that the independent functioning of the world's mechanism gives expression to the perfection of its divine author and of his work. In the early eighteenth century Protestant theologians realized the danger, however, that in this way God would be separated from the creation. J. F. Buddeus argued that in the final analysis this amounts to a denial of God's very existence, because God becomes superfluous.

It was the same reason that induced Isaac Newton to reject Descartes' reduction of movement to the concept of body and to replace it by his conception of force as *vis impressa*, as a force that may impress movements upon bodies even over great distances in space. But at this point, with his general conception of force, Newton was not successful, at least not in the judgment of his own age. Instead, the combination of Newton's interpretation of inertia in terms of a force that is inherent in bodies with the reduction of force to a body and to its mass contributed in a decisive way in the course of the eighteenth century to the removal of God from the explanation of nature.

The Concept of God as an Explanation of Nature?

Protestant theology since the early nineteenth century, in Germany at least, developed an attitude of resignation over against this development. In order to explain this fact, it is important to see that there were also theological reasons at work. The rapid development of historical-critical investigation of the biblical writings had dissolved the traditional understanding of the authority of the Bible based upon the divine inspiration of its wording. The biblical authors' conceptions of the order of nature came now to be interpreted as an expression of a primitive understanding of the natural order, as an expression of some archaic, "mythical" conception of the world, or even the perspective of cultic life, as found in the biblical seven-day scheme of creation. Therefore, as early as 1814 even a rather traditional theologian like Karl Gottlieb Bretschneider considered it "a lost effort to try a physical demonstration of the words of creation as reported by Moses."[2]

After that time, theological apologetics increasingly abstained from theological interpretation or criticism of the foundations of natural science and embarked on the unhappy strategy of looking for the gaps in the scientific explanation of nature. It was largely because of this strategy that Darwin's theory of evolution could be perceived and rejected as a fundamental challenge of faith in God. When the theory of evolution had come to prevail in the scientific world, many theologians in Germany withdrew to a position claiming an incomparability of the theological and the scientific descriptions of the world. This was quite contrary to the situation in England and in America, where an early breakthrough to a positive interpretation of natural evolution took place. The most remarkable example of the theological retreat from a discussion of the scientific description of nature was Karl Barth, who in the preface of his doctrine of creation in his *Church Dogmatics*[3] decided that in principle a theological doctrine of creation should not concern itself with scientific descriptions and results.

One may point to the work of Karl Heim as an example of a different attitude in German theology. Yet even Heim, for all his competence in conversations with scientists, was more concerned to relativize the level of scientific conceptualizing and description of nature *in toto* by presenting it as a form of thought, over against which theology represents a quite different form of thought. The two forms of thought are not "polarized" but, as Heim said, "superpolar." Therefore, even Heim did not really enter into a theological appropriation and critique of the conceptual foundations of natural science. In order to do so he would have needed a clear perception of the interrelations between the history of philosophy and the history of the formation of scientific conceptuality; and in this area he did not employ the necessary information. In positive contrast to Barth, nevertheless, Heim was aware of the fact that theological talk about God as creator (and, therefore, any talk about God) remains empty, if it is not relatable to the scientific description of nature.

In the modern world, scientific theories have achieved such a high degree of common recognition of validity that in public consciousness the primary, if not exclusive, competence for valid assertions about the reality of the world is attributed to the sciences. It is impossible to change this fact by mere decree. If theologians want to conceive of God as the creator of the real world, they cannot possibly bypass the scientific description of that world. Certainly, theological assertions concerning the world are not formulated on the same level with scientific hypotheses of natural law. Nevertheless, they have to be related to scientific reasoning. Whether this is possible or not must be discussed on the level of philosophical (or maybe theological) reflection on the assertions of the natural sciences. Of course it is possible to suspect that such a reflection may remain something secondary and arbitrary in comparison to the scientific statements themselves. It may be considered a form of thought that remains irrelevant on the level of the demonstration and validity of scientific hypotheses and theories. Positivistic philosophy of science used to describe the situation in such a way.

Now research in the history of science has suggested a different perspective. In contrast to other positivists, Karl Popper even in his earlier period admitted that metaphysical convictions of innovative scientists may belong to the subjective factors conditioning the formation of their scientific hypotheses and theories. Yet his former student William Berkson uses the history of field physics to show that certain metaphysical conceptions not only have individual importance but also accompany or even guide the development of entire branches of natural science. If this is so, the philosophical origin of scientific conceptuality can no longer be regarded as something external and irrelevant as far as the scientific theories themselves are concerned. Certainly, the demonstration of the scientific usefulness of such conceptualities and of their use in scientific formulas has to operate on a different level; but even so they remain dependent on the broader philosophical intuition from which they were derived. The interrelation of scientific and philosophical conceptuality determines the framework for a rational discussion of the question whether theological assertions about the *world as creation* are relatable to the scientific description of the natural world.

The rest of this chapter intends to suggest how the subject matter of the theological doctrine of creation implies that it is impossible to appropriate the scientific description of the world of nature in the way just indicated. It is not my intention, however, to discuss the claims of an alternative "creationist" science. I do not think that the creationists are really in a position to challenge the established theories of modern science. Theology has to relate to the science that presently exists rather than invent a different form of science for its own use.

Creation and Contingency

The traditional doctrine of creation distinguishes between creation as an act of God and creatures as the products of divine activity. In dealing with creation as an act of God the correspondence between creation, conservation, and the divine government of the world was discussed along with questions such as the meaning of the participation of Christ or the divine *Logos* and of the Holy Spirit in the work of creation. The theological treatment of the different creatures is traditionally concerned with the order of creation in the sequence of the divine production following more or less the biblical presentation of the work of creation taking place in a sequence of seven days. The attribution of certain creatures to a certain "day" of creation has been the dominant form in theological tradition of conceiving of an order of nature.

Obviously there are connections—not only correspondences but also differences—between the traditional theological account of the formation of the world and the scientific description of nature, especially with reference to the description of the different creatures and the sequence of their appearance or emergence. There are also such connections already with the theological doctrines of creation, conservation, and government of the world, and these raise fundamental questions regarding our understanding of the world. Therefore, the following considerations focus primarily on these issues.

In the first place the theological affirmation that the world of nature proceeds from an act of divine creation implies the claim that the existence of the world as a whole and of all its parts is contingent. The existence of the whole world is contingent in the sense that it need not be at all. It owes its existence to the free activity of divine creation. So does every single part of the world. In the second place, there is a close tie between this contingency and the structure of time insofar as the possibility of existence is tied to the future. The structural modes of reality are rooted in temporality.

Affirmations about the contingency of the world at large and of all its parts already imply a close connection between creation and conservation. The world was not simply put into existence once, at the beginning of all things, in such a way that it would have been left to its own afterward. Rather, every creature is in need of conservation of its existence in every moment; and such conservation is, according to theological tradition, nothing else but a continuous creation. This means that the act of creation did not take place only in the beginning. It occurs at every moment. Accordingly, in the traditional theological doctrine of creation the activity of every creature is dependent upon divine cooperation, a *concursus divinus*. There is no activity and no product of creative activity in the world without divine cooperation.

The divine activity operates without detriment to the contingency and immediacy of singular actions, which has been identified in the theological tradition with the idea of divine governance of the world. It is due to this divine government of creation that the sequence of contingent events and created forms takes the shape of a continuous process toward the divine goal of an ultimate completion and glorification of all creation.

The three aspects of conservation, concurrence, and government have been often taken together into the concept of divine providence. The difference, however, between the act of creation in the beginning and the activity of divine providence in the course of an already existing world, as well as further subdistinctions of the concept of providence itself, must not obscure the unity of divine action in all these respects.

This entire conception of God's creative activity was deeply challenged in the seventeenth century due to the introduction

of the principle of inertia. The German philosopher Hans
Blumenberg[4] has repeatedly put his finger on this remarkable
event, an event of far-reaching importance in the history of
modern times. The principle of inertia as formulated by
Descartes means that no longer is the continuous existence of
any given state of affairs in need of explanation, but only the
occurrence of any changes of this status. This principle does not
yet abolish the notion of a creation in the beginning, but a
continuous conservation of what once was created becomes
unnecessary. This consequence seems to be inevitable, if
inertia in contrast to Descartes is understood as a force of
self-preservation inherent in the body, a *vis insita*. On this
basis, a transcendent conservation *(Fremderhaltung)* of nature
becomes indeed superfluous. In a similar way the mechanical
interpretation of the changes occurring to the bodies in terms of
a transfer of movement renders the assumption of a divine
cooperation in the activities of the creatures superfluous. Thus
deism must be seen as the consequence of the introduction of
the principle of inertia in modern physics.

   In view of the historical importance of this development, any
contemporary discussion between theology and science should
focus in the first place on the question of what modern science,
and especially modern physics, can say about the contingency
of the universe as a whole and of every part in it. This is, of
course, a more general formulation of the basic issue inherent
in the affirmations of the dependence of the natural world on its
creation and conservation by God.

   A discussion of this question of contingency in natural
science took place at the Protestant Academy of Research at
Heidelberg during the 1960s. The subject was treated by way of
reflection on the character, range, and limits of scientific
language and especially on the correlation of law and
contingency. There was a resulting agreement to the effect that
each scientific hypothesis of law describes uniformities in the
behavior of the object of such affirmations. The object itself,
however, is contingently given in relation to its hypothetical
description as a case where the affirmed law obtains. This
element of contingency in the givenness of the object,

however, is usually not explicitly focused upon in scientific statements. The focus is rather on the uniformities that can be expressed in equations. It is accepted as fact that those uniformities occur in a substratum that is not exhausted by them.

On reflection, however, the applicability of scientific formulas to concrete cases of natural processes requires initial and marginal conditions that are contingent in relation to the uniformity affirmed in the equation as such. Also, the natural constants that become part of the equation are considered contingent factors. This means that the description of nature by hypothetical statements of natural law presupposes their material as contingently given. The scientific formulas do not focus on this contingency, therefore, because their intention is to formulate uniformities that occur in the natural phenomena, their contingency notwithstanding. This focusing on the aspect of law constitutes the specifically abstract character of a scientific description of natural processes.

If this consideration is correct, it yields far-reaching consequences: The scientific affirmations of law cannot be considered as complete and exhaustive descriptions of the natural processes. They are only approximations, although they may be more than sufficiently precise for most practical purposes. The connection between events admits, however, another form of description which does not focus on uniformities in abstraction from the unique and contingent sequence of singular events. Rather, it describes the kind of connection that is to be constituted in the course of the contingent sequence itself and that can be perceived, therefore, only at the end of the sequence in question. In the perspective of such a description, the sequence of events is not considered as exchangeable cases, where a common formula of law applies according to the scheme: "if A, then B." Rather, the sequence is here perceived as a historical sequence, as a unique and irreversible process.

The two descriptions do not necessarily relate to different kinds of processes. The same process admits the description of cases of general laws as well as the description of individual, historical sequences. The description of a sequence of events as a historical process may be less abstract than its scientific description; but it presupposes more information about the individual sequence and its phases, while the description of the same sequence as a case of general law presupposes a knowledge of other comparable processes.

In theological discourse—in distinction from scientific descriptions, with the possible exception of the discipline of natural history—the sequence of events is taken as a historical sequence. The preference of theology for historical presentation of reality is related to its interest in nature's contingency. This does not necessarily mean that theology should treat everything in a "narrative" form. Rather, much analytic and constructive reflection is necessary before the theologian can hope to tell the story of God's creation with any degree of plausibility. Even historical narration presupposes a prior reconstruction of the process the historian reports.

The particularity of theology in looking at the world as history also applies to the uniformities that occur in the course of natural processes and to the enduring forms of natural reality that emerge on the basis of such uniformities. In the theological perspective such uniformities, a substratum of the hypothesis of natural law, as well as the enduring forms of natural reality are considered as contingent in the same way as any single event. The laws of nature appear to the theologian as contingent products of the creative freedom of God. The unity of contingency and continuity in the creative activity of God as well as in its products is rooted, according to a theological interpretation of the world, in God's faithfulness. Although God's action is contingent and underivable in each singular moment, still it keeps a connection to what happened before, while the future form of manifestation of God's faithfulness remains unforeseeable.

Field and Spirit

The reflections on the interrelation of contingency and natural law provide only a very abstract and formal framework for the interpretation of scientific and theological statements about the world of nature. These considerations do not yet relate to the specific object of natural science. If one remembers the history of modern science, it is obvious that its theories have been related in the first place to the task of describing the movements and changes in natural phenomena. For this purpose modern physics developed the concepts of force and energy that act upon bodies and produce changes within them. By introducing the concept of force, Newton modified Descartes' interpretation of the changes in natural bodies as a result of movement. On the one hand, this modification broadened the concept of mass, so that the product of mass and acceleration now allows for the measurement of force; but, on the other hand, and above all, the basic concept of force itself took the general form of *vis impressa*. In contrast to Descartes, Newton took into account the possibility of immaterial forces that act in a way analogous to the activity of the soul upon the body. He took gravitation as an example of such a form and considered it as an expression of the immaterial activity of God moving the universe by means of space (A. Koyre).[5] Apparently it was precisely these theological implications of Newton's conception of immaterial forces causing material changes that provoked the criticism of his idea of force through the eighteenth century and further until the work of Mach and Hertz, as Max Jammer suggested.[6] The tendency on a certain line of the development of modern physics to reduce all forces to bodies or "masses" (Hertz) had anti-theological implications: If all forces would proceed from bodies or masses, then the understanding of nature would be so thoroughly separated from the idea of God—who is not a body—that theological language about a divine activity in the processes of the natural world would become simply unintelligible and absurd.

After this has been said, the implicit theological relevance of the field theories of Michael Faraday and his successors becomes evident. The main point of the field concept was to turn around the relation between force and body. To Faraday the body was but a manifestation of the force that he conceived as an independent reality prior to the body, and he did so in conceiving forces in terms of fields. His vision was to reduce all the different forces to a single field of force that determines all the changes in the natural universe. In 1974, William Berkson showed that this metaphysical vision formed the basis of Faraday's field physics and the point of departure for the different experiments he devised and for the relatively limited demonstrations of the reality of fields that he achieved by those experiments. The decisive point in Faraday's grand vision was to conceive of body and mass as secondary phenomena, a concentration of force at particular places and points of the field. The material particle appears as the point where the lines of force converge and form a "cluster" that persists for some time.[7]

The turn toward the field concept in the development of modern physics has theological significance. This is suggested not only by its opposition toward the tendency to reducing the concept of force to bodies or masses, but also because field theories from Faraday to Einstein claim a priority for the whole over the parts. This is of theological significance, because God has to be conceived as the unifying ground of the whole universe if he is to be conceived as creator and redeemer of the world. The field concept could be used in theology to make the effective presence of God in every single phenomenon intelligible. But does not such a use of the field concept ask too much of a term of natural science? Would its use in theology amount to more than equivocal language which had little in common with the meaning of the word in physics? And, in addition, does not such language misuse the idea of God as if it referred to a factor in the explanation of the world, if not even to one physical force?

The answer to scrupulous questions such as these can refer to the fact, in the first place, that the field concept was originally a metaphysical concept. The metaphysical idea of a field that inspired the modern field theories from Faraday to Einstein is traceable back to the pre-Socratics. It is to be found in Anaximenes who conceived of the air as cause and origin of all things, which supposedly had been built as concentrations of this thin element. It was Max Jammer who identified here the historical origin of all field theories, in the German dictionary of the history of philosophical terms.[8] Now in the Greek language, air was also named *pneuma*, and it is not by accident that in one of the fragments of Anaximenes *pneuma* and *aer* are used side by side.[9]

According to Max Jammer, the direct predecessor of the field concept in modern physics was the Stoic doctrine of the divine *pneuma*, which was conceived as a most subtle matter that penetrates everything and holds the cosmos together by the powerful tension between its different parts, that accounts for their cohesiveness as well as for the different movements and qualities of things. The Stoic doctrine of *pneuma* had an important impact on the patristic theology of the divine spirit and especially on its descriptions of the cosmological function of the Spirit in creation. From the point of view of the early Christian fathers there was only one major difficulty connected with the Stoic conception of the *pneuma*: The Stoics conceived of it as a subtle material element. This was unacceptable to the Christian theologians, because they could not imagine God to be a material body. They rather opted for the Platonic conception of the divine reality as purely spiritual.

Difficulties of this sort no longer burden the field concept of modern physics, at least if no ether is considered necessary for the expansion of waves within the field. Thus the major theological difficulty with the Stoic field concept has been removed by its modern development; and since the field concept as such corresponds to the old concept of *pneuma* and was derived from it in the history of thought, theologians should consider it obvious to relate also the field concept of modern physics to the Christian doctrine of the dynamic presence of the divine Spirit in all of creation. Such a way of using the field concept would certainly correspond to the connection that Christian patristics established between the biblical affirmations about the divine Spirit as origin of all life and the Stoic doctrine of the *pneuma*.

In substance there is a much closer connection here than that with the Aristotelian doctrine of movement which gained such a fatal significance in medieval scholasticism and in early modern theology. It was the reduction of movement to bodies in Aristotelian physics that became a point of departure of the mechanical doctrine of movement in early modernity and consequently of the difficulties it created for theology. In contrast to the mechanical model of movement by push and pressure the field concept could be celebrated as inauguration of a spiritual interpretation of nature.

This is particularly true in the case of Faraday's vision of reducing all material phenomena to a universal field of force.[10] However, the metaphysical intention of Albert Einstein took a different direction aiming at a reduction of the concept of force to a geometrical interpretation of gravitation that reduces the concept of force to a geometrical description of forceless movement of bodies in curved spaces.[11] In this connection one may remember Einstein's skeptical remark on the indeterminacy of quantum physics: "The old one doesn't play at dice." According to the presentation of Einstein's doctrine by Berkson, he was primarily interested in keeping the laws and properties of field invariant. Could it be that religious options were effective in the background of the conceptual differences between Faraday's concept of a field of force and Einstein's idea of the geometrical character of cosmic field? Could these be different interpretations of the Jewish idea of creation either in the line of the immutability of the law of the cosmos or in the line of God's powerful presence in the world?

To be sure, even a cosmic field conceived along the lines of Faraday's thought as a field of force would not be identified immediately with the dynamic activity of the divine Spirit in creation. In every case the different models of science remain approximations in that they are all conceived under the point of view of natural law, of uniform structures in natural processes. Therefore, theological assertions of field structure of the cosmos activity of the divine Spirit will remain different from field theories in physics. The difference may be illustrated by two examples, one of them connected with the question of how the different parts of the cosmic field are related to the field itself and the other one dealing with the role of contingency and time in the understanding of a cosmic field.

The first example carries the theologian into the territory of the old dogmatic doctrine of angels. This fact alone could be sufficient to distinguish the theological use of the field concept from that of physics. Traditional theology conceived of angels as immaterial, spiritual realities and powers who in distinction from the divine Spirit are nevertheless finite realities. Their activities were related to the natural as well as to the historical world of human beings, either as messengers of God or as acting in God's authority or by way of demonic emancipation from God. From the point of view of the field structure of spiritual dynamics one could consider identifying the subject matter intended in the conception of angels with the emergence of relatively independent parts of the cosmic field. However, according to theological tradition angels are personal spirits who decide for or against God. One need only recall the fact that the concept of person in phenomenology of religion is related to the impact of more or less incomprehensible "powers," the direction of which toward human beings and their world is taken as evidence of a kind of "will," which, however, must not suggest further anthropomorphic features. If one considers this background of the biblical language about angels as personal realities, they may very well be related to fields of forces or dynamic spheres, the activity of which may be experienced as good or bad. Still, the difference of such a conception of angels from the later doctrines of medieval scholastics as well as Protestant orthodoxy would be obvious.

Space and Time

The other example concerning the relation of a theological use of the field concept to time leads to even more complex problems. This is so, because the field concept is closely related to space. Now there are a number of good reasons—suggested by both philosophical as well as scientific thought—to consider time and space as inseparable. Einstein's field concept comprises space, time, and energy. It takes the form of a geometrical description, and this seems to amount to a spatialization of time. The totality of space, time, and energy or force are all properties of a cosmic field.

Long before our own age a theological interpretation of this subject matter had been proposed, and it was Sir Isaac Newton who offered this proposal. It too referred everything to space or, more precisely, to the correlation of space and force as in the case of a force like gravitation acting at a distance. Newton's well-known conception of space as sensory of God *(sensorium Dei)* did not intend to ascribe to God an organ of perception, the like of which God does not need according to Newton because of divine omnipresence. Rather, Newton took space as a medium of God's creative presence at the finite place of his creatures in creating them. The idea of Newton was easily mistaken as indicating some monstrously pantheistic conception of God similar to that found in Leibniz's polemics against Newton.

The basic argument of Newton or his spokesman Samuel Clarke was, however, widely discussed in the eighteenth century and has been taken up even in Kant's *Critique of Pure Reason*. In its first part, the transcendental aesthetics, the priority of infinite space over every conception of partial spaces was Kant's decisive argument for the intuitive character of space. The theological implications of this idea, however, were not even mentioned by Kant in this connection. More comprehensive consideration of the priority of the infinite over every finite experience had been affirmed already by Descartes' decisive argument in his thesis that the idea of God is the prior condition in the human mind for the possibility of any other idea, even that of the ego itself. If Kant had considered the full implications of the priority of the infinite over a finite conception, his phenomenalism would have become impossible because the subject of experience itself belongs to those things that become conceivable only on the basis of the intuition of the infinite.

Samuel Alexander was quite correct to challenge Kant at this point in his book, *Space, Time and Deity*.[12] Alexander himself, however, in distinction from Newton, conceived of infinite time and space in such a way as to attribute priority to time. The weakness of Newton's contribution to the subject matter is in the first place due to his deficient conception of time simply in terms of duration. Perhaps this deficiency is even responsible, at least in part, for Newton's poor appreciation of the doctrine of the Trinity. In any event a trinitarian interpretation of the relation of God to the world is closely connected with time and history in the divine economy of salvation.

A discussion of the concept of time and of its importance in the field concept requires considerations that can be hardly touched upon in the context of the present reflections. But this much may be said: In Kant's transcendental aesthetics—in the case of time as well as in the case of space—the infinite has priority over any finite part. In the case of time this brings Kant's argument into close contact with Plotinus' conception of time in distinction from the Aristotelian one. Plotinus argued that only on the basis of the perfect wholeness of life, an understanding of the nature of time is possible.[13] Now the whole of time, according to Plotinus, cannot be conceived as the whole of a sequence of moments, because the sequence of temporal moments can be indefinitely extended by adding further units. But according to Plontinus, time and the sequence of its units are understandable only under presupposition of the idea of a complete wholeness of life, which Plotinus conceived under the name of eternity (αἰών). In his conception the total unity of the whole of life is indispensable in the interpretation of the time sequence, because it hovers over that sequence as the future wholeness that is intended in every moment of time, so that the significance of eternity for the interpretation of time in Plotinus results in a primacy of the future concerning the nature of time. Not before Martin Heidegger's analysis of time was this insight rediscovered, and even here in only a limited way, limited to the experience of time in human existence.

The theological significance of the priority of eternity in the conception of time and of the consequent priority of the future is obvious, obvious at least in the contemporary context of theological discussion under the impact of the rediscovery of the meaning of eschatology in the message of Jesus and in early Christianity in general. When Augustine adapted Plotinian ideas about time, the situation was different. The primacy of the eschatological future in the understanding of time was not considered important; instead Augustine focused upon the relation of the individual soul to time and eternity. His concentration on the subjective experience of time provided the direction for subsequent discussions of the subject all the way to Kant and Heidegger. Yet Augustine's psychological analysis of he experience of time presupposes the Plotinian ontology of time. This is particularly evident in Augustine's famous idea that the soul is the place of some continuous presence in the flow of momentary events. His account of this continuous presence in terms of a distension of the soul *(distentio animi)* stretching across the remembered past and the expected future conceives the duration of the soul as a form of participation in eternity.

This brings us back to the relation between theology and science in the understanding of time. If space is to be described as the form of simultaneity of phenomena, then the spatialization of time in physics—already in the preparation of a homogeneous time by the scientific techniques of time measurement and further then in the model of space-time or of a universal field comprising space, time, and energy—may be described as an extrapolation of all limited participation in the eternal presence of God, a participation that is granted to us in the experience of our duration in the flow of time. Spatialization, then, is not a mere fiction, as H. Bergson suspected. Rather, it is rooted in the experience of "duration," the experience that was basic in Bergson's own thought but is also to be understood as constitutive of simultaneity in space as well as of continuity in the sequence of day and night, of summer and winter, all of which were early related to the movements of the skies. The cosmic clocks of the seemingly circular movements of the stars, especially of sun and moon, form the basis for our human division of time into equal segments. Nevertheless, no part of time is completely

homogeneous in comparison to any other. This is a consequence already of the irreversibility of the time sequence.
Therefore, the spatialization of time in physics remains a mere
approximation, even in the model of cosmic field, to the
comprehensive unity of the process of the universe in the
irreversible sequence of its history as seen from the perspective
of divine eternity.

In distinction from the perspective of physics, the theologian
looks at the universal field with the dimensions of space, time,
and energy from the point of view of the eschatological future.
Certainly, this theological perspective is in its own way limited
to approximations. This is obvious in view of the inevitable lack
in theological descriptions of the kind of precision available to
science. This lack of precision is due to the fact that theology
concerns itself with the contingent historicity of reality and
with its contingent origin in the incomprehensible God who is
incomprehensible precisely in his creative transcendence.
Duns Scotus already recognized the limitation of theological
knowledge in the fact that all theology knows God as well as
other individual realities only through general concepts, while
God's knowledge (if we are entitled to use that term in relation
to God at all) grasps the variety of individual existence in one
simultaneous act, in the form of an intuitive knowledge.

The Creatures of Creation

It seems appropriate to conclude this survey of problems
connected with the doctrine of creation by turning at least
briefly to the other side of that doctrine, to the products of the
divine act of creation and to the emerging sequence of
creatures.

The Priestly report on creation in the Bible presented the
order of creation already as a sequence of creatures that are
related to the sequence of days within the week of God's work.
They rise one after another: first the light of day in distinction
from the darkness at night, then water and the vault of heaven,
then earth, vegetation, and the stars, followed by the animals of
the sea and birds, until finally animals appear and populate the
land, and at last the human being. In the perspective of
contemporary information about the course of nature the

sequence of forms would have to look different in certain particular cases. The Priestly report is, of course, colored by the natural science of its own day. A telling example of this is the conception of a separation of the waters by the massive building of the "vault of heaven." This vault separates the waters below from those above and provides the initial condition for a mechanical process, i.e., that the waters below the vault, because their continuous supply from the upper ocean in heaven is cut off, recede to the deeper places, so that the solid ground shows up (Gen. 1:6, 9 ff.). The same mechanism works the other way, when the "windows" that had been placed in the "vault of heaven" get opened (Gen. 7:11). The consequences are reported in the story of the flood.

The cosmology that comes to expression in this idea of a vault of heaven is very impressive, but need not oblige the believer of the twentieth century. The theological doctrine of creation should take the biblical narrative as a model in that it uses the best available knowledge of nature in its own time in order to describe the creative activity of God (E. Schlink). This model would not be followed, if theology simply stuck to a standard of information about the world that became obsolete long ago by further progress of experience and methodical knowledge.

The features that show in particular the historical relativity of some information in the Priestly reports include the relatively late creation of stars. That they appear as late as in the fourth day (Gen. 1:14 ff.) and only in the utilitarian function of "lamps," is certainly due to the struggle of Israel's faith against those gods of the ancient Orient who were connected with sun or moon or other heavenly bodies. A certain degree of overreaction is also obvious at this point. In our present situation this is no longer an urgent problem of theology. Much more remarkable, however, than the necessary revisions in detail concerning the sequence of creative forms as reported in the first chapter of the Bible is the extent of substantial analogies between our contemporary and those ancient ideas about the origin and development of creation: the light in the beginning; human beings at the end of the sequence; the beginning of vegetation as a presupposition of animal life; the close kinship between human beings and mammals (the land animals) as creatures of one and the same, the sixth, day of creation. Above all, the scheme of a sequence of steps is still shared by the modern view. Certainly the sequence of steps appears from a modern perspective as an evolutionary process leading from primitive to more complex or higher organized forms. It is at this point that we identify the deepest difference between the biblical and modern conception of a sequence of forms in the process of the creation.

The resistance of many theologians during the nineteenth and early twentieth centuries against the doctrine of evolution was largely caused by their apprehension that the doctrine of evolution would do away with all immediate dependence of the particular creatures on God's activity by deriving the higher forms from their predecessors. This discussion is no longer important at present, not only because the doctrine of evolution has been victorious in shaping the cultural consciousness, but also because a further development of the doctrine of evolution itself went beyond that dispute. Presently, the proponents of an epigenetic interpretation of evolution in terms of an "emergent evolution" emphasize that later forms cannot be simply derived from earlier and lower ones. A. Lloyd Morgan's title *Emergent Evolution* of 1923 has almost become the catchword of a metaphysical concept of nature, because "emergence" means that on each level of evolution something new and underivable arises. Theodosius Dobzhansky could even call evolution "a source of novelty."[14]

In his *Ecumenical Dogmatics*, the Lutheran theologian Edmund Schlink identified the difference between the modern understanding of the sequence of natural forms and that of the Priestly report in the Bible to be rooted in the fact:

> That, according to the biblical conception, the autonomous activity of the creatures is bound to the framework of their concrete order which was given to them in the beginning, while the picture emerging from modern research has been increasingly such that the concrete species of reality developed from the autonomous activity of the creatures before them.[15]

Even the Priestly report, however, knows and uses the idea that God's creative activity can be mediated through creatures. This is said especially with respect to the earth which, according to God's demand, produces the different forms of vegetation. This shows that there is no opposition in principle between the biblical conception of God's creative activity and the idea that this activity is mediated through creatures.

Something else, however, is missing completely in the biblical report, something that has become extremely important in the modern description of nature. This is the derivation of more complex forms from elementary processes, a method of looking at things that is rooted in Democritus' theory of atoms. Democritus had already envisioned all complex forms as consisting of elementary components of similar kind and as distinct only because of the different number and connection of those components. It was this idea that influenced decisively the interpretation of nature and modern science. Without this idea, the evolutionary theories, including that of living forms, would be no longer conceivable. This is completely different from the biblical conception of the sequence of created forms. Nevertheless, this is not sufficient to conclude the basic contradiction to the implicit intentions of the biblical report and of the idea of creation in general. There is no such contradiction as long as the contingency of each of the newly emerging forms is preserved, as it is certainly the case in the doctrine of emergent evolution.

If the contingency of new forms is so important, the question must arise how contingency is to be reconciled to the peculiar logic suggested by the course of evolution moving in the direction from simple to more complex forms. Again and again philosophical and theological reflection on this phenomenon has arrived at the idea of some intrinsic teleological direction in the evolutionary process. The ideas of Teilhard de Chardin on this matter became widely known, but also became the object of serious criticism.[16] Personally, I consider more plausible the vision of Michael Polanyi, who argues for the interpretation of the emergence of more or less durative forms of finite reality in terms of phase of equilibrium within the context of a field. He consequently perceives the evolutionary processes of ontogenesis as well as phylogenesis as field effects.[17] In this perspective, the evolutionary processes of phylogenesis as well as of ontogenesis are accounted for on the basis of determinants that are not only localized within the individuals in question or the genes as the models of socio-biology suggest today, but rather the future of the evolving forms is conceived as dependent on the overall status of a field that functions as the environment of individuals and species. Ideas of this kind that have been developed by Polanyi in more or less speculative ways are convergent with Alister Hardy's concept of "organic evolution." Furthermore, they do not only recommend themselves because they allow a description of organic and inorganic nature on the basis of the same fundamental conceptuality, but they also offer to the theologian a description of life processes in analogy to the biblical intuition of an origin of all life from the activity of the creative spirit of God.

Conclusion

In this chapter, I have suggested that the theologian cannot in good conscience simply accept as exhaustive the description of nature given us by the natural scientist. There is more to nature than simply what the scientist, working within the confines of the established disciplines, have been able to report. The reality of God is a factor in defining what nature is, and to ignore this fact leaves us with something less than a fully adequate explanation of things. The recognized contingency within natural events helps us perceive the contingency of nature's laws, and this cannot be accounted for apart from understanding the whole of nature as the creation of a free divine creator. The concept of the force field, both in terms of its historical antecedents as well as its systematic implications, needs careful assessment by the theologian. The concept of a field of force could be used to make effective our understanding of the spiritual presence of God in natural phenomena. Einstein's field theory comprises space, time, and energy in such a way as to make thinking about the whole of time intelligible. This, it seems, would give priority to eternity in our conception of time.

Our task as theologians is to relate to the natural sciences as they actually exist. We cannot create our own sciences. Yet, we must go beyond what the sciences provide and include our understanding of God if we are properly to understand nature.

NOTES

1. *D. Martin Luthers Werke,* Kritische Gesamtausgabe (Weimar, 1883), IV:4638.
2. Karl Bretschneider, *Handbuch der Dogmatik der evangelisch-lutherischen Kirche* (Leipzig: Barth, 3rd ed., 1828), 1:587.
3. Karl Barth, *Church Dogmatics* (Edinburgh: T. & T. Clark, 1936–1962), III:1:Preface.
4. Hans Blumenberg, *The Legitimacy of the Modern Age,* trans. Robert M. Wallace (Cambridge: MIT Press, 1983).
5. Alexandre Koyre, *Von der geschlossenen Welt zum unendlichen Universum* (Frankfurt: Suhrkamp, 1969), trans. from English, *From the Closed World to the Infinite Universe* (Baltimore: Johns Hopkins University Press, 1957), pp. 163-64.
6. Max Jammer, *Concept of Force* (Cambridge: Harvard University Press, 1957).
7. William Berkson, *Fields of Force: The Development of a Worldview from Faraday to Einstein* (New York: Wiley, 1974), pp. 52 ff.
8. *Historisches Wörterbuch der Philosophie,* ed. Joachim Ritter, 6 vols., (Basel: J. Ritter, 1971–1984), II:923.
9. Hermann Diels, *Die Fragmente der Vorsokratiker, griechisch und deutsch,* 3 vols. (Berlin: Weidmann, 1934–1938), 13:B:2.
10. Berkson, *Fields of Force,* p. 317.
11. Ibid., p. 318.
12. Samuel Alexander, *Space, Time and Deity,* 2 vols. (London: Macmillan, 1920), I:39,n.1; cf. p. 147.
13. Plotinus, *Enneads,* III:7, 3, 16-17 and II:7, 11.
14. Theodosius Dobzhansky, *The Biology of Ultimate Concern* (New York: New American Library, 1967), p. 33.
15. Edmund Schlink, *Ökumenische Dogmatik* (Göttingen: Vandenhoeck & Ruprecht, 1983), p. 93.
16. Pierre Teilhard de Chardin, *The Phenomenon of Man* (New York: Harper and Bros., 1959).
17. Michael Polanyi, *Personal Knowledge* (New York: Harper & Row, 2nd ed., 1962).

FIVE

Cosmology, Creation, and Contingency

ROBERT JOHN RUSSELL

"The existence of the world as a whole and of all its parts is contingent. . . . It owes its existence to the free activity of divine creation."   *Wolfhart Pannenberg*

We live in an age of boundless discovery. More knowledge has been learned about our world in the last few decades than had been learned over the previous millenia of recorded history. Our generation cut its teeth on Apollo 12 and the microchip, Einstein and Crick, the artificial heart, the laser and nuclear fission. Yet we are a people of tradition, rooted and growing in the biblical witness to a creator God whom we worship and proclaim in our churches and in our lives. What then does it mean to believe that the God who acts in history is the creator of the universe, "maker of heaven and earth"?

The gleaming goal of consonance with its intense joy—and the dusty reality of dissonance with its eroding disappointment—mark the lives of so many of us caught "far from equilibrium" in the intellectual and spiritual milieu of "science

Robert John Russell is associate professor of theology and science, in residence, at the Graduate Theological Union, and also director of the Center for Theology and the Natural Sciences in Berkeley.

and religion." To continue to demark one from the other, as has been tried for centuries, no longer seems fruitful.[1] Yet what are our options?

I believe we stand at the brink of a new Reformation, one in which all we think and believe will be rethought in new terms. If it is to be faithful to its mission, the church can no longer ignore this crisis of meaning—or the opportunity for renewal. We must begin to make sense of our theology in terms of the implications of today's science if we do not want to lose our most cherished traditions. But if the risk is great so too is the reward: a new era of exchange between our knowledge of the universe and our belief in God, a new awakening of spiritual insight and ethical motivation.

Fortunately there are a few who feel the urgency of this situation. One of the leaders is Arthur Peacocke, British biochemist and Anglican theologian. Peacocke urges, "Any affirmations about God's relation to the world, any doctrine of creation, if it is not to become vacuous and sterile, must be about the relation of God to, the creation by God of, the world which the natural sciences describe. It seems to me that this is not a situation where Christian, or indeed any, theology has any choice."[2]

In this spirit I will explore the doctrine of creation in the context of contemporary physical cosmology.[3] The first step will be to survey both the creation tradition and Big Bang cosmology, looking for the role of contingency as a concept common to each, and articulated in terms of origins, finitude, dependence, and the future.

The Christian Creation Tradition

The central affirmation of Jews and Christians is that the God who saves is the God who creates. As the Psalmist writes, "Help comes from the Lord, who made heaven and earth" (Ps. 121:2). Throughout the Hebrew Scriptures, the God who works through the history of Israel, freeing the Jews from captivity in Egypt and bringing them to the Promised Land, hearing their prayers in Babylon, and releasing them from

Exile, is not only a tribal God but the very God who created "the heavens and the earth." Christians, celebrating the New Creation in Jesus the Christ who gives victory over death, proclaim this Jesus as the same Word of God by which all things are created, the life and light of the world. Though expressed in the context of, and often opposed to, indigenous cosmologies of its period, the underlying vision of scripture is "God as creator" and "the world as creation."

In the early church the creation tradition was articulated in two distinct models: *creatio ex nihilo* (creation out of nothing) and *creatio continua* (continuing creation). The former dominated patristic thought as it sought to reject Platonic and Neoplatonic cosmology. Continuing creation was rooted in this period but remained less developed during the history of Christian thought. The difference as well as the similarity of these traditions is worth noting.

Creatio ex nihilo

The *ex nihilo* tradition has remained relatively unchanged from its inception, though it has been expounded by Catholic and Protestant of every intervening period.[4] In its contest with Greek culture, the church sought to reject both metaphysical dualism, in which the world was an eternal divine substance equal to and over against God; moral dualism, in which the world was an evil power resisting a good God; emanationism, in which the world emerged from and was the body or substance of God; and monism (or pantheism), in which the world was God.

Hence the *ex nihilo* argument first of all affirms that God alone is the source of all that is, and God's creative activity is free and unconditioned. For example, the world was not merely shaped out of preexisting matter by the Demiurge who gazed at a set of transcendent forms, as Plato taught in the *Timaeus*. Neither the material of this world, nor the set of possible patterns it can assume, existed prior to God's creative activity; rather, these were created by God in the process of creating the world. And while God is the source of the world, the world is not just a part of God, a direct emanation of God's being. Rather it is an autonomous and distinct reality *created* by God. Hence though the world is real and good, it is neither God nor anti-God. The world is contingent, finite, temporal, and relative, for only God is necessary, infinite, eternal, and absolute. Finally as a creation by God, the world is characterized by freedom, purpose, and beauty.

A corollary to *creatio ex nihilo* which is pertinent to our subject is the point frequently made about the roots of the empirical method. Since God creates freely, under no jurisdiction or rule of necessity, the world is radically contingent: it need not be at all and it need not be the way it is. Hence for us to know the world we must set out on the path of discovery. Empirical science embodies as its methodological presupposition this Judeo-Christian view of nature framed in the doctrine of creation.

Creatio continua

The notion of *creatio continua* stands for God's continuing involvement with the world. Not only does God relate to creation as a whole but also to every moment, and God's fundamental relation is as creator. Hence God not only creates the world as a whole but every part of it. Though older than the *ex nihilo* tradition, *creatio continua* is a less developed doctrine of creation.

In the static cosmologies of medieval, Renaissance, and Enlightenment periods, the term "creation" was usually intended to mean "creation at the beginning," and God's present relation to the world was understood in terms of divine providence, concurrence, and government. However, with the rise of modern geology, evolutionary biology, and thermodynamics in the nineteenth century and Einsteinian cosmology in the twentieth, as well as the changing climate in philosophy, a new theological perspective is now emerging—at least in some circles. A growing number of theologians now stress the dynamics, indeterminacy, and novelty of nature (*including* human nature) as critical loci of God's participation in the universe. In this perspective God is continuously creating the world anew, guiding and urging humankind toward fulfillment and consummation in the Spirit.

So whether as a relatively separate tradition, as Ian G. Barbour[5] and Arthur Peacocke[6] suggest, or as a subordinate part of the *ex nihilo* tradition, as Phil Hefner,[7] Wolfhart Pannenberg,[8] and Jürgen Moltmann[9] suggest, an increasing number of theologians working to appropriate a scientific perspective seem to agree on the emerging vitality and importance of *creatio continua*.[10]

Contingency in Creation Theology

As we see in both Roman Catholic and Protestant thought, the philosophical sense of the dependence of the finite world on God is taken up into the concept of *contingency*. States of affairs or things are contingent when they are neither self-evident nor necessary. According to Karl Rahner, "Contingency is the . . . philosophical counterpart of the theological notion of createdness, since this latter more explicitly grasps the free production of the contingent and knows that the 'first' creative defficient cause is identical with the living God whom man encounters in saving history."[11] Similarly, Paul Tillich identified contingency with creatureliness when he wrote: "Man is a creature. His being is contingent; by itself it has no necessity, and therefore man realizes that he is the prey of nonbeing."[12] Finally, the connection between contingency, dependence, and finitude is evident in Langdon Gilkey's summary of the creation tradition: "Creatures, i.e., the finite world of created things, have a being or existence which is at one and the same time dependent upon God, and yet is real, coherent and 'good.' "[13]

In *ex nihilo* theology the concept of contingency tends to denote finitude and purpose while the *continua* tradition focuses attention on the contingent in the emergence of novelty and an orientation toward future fulfillment. Of course there are important thematic differences between the two creation models. For example, *creatio ex nihilo* tends to emphasize

God's transcendence of the world, while *creatio continua* suggests the presence and immanence of God at the heart of nature. Yet in both traditions we find the total dependence of all-that-is on God. The finite world depends on God for its very being as such, and for its being, moment by moment.

Given the centrality of contingency in creation theology, its meaning and significance in contemporary cosmology becomes a key question, as Wolfhart Pannenberg argues: "Any contemporary discussion between theology and science should focus in the first place on the question what modern science and especially modern physics can say about the question of the contingency of the world as a whole and of every part in the universe."[14]

But does it make sense to talk of the universe as contingent in the context of contemporary science? Let us pursue this by turning to Big Bang cosmology.

The Big Bang: A Brief Look

In his special theory of relativity (1905), Albert Einstein took the first step in establishing modern cosmology. In this theory, space and time are put on an equal footing, combined as a four-dimensional continuum called space-time. With the new arena of space-time our intuitive notions of the simultaneity of events and of the lengths of objects are altered. Here space or time measurements alone, such as the size of a soaring rocket or the rate at which a moving watch ticks, lose their individual meaning, blending together in a deeper space-time whole. Like the shadow of a rotating ruler, they seem to contract and expand—though the ruler does not.

Einstein's subsequent work, the general theory of relativity (circa 1915) is a theory of gravity. For Newton gravity was a force exerted between masses as they moved about in space. Einstein took a radically new approach. Whereas the space-time geometry of special relativity was "flat" (or pseudo-Euclidean), in general relativity theory, space-time is allowed to curve. Instead of particles being forced into curved paths by the force of gravity as Newton suggested, Einstein depicts the natural motion of particles by the naturally bent paths of curved space-time. What determines the curvature of space-time? For this Einstein turned back to matter and created a "closed circuit" between the two great ideals of natural order: form and content. In Einstein's view, the structure of space-time, its size, shape, and texture, is dependent on the distribution of matter, while the motion of matter is determined by the local curvature of space-time. In the phrase of Misner, Thorne, and Wheeler: "Space tells matter how to move; matter tells space how to curve."[15]

Given general relativity, what sort of predictions could be made about the nature and history of the universe? Imagine trying to describe a universe of a trillion trillion stars with one or two simple equations, yet this was precisely what scientists did early in this century. They returned to the mathematics of Einstein's theory and explored two different models which could apply to the universe as a whole. Both of them are expanding in time from a singularity of zero size and infinite density at $t = 0$ (where t is physical time). In the so-called open model, a saddle-shaped surface, *infinite* in size, expands forever, while in the "closed" model, a spherical-shaped surface, *finite* in size, expands up to a maximum radius, then recontracts to the final singularity.

But these are just mathematical models. How can we relate them to the data astronomers give us? First, we shouldn't miss the fact that even the visible portion of our universe is *enormous:* there are at least one hundred billion stars in our galaxy alone and easily a trillion such galaxies within the limits of present-day telescopes. Still, astronomical observations show that galaxies are grouped in the form of clusters, each containing on the average 100 million million stars, and that these clusters are distributed *evenly* throughout space-time! Moreover in the 1920s, Edwin Hubble discovered that light from these is redshifted, and hence that these galactic clusters are *receding* from us and from one another. The expansion of the *universe* had been discovered!

This is a staggering fact! Modern cosmology depicts the universe as radically historical, evolving from an initial point

15-20 billion years ago. Moreover, its expansion is slowing down. If the closed, finite model is correct, the slowdown will continue until the universe reaches a maximum size, after which contraction will begin until the universe is once again arbitrarily small some 50-100 billion years from now. If, however, the universe is open and infinite in size, as most evidence currently suggests, it will continue expanding forever, growing steadily colder and more dilute.

Now I wish to try to draw out the implications of Big Bang cosmology for creation theology. I will do so by posing four questions: (1) What about the beginning? (2) Is the universe finite? (3) Is the universe necessary? and (4) Does the universe have an eschatological purpose?

Implications for Creation Theology

1. "In the beginning . . . "? "Gravitational collapse confronts physics with its greatest crisis ever. At issue is the fate, not of matter alone, but of the universe itself."[16]

To many, the most profound claim of modern physical cosmology is the seeming discovery of an absolute beginning at $t = 0$. Within science this claim cannot be dismissed casually because as we approach the singularity at $t = 0$, gravitational tidal forces, densities, and temperatures increase without limit. Moreover, it is an irremovable mathematical feature of these models[17] and, given their enormous explanatory power, these models cannot be dismissed easily. They provide an integrative framework that links together the results of evolutionary biology, physical chemistry, geology, solar physics, galactic astrophysics, the relative abundances of elements in the universe, and many other disparate areas of physical science into a consistent framework. The ages of each system under study nest properly: the geological age of the earth is consistent with the age of the sun. Physical cosmology gives a unified interpretative scenario through which the universe developed from an embryonic fireball into the present composition. Recent work in high energy physics when projected back to the temperatures of the earliest epoch of the universe suggest even more unified scenarios for all of fundamental physics.

Meanwhile, physics gives little room for speculation for what could lie before $t = 0$, where tidal forces, temperature, and density become infinite. All that is seems to be the outcome of initial conditions at an initial starting point which, within these models, is without physical precedent or cause, and which therefore seems outside of scientific study. To many physicists, the embarrassing thing about modern cosmology is its seeming inability to eternalize matter. What then are we to make of the initial singularity? Should theology be enlisted in some way?

Amazingly, some secularists attribute to $t = 0$ a direct religious implication. The June 1978 issue of *New York Times* contained an article by NASA's Robert Jastrow, an avowed agnostic, entitled "Found God?" Here Jastrow depicts the theologians to be "delighted" that astronomical evidence "leads to a biblical view of Genesis." The article ends by describing the beleaguered scientist who, as in a bad dream, after scaling the highest peak of discovery finds a "band of theologians . . . [who] have been sitting there for centuries."[18] I recently heard him speak about this issue. Though claiming to be agnostic, he argued without reservation for the religious significance of $t = 0$: it is beyond science and leads to some sort of creator.

A more subtle but strongly positive response came from the Vatican in 1951. In an address to the Pontifical Academy of Science, Pope Pius XII praised cosmologists for disclosing astrophysical evidence which is "entirely compatible" with theological convictions about divine creation. Although prescinding from a claim of "absolute proof" throughout the text, in a final effluence of praise the pope concluded: "Thus, with that concreteness which is characteristic of physical proofs, it has confirmed the contingency of the universe and also the well-founded deduction as to the epoch when the cosmos came forth from the hands of the Creator. Therefore, God exists!"[19] Conservative Protestant circles have also welcomed Big Bang cosmology as supporting a historical interpretation of the doctrine of creation.

On the other hand there have been numerous critics of these theological overtones within scientific *and* religious circles. Here one thinks of the Roman Catholic cosmologist and key architect of contemporary cosmology, G. Lemaitre, who disavowed the papal endorsement of its theological implications. Many other scientists rejected the religious overtones of $t = 0$ and even challenged the scientific standing of Big Bang cosmology itself because of these overtones. Most notable among these is Fred Hoyle, who helped construct an alternative model precisely for this reason. In Hoyle's "steady state" model the universe has an infinite past and continues to expand forever. Since its predictions include matter spontaneously "popping" into existence from time to time to keep the cosmic density constant, this has frequently been called (ironically!) the "continuous creation" model. It was eventually abandoned after the discovery of the microwave background radiation that strongly favors the Big Bang theory. Nevertheless, the fact that a scientifically acceptable alternative cosmology was possible should make us at the very least cautious of using cosmology (Big Bang or steady state) to give direct support to *any* theological position whether that position be theistic *or*, as with Fred Hoyle, atheistic.

Indeed, one could take the approach within theology that *any* physical cosmology that science generates, including one without an initial singularity or a finite age, is at least compatible with the heart of the Christian creation tradition in its insistence on the *ontological* dependence of all-that-is on God. Neoorthodox, existentialist, and liberal theology have stood passionately and uncompromisingly for the radical separation of science and religion and hence the complete independence of religious doctrine from secular cosmology. One need only think of Karl Barth and Paul Tillich to gauge the sweeping power of this position in contemporary theology. And such a separation is, naturally, advocated by most professional scientific societies, including the prestigious American Academy of Sciences.

There are of course deep philosophical and scientific grounds for caution. The method of science is based on causal explanation, whether deterministic (in the extreme case, Laplacian) or statistical (either for mathematical or physical reasons). From this point of view $t = 0$ cannot finally refer to a physical state but at best it can represent a mathematical limit in the theory, suggesting the need for a new cosmology to replace it. Indeed, Newtonian cosmology gave way to Einsteinian, and the latter will eventually be replaced since it does not take into account quantum effects—the physics of the microscopic. Inflationary cosmologies are already being explored, which account for many of the "inexplicable" features of our universe, such as its homogeneity and isotropy. Though I cannot extensively discuss quantum physics in this essay, it is clear that such effects in cosmology become critically important near $t = 0$, precisely at the initial moments of the universe, since then the size of the universe is microscopic. Will new cosmological models influenced by quantum gravity predict a "bounce" and hence an "oscillating" universe, infinitely old already, with an infinite set of oscillations in the future? If our current views could so radically change, what is there about present cosmology that will survive the change—and how can we know what it is in advance?[20]

Alternatively, if we identify $t = 0$ as having religious significance, how can we simply ignore other striking features of the *same model?* If the universe is describable in terms of an open Big Bang model, wouldn't we have to deal with the prediction of an infinite future? Such a model makes the universe infinite in size. What does this do to other theological issues such as the doctrine of God or eschatology? Moreover, like all models in Einstein's general relativity, it is highly deterministic. Though the astronomical data provide an empirical arrow of time (the red shift means the universe is expanding whereas a blue shift would mark a contracting universe), the model itself is time reversible. What then do we do with our subjectivity, based irreducibly on duration and the distinction between past and future? We will be in a very awkward position if we "pick and choose" after the fact, selecting those features that favor our theological perspective and ignoring those that count against it.[21]

So caution is clearly in order. Nevertheless one is still tempted to seek out some positive relation between scientific results and theological affirmations. Notre Dame philosopher Ernan McMullin suggests what might be the narrow path between extremes. He believes we should aim at a "coherence of world-view" in which theology and cosmology are "consonant in the contributions they make to this world-view" although this consonance is always in "slight shift." Applied to the problem of the ultimate beginning, he concludes: "What one *could* readily say, however, is that if the universe began in time through the act of a Creator, from our vantage point it would look something like the Big Bang that cosmologists are now talking about. What one cannot say is, first, that the Christian doctrine of creation 'supports' the Big Bang model, or second, that the Big Bang model 'supports' the Christian doctrine of creation."[22]

Can we generalize McMullin's position on consonance? In succeeding sections I will try to do so by trying out several tentative hypotheses about cosmos and creation. The first step is to reframe the question of $t = 0$ in terms of the *space-time* character of Einstein's work.

2. Is the universe finite? The idea of the origin of the universe at $t = 0$ is only one aspect of the more general concept of finitude. Related to its age, we can ask if the universe is finite or infinite in size and whether it will go on forever or someday end.

Of course we can only answer questions like these within one or another model of the universe. No data is sufficient to force us into univocal answers as to its age, size, or future. Within the two options afforded by the standard Big Bang models, most scientists presently believe that the data indicate that the universe is marginally open, though many still hope it will turn out to be closed for theoretical reasons. This conclusion is based on estimates of the average density of matter in the universe that in turn comes from observing galactic clusters, estimates of dark matter, assuming that certain elementary particles such as neutrinos are massless, and other factors. If this is the case the universe is already infinite in size and will expand forever. If neutrinos are in fact massive, the universe would probably be closed. Clearly the issue is far from settled!

Yet from a space-time perspective, the size or finitude of the universe becomes an even more intriguing and elusive concept since space and time are really more like directions on a four-dimensional "object."[23] From this perspective we can ask whether space-time stretches in all directions to infinity, or whether it has edges along some directions or folds back smoothly onto itself like a sphere along others. Since the closed universe is spatially finite and since it has a finite past and a finite future, as a space-time model it can be classified as *homogeneous* or strictly finite. Its spatial sections are smooth spheres, finite in size with no edges, but in reaching back into the finite past or forward into the finite future, we come to a singularity whose structure, at least in some mathematical representations, is like an edge. Hence its finitude is bought at a price: the essential singularity that poses the greatest crisis physics has ever faced, according to John Archibald Wheeler.[24]

Strange as this may be, the open model raises an even more intriguing paradox about infinity. In this model the universe is spatially infinite and its future is infinite; yet like the closed model its past age is *finite!* Therefore as a space-time model it is *heterogeneous* or mixed, displaying both finite and infinite characteristics!

Actually theoretical cosmology includes still other possible combinations of finitude and infinity if we modify Einstein's equations of general relativity to include a so-called cosmological constant, to which he ascribed the symbol *lambda*. This constant was originally introduced by Einstein because his initial calculations showed that even the simplest models of the universe were time dependent: expanding or contracting, features that he considered unacceptable. Later after the red shift of distant galaxies was discovered, indicating that the universe actually was expanding, Einstein retracted the cosmological constant. Recently, however, a number of theorists have argued for its reinclusion because of technical problems with the early universe.

If we include a non-zero value for the cosmological constant, seven theoretical models are permitted by general relativity, and they may be classified according to the kind of infinities they assign to the past, future, and size of the universe, as summarized in the following figure:

Figure 3.

TYPE	TIME PAST	FUTURE	SPACE	LAMBDA	TOPOLOGY/ NAME
I	finite	finite	finite	o	closed (standard model)
II	finite	INFINITE	finite	+	closed ("hesitation")
III	INFINITE	finite	finite	+	closed
IV	INFINITE	INFINITE	finite	+	closed ("turnaround)
V	finite	INFINITE	INFINITE	0, +	open (standard model)
VI	INFINITE	finite	INFINITE	0, +	open
VII	finite	finite	INFINITE	—	open
VIII	INFINITE	INFINITE	INFINITE	——	open ("steady state")

Eight types of cosmological models classified by their temporal and spatial infinities. Types I-VII are consistent with Einstein's *general relativity* (if we include a non-zero cosmological constant lambda in some cases). Type VIII, and a special case of type V (see note 25), represent the kind of homogeneous infinity found in Fred Hoyle's steady-state cosmology.

Here types I (closed) and V (open) are the standard Big Bang models (with lambda equal to zero). Types II (the closed "hesitation universe"), III (a closed contracting universe, the time reversal of type II), and IV (the closed "turnaround universe") are extensions of the closed model type I with positive lambda. Types VI (a contracting time-reversed version of type V) and VII are extensions of the open model for non-zero lambda. Except for type I, all of these models are *heterogeneous*. Interestingly, though one can have a homogeneously finite model, no *homogeneously infinite* model, such as Fred Hoyle's steady-state model (represented here as type VIII) is possible in standard general relativity![25]

The pedigree of these models is clear: they arose out of a dominant paradigm in twentieth-century physics. Their value for us lies in that they offer a set of mathematically self-consistent representations of finitude and infinity within the framework of a dominant scientific paradigm. Of course the radical differences they suggest about the kind of universe we live in could lead one to abandon the attempt to draw theological conclusions from cosmology. Moreover, since most of these models have been rejected on empirical grounds one could object that they are irrelevant to theology and science today.

However what *is* significant for our purposes is not the present empirical status of any particular model, since that *will* constantly change. Instead the advantage of inspecting a set of recent, historical models is that the lessons gained may help us with the much more complex question of working at our own present frontier. Here too there lies a wealth of competing models, but we do not have tomorrow's hindsight in weeding out weak candidates among our current competitors. Moreover the most relevant factor for theology may not, indeed should not, be linked to a precise characteristic of the model that prevails but on something more general that characterizes all those models in competition at one time. In other words my view is that, while we ought not to expect a direct relation between $t = 0$, temporal finitude, or any other individual feature in cosmology and theology, a concept such as contingency, operating at a more abstract and general level, can provide a common framework for relating creation theology and scientific cosmology. Hence I suggest that through the element of contingency the Einsteinian models we are considering do share something in common which could offer a fruitful element of consonance with theology, something that may continue to be in consonance even as we move into the future and discover new cosmologies beyond our present horizon.

In this spirit I would venture a first working hypothesis: *The particular elements of contingency in a given cosmological model both interpret and limit the theological claim that creation is contingent*. We can test this hypothesis by a specific question, If finitude is an element of contingency, how do the various types of cosmologies interpret the temporal and physical meanings of finitude and what sorts of trade-offs qualify these meanings?

To unpack this further let's start with the notion of a finite past as the correlate of the theological affirmation of finite creation. Recall McMullin's argument: if we claim that "the universe began in time through the act of a Creator," and if we work within standard Big Bang cosmology, then such a finite past might provide a fruitful interpretation of divine creation; or, as he put it, "from our vantage point [the universe] would look something like the Big Bang that cosmologists are now talking about."

However, looking more closely at our cosmological models, we find that there are not one but four different models that depict the past as finite: I, II, V, and VII. *As far as a finite past is concerned, these models are equivalent:* they would all "look something like the Big Bang that cosmologists are now talking about," to use McMullin's phrase. Yet the kind of *future* they depict includes both varieties: finite (I and VII) and infinite (II and V). Similarly their *spatial size* includes both finitude (I, II) and infinity (V, VII). (They also vary in terms of the cosmological constant, lambda; in fact, in a deeper mathematical sense this is what accounts for their variety.)

Alternatively we might start with the requirement of a *finite size* as the correlate of theological finitude and hence contingency. Now we find a different set of appropriate models: I, II, III, and IV. Moreover in this case we couldn't be guaranteed of the finitude of time since some of these models involve temporal infinity (II, finite future; IV, infinite past and future). Figure 4 summarizes these results.[26]

What this analysis suggests is that we cannot equate contingency with something as loosely defined as finitude; we need to specify further what we mean by the claim that creation

Figure 4.

*Combinations of finitude and infinity in
Einsteinian cosmological models.*

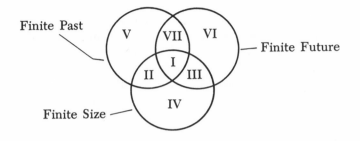

The circles in this graph represent the properties of finite past, finite future, and finite spatial size, respectively. Models lie in the areas that represent their finite properties. Hence type I, being homogeneously finite, lies in the intersection of all three circles. Types II, III, and VII are finite in two aspects; for example, type VII is finite in both past and future and hence lies in the area common to both upper circles but excluded from the lower circle. Types V, VI, and IV are finite in only one aspect.

is finite, or that finitude is a mark of contingency. Moreover, when we specify what we mean by finitude in terms of time or space, contemporary cosmology both interprets and limits our terms: it admits temporal and spatial interpretations of finitude but it limits them by showing that we cannot claim that the universe is contingent in terms of *both* temporal and spatial finitude. The only exception is the fully finite model, type I. If we then move to identify contingency as finitude with type I uniquely, we run the perennial risk of tying creation theology to a particular physical model, the outcome we were trying to avoid by abstracting to the level of contingency.

Hence if we want to avoid a direct linkage between a specific cosmology (such as type I) and a particular interpretation of theological terms we must allow for a degree of dissonance as well as consonance between theological and scientific claims (e.g., that the universe is in some respects infinite as well as finite). So we must extend McMullin's suggestion and define consonance more carefully: If we look for consonance in terms of the temporal past, so that the Big Bang that cosmologists are now talking about would count as a correlate to the theological concept of finitude in terms of a beginning in time through the act of a creator, then from our vantage point we cannot expect the future or the size of the universe within the same Big Bang cosmology to show a similar correspondence with the theological concept of finitude in terms of the future or the plenitude of creation. In sum, we must choose between alternatives: *consonance over the past but dissonance over the future and size, consonance over the future but dissonance over the past and size, and so on.*

One might be tempted to raise this sort of trade-off to a tentative epistemological principle: *When comparing theological and scientific models of more abstract concepts, there will always be some agreement between some features of the theological and scientific models, but one cannot expect simultaneous agreement between all such features.* The contradictions (dissonances) as well as agreements (consonances) are beneficial: without contradiction one would be open to reductionism or idolatry[27]; of course, without agreement one would be back in the problem of fully compartmentalized language games and non-intersecting spheres of rationality that we set out to overcome. The method then is to find the appropriate balance between abstraction and ordinary language; we must carefully tune our instruments so they ring with consonance *and* dissonance.

3. *"The best of all worlds . . . "?* Just as $t = 0$ and finitude lead to one form of contingency, so too does the idea that nothing in the universe seems totally self-sufficient or absolutely necessary. As Paul Tillich put it, "Man is a creature. His being is contingent; by itself it has no necessity, and therefore man realizes that he is the prey of nonbeing."[28]

If we generalize this same form of contingency and consider the universe as a whole we are led to ask, Why does the universe exist and why does it exist in precisely the way it does? Could things have been different?[29] The theological response, coming out of the creation tradition, has been to affirm the aseity and freedom of God as utterly distinct from the absolute dependence of all creation. In other words the church claims that the universe is contingent both *ontologically,* since nothing need be at all, *and existentially,* since the particular way it exists seems arbitrary. Traditionally anything less than this would appear to undermine the claim that God alone is both necessary being and free creator.

The consensus behind this position is underscored by a recent document of the World Council of Churches (circa 1975): "Nothing—not even space, time, matter, or the laws of physics—is self-explanatory. This is the most radical contingency imaginable. . . . The cosmos did not have to be at all. . . . Such questions have no answers within science, and their contemplation leads to some sort of theological inquiry."

But do these questions lie entirely outside of science? The surprising answer is that contemporary cosmology does seem to address this issue—and precisely by combining new scientific perspectives on the ontological and existential dimensions of global contingency! Even with the unimaginable vastness and complexity of the stars and galaxies in our universe, it now seems that the universe as a whole possesses some overall simplicity, some unifying features, that we can use to classify and compare our universe with other theoretically possible universes. If so, we can then ask whether these global features of our universe are arbitrary or whether there is some fundamental reason why they must be as they are. Perhaps the actual *existence* of our universe is connected to its own *particular* global characteristics!

First we must find a way of characterizing our universe as a whole, and then we can consider what alternative universes would be like. It turns out that there are fundamental constants scattered throughout the laws of physics which play a quixotic role in determining the most general features of, and hidden connections within, nature as a whole.[30] These include: Planck's constant, the speed of light, the charge of the electron, the proton and electron masses, the gravitational constant, and the Hubble constant. With a few simple combinations of just these fundamental constants we can characterize most of the global features of the universe! So one way to approach the question of contingency, then, is to ask why the values of these constants are what they are.

The Anthropic Principle

Surprisingly, the answer is connected with the fact that our universe is one in which life has evolved. Pervading recent literature, the so-called Anthropic Principle[31] was first developed by B. Carter in 1974. According to this principle, the fundamental constants of nature must be such that "what we expect to observe must be restricted to the conditions necessary for our presence as observers. . . . The universe must be such as to admit the creation of observers within it at some stage," and this places *very stringent* restrictions on those physical constants mentioned already.[32]

To see this argument, consider all possible universes, characterized by different values of the physical constants. Which of these universes could produce life, at least as we know it? Carter argues that only a small subset of them could be such as to *ever* produce life. For example, the age of the universe must be consistent with the rate of stellar evolution, the production of heavy elements in stars and then novas that spill these elements into the surrounding space, the birth of a second generation of stars and planets, the evolution of life on these planets. Hence a much younger universe would not yet have produced life; a much older one would be long since barren and cooling.

Perhaps Leibniz was correct in arguing that, even in spite of evil, this is the best of all possible worlds, since, if the Anthropic Principle is correct, it is the only one in which life is at all possible! In a marvelous passage from his autobiography, *Disturbing the Universe,* Freeman J. Dyson writes: "The more I examine the universe and study the details of its architecture, the more evidence I find that the universe in some sense must have known that we were coming."[33]

Does this lead to a new argument from design? Granted that life arose on earth through evolutionary processes from primordial matter, i.e., through processes explained by and within the domain of science, why should such processes have occurred in the first place? Is this universe *as a whole* designed? And what kind of designer would this suggest?

Although an intriguing and sophisticated case can be made for a type of generalized design argument leading to a Neoplatonic, aesthetic/ethical divine principle,[34] I do not want to make such a case nor do I want to argue directly from nature to a concept of the divine. One reason is that, like the problem of $t = 0$, the Anthropic Principle is highly subject to changes in science. Even its standing within science remains extremely controversial, as indicated by the critical and often negative reaction to the massive study on the subject by John Barrow and Frank Tipler.[35] Another reason is that design-type arguments rarely carry significant theological pay-dirt, since it is far from clear whether the God that emerges from them is related to the biblical Creator. Still we may now be able to find a degree of consonance between our theological perspective, informed by its primary sources, our evolutionary perspective on biological existence, and our emerging cosmological perspective on the universe as a whole.

Such a perspective might come from first appreciating the counterarguments to design which most physicists advance. Granting that our universe may be the only universe consistent with life, the real question becomes whether our universe is the only *actual* universe. The design argument seems, at face value, to assume that the only actual universe is one that happens to be—miraculously—consistent with life. But suppose an infinity of universes actually exist. Inflationary cosmologies, for example, suggest that countless bubbles were thrown out in the early cosmic epoch, each forming its own universe. Our bubble universe, with its four dimensions and particular natural constants, is like a special, fragile, and fragrant island surrounded on all sides by an infinite lifeless sea of islands. But suppose *all such universes exist?* What would this imply about design and contingency?[36]

Interestingly, physicist Jim Trefil writes: "For myself, I feel much more comfortable with the concept of a God who is clever enough to devise the laws of physics that make the existence of our marvelous universe inevitable than I do with the old-fashioned God who had to make it all, laboriously, piece by piece."[37] Similarly, in an extraordinary series of recent lectures, theologian and biochemist Arthur Peacocke invents grand metaphors of God the creator, articulating each possible world as a bell-ringer "rings the changes" and as a composer "elaborates a fugue."[38] Tom Torrance makes the similar claim: "Since (the world) was created out of nothing, it might have been quite different from what it is, but now that it has come into being, it has a contingent necessity in that it cannot not be what it now is. Considered in itself, then, there is only *the* world, this world that has come into being, but considered from the side of God's creation it is only one of all possible worlds."[39]

On reflection what Peacocke and Trefil seem to imply is that we need not choose merely between a many-worlds theory and a design argument. Instead the design argument can be cast at a series of meta-levels that include the many-worlds option as part of the design! To make this explicit, we can imagine a series of levels of design contingency:

Figure 5.
Levels of Design Contingency

Designer?

LEVEL 4: ???
LEVEL 3: different logical systems; same ???
LEVEL 2: different physical laws; same formal logic
LEVEL 1: varying constants; same physical laws

Levels of design contingency include the space of all possible laws of physics (of which our laws, representing our and all other universes consistent with them, are one point); the space of all possible logical systems, each of which generates a space of possible laws of physics; and so on. Does the sequence of levels point to a designer? Is every level designed?

1. Level one, representing the standard form of the Anthropic Principle, is the space of all possible universes in which the same laws of physics apply but in which the constants vary. Each point in this space is one possible universe, and various regions of this space include universes consistent with life. Our universe is represented by a particular point in such a region, apparently of vanishingly small area, if the tight limits set by Anthropic Principle arguments on the size of the variation in the constants consistent with life are correct.

2. Level two, the first type of meta-Anthropic Principle, is the space of all possible laws of physics. Each point in this space represents a particular set of physical laws. Level one is thus a particular point in this space in which the physical laws are those that govern our universe. Each point in level two, being a level-one type space, contains an infinite set of possible universes consistent with that type of physical laws.[40]

3. Level three, the next level of meta-Anthropic Principles, is the space of all possible formal logical systems. Each point in this space represents one particular type of logic. The point representing traditional two-valued logic contains level two, since all known laws of physics are governed by this form of logic. Other points in level three represent multi-valued logic, non-distributive logic, and so forth. For each point there is an infinite set of possible physical laws, and for each such set an infinite set of universes distinguished by the values of the natural constants.

4. Similarly one could generalize to levels four, five, six, and so on.

What I find interesting about this generalization of the standard Anthropic Principle is that each level involves an option between contingency (leading to design) and necessity (many-worlds); but the latter in turn leads to the next higher level with its own choice between contingency and necessity. For example, consider level one. Here one pursues the standard argument: either our universe is the only actual universe, leading to a design-type argument to account for why this should be, or one assumes that all possible universes actually exist, consistent with the same laws of physics but differing in the values of their natural constants (the many-worlds option), thereby eliminating the novelty of our solitary existence.

But now note that we simply move to level two; after all, why should the laws of physics that govern level one be what they are? At level two these particular laws become one of an infinite set of possible laws, and again we have two options: either they are the only set of actual laws, and a design argument is invoked to account for them, or else all possible laws are in effect, each producing their own space of level one–type possible universes.

If the latter is assumed, eliminating level-two contingency, we can still move to level three where these sets of laws are all the realization of a unique type of logic. Do other types of logic exist, leading to other types of laws, other types of constants, and other types of universes, or is only one kind of logic realized in all possible universes? If so, why? In this manner we can continue to move up the ladder of levels, finding a choice at each level: either at a given level the series terminates in a unique point whose contingency serves as the basis of a design argument, or a given level is granted a many-worlds status, eliminating the contingency of any particular point in the level but leading to the next level and the same type of option. Even if the series of levels never ends, the series itself suggests its own form of design argument.

It is crucial to recognize that this particular series is not unique. A different, but equally valid, series could be constructed; for example, one in which we first generalize the laws of physics before the values of the constants. Clearly the levels in a particular series are not really successive abstractions from nature, since the higher levels in one series can always occur as the lower levels in another. Rather they are alternative ways to organize the meaning of contingency within a particular scientific theory, such as Big Bang cosmology, and they provide alternative perspectives on the complex of inherent contingency in the physical universe.

I believe this kind of analysis tells us two things about constructing a theology of creation. *First,* no matter how strong an explanation science can give of "the way things are," an element of the unexplained always remains; hence science will never eliminate the meaningfulness of contingency in the creation tradition. Indeed, since empirical science is based on the contingency of the world, every scientific theory will be compatible, at some level, with theology. In this sense one is never forced to choose between faith and science. *Second*, the kind of contingency which exists in each particular scientific theory provides a special context of meaning for our understanding of divine creativity. For example, if convincing arguments are given for preferring a many-worlds theory in level one, we should both accept the limitation this places on the theological meaning of contingency and yet press for the possibility of contingency at another level of generalization, perhaps one involving the laws of physics or the form of logic. In this way the discoveries of science are essential to the task of theology as *fides quaerens intellectum,* for science gives concrete language for our deepest insights about God's relation to creation.

4. Does the universe have an eschatological purpose? We have looked at the contingency of the universe in terms of its origins, finitude, and global character. What about the future? Will time have an end? What will the future bring? What about life and the fulfillment of history? What is the ultimate future of the universe? Is the far future eschatologically contingent?

Standard cosmology presents two options for the far future: an open universe, expanding and cooling forever, or a closed universe, eventually recontracting and heating to lifeless incandescence. The seeming futility of life in an uncaring cosmos has prompted expressions of anguish in much of our modern consciousness. As early as 1903, Bertrand Russell wrote: "All the labours of the ages, all the devotion, all the inspiration, all the noonday brightness of human genius, are destined to extinction in the vast death of the solar system, and . . . the whole temple of Man's achievement must inevitably be buried beneath the debris of a universe in ruins."[41] In a similar mood, Steven Weinberg closes his book, *The First Three Minutes,* with this passage: "It is very hard to realize that this all is just a tiny part of an overwhelmingly hostile universe. It is even harder to realize that this present universe has evolved from an unspeakably unfamiliar early condition, and faces a future extinction of endless cold or intolerable heat. The more the universe seems comprehensible, the more it also seems pointless. . . .The effort to understand the universe is one of the very few things that lifts human life a little above the level of farce, and gives it some of the grace of tragedy."[42]

What can we say theologically in light of the end of all life in the universe, even of the universe itself? If modern cosmology has seemed to suggest positive features for a creation theology, what can we do with this view of a hopeless future?

Freeman J. Dyson has made an extremely valuable contribution to this problem in his recent paper, "Time without End: Physics and Biology in an Open Universe."[43] He opens with this remark: "I hope . . . to hasten the arrival of the day when eschatology, the study of the end of the universe, will be a respectable scientific discipline and not merely a branch of theology." With this, Dyson begins a detailed study of life in the far future of an open (infinitely expanding) universe. Dyson first argues that physical processes will continue to occur into the surprisingly distant future, opening up the time scales enormously. Here Dyson is talking about time scales like $10 \, (\exp 10 \, (\exp 30))$! Second, by a process of massive and intentional biological adaptation to the lowering ambient temperature, life can continue almost indefinitely, transforming itself through a series of appropriate biological vehicles to meet the changing physical environment.

In addition, if one defines subjective time carefully, one can envisage consciousness continuing indefinitely and life communicating by growing networks across even intergalactic distances that ultimately embrace the visible universe. Thus in Dyson's view, life can continue into the infinite future, conscious of its history, processing new experiences and storing them through new forms of memory. Hence, "an open universe need not evolve into a state of permanent quiescence. Life and communication can continue forever, utilizing a finite store of energy. . . . So far as we can imagine into the future, things continue to happen. In the open cosmology, history has no end."

Dyson concludes by recalling the model of the universe as suggested by Weinberg in which the universe seems "pointless." By contrast, Dyson has "found a universe growing without limit in richness and complexity, a universe of life surviving forever and making itself known to its neighbors across unimaginable gulfs of space and time. Is Weinberg's universe or mine closer to the truth? One day, before long, we shall know. . . . I think I have shown that there are good scientific reasons for taking seriously the possibility that life and intelligence can succeed in molding this universe of ours to their own purposes." Though Dyson's vision of the future is *prima facia* different from the future of traditional eschatology, there are many striking features in common: life, hope, community, discovery, fulfillment.

To borrow a phrase from Phil Hefner, the doctrine of creation asserts that "life is trustworthy." But we must generalize this and ask, Is the universe trustworthy? At least in Dyson's scenario the answer seems to be yes! The future of the open universe from a scientific perspective may once again be compatible with our deepest religious values and visions, the unending creation of new forms of life and society, the continuing of experience, memory, and hope without limits. But what about the closed universe, with its prognosis for eventual recontraction?[44]

Interestingly, there is one theoretical candidate that could provide a scenario something like Dyson's for the open model, although it is not a likely candidate given current astrophysical data. If the cosmological constant is *negative*, one can find a closed model that expands forever: the "hesitation" model described previously. When I asked Professor Dyson about this possibility, he answered with characteristic humor, and without a pause: "It would be boring!" His remark is, of course, right on target. Since this is a closed model, the universe is *always* finite in size even though it expands indefinitely! Eventually we'd run out of new planets to explore, new neighbors to meet.

But the question can go another step. It is possible that life so radically "terraforms" ("cosmoforms") the universe as to change its *topological* properties? Could life change a closed universe into an open universe? Just such a question is being raised in the discussion of the Anthropic Principle. In an extraordinary theorem, Barrow and Tipler prove the following assertion: "Certain global properties of the universe—openness vs. closure, and re-collapse vs. expansion forever—cannot be changed from one to the other by *any* sort of operation by intelligent life, provided the laws of physics as we now understand them are correct."[45]

Is it true that our theological convictions are consistent with *any* cosmology science produces, or are there cosmologies that do seem to preclude a theology of creation? Perhaps the answer lies in a trade-off between theological convictions that can and cannot be interpreted within a given scientific cosmology. The *ex nihilo* doctrine emphasizes finitude and purpose; *creatio continua* stresses the dynamic of God's relation to the universe. Dyson has shown how an open model can provide a scenario for the continuing unfoldment of life and purpose—at least intracosmically. But this is necessarily linked to the infinity of the open model, infinity in both size and (future) time. My interest in the hesitation model as a theoretical alternative is because of its finite size and infinite future. Of course I am *not equating* the finitude of a physical model of the universe and the meaning of finitude in theological/philosophical contexts. Nevertheless it is interesting theologically to learn that one cannot consistently attribute *both* purpose and finitude to the universe within theoretical Big Bang models.

In the spirit of McMullin's remark about cosmogony, this trade-off could be phrased as a hypothesis: To the extent that our universe can be described by standard Big Bang cosmology, we seem forced into the following trade-off: *If the open model proves valid we can find a Dyson-type scientific correlate for eschatological purposes but we will have to yield on the theological claim of finitude; alternatively, if the universe is in fact closed, the consonance over claims of finitude would entail a loss of eschatological purpose.*

Conclusion

In this paper I propose that the concept of contingency is central to the doctrine of creation, both as *creatio ex nihilo* and *creatio continua,* and to contemporary scientific cosmology. Working primarily within Big Bang cosmology (and hence setting aside questions of quantum mechanics, thermodynamics, and other relevant areas of physics), I suggest various tentative hypotheses about $t = 0$, finitude, design, and the eschatological future. These results are aimed at consonance between theology and science in which the empirical test of science will strengthen and trim the theological meaning of contingency.

The common role of contingency in both fields leads to a fresh perspective on why science and theology can be consistent with each other and need not be compartmentalized. *Every* scientific cosmology must include an element of contingency since it is precisely the role of these contingent elements in the theory to exclude that which is ultimate, absolutely necessary, *a se,* and hence to exclude "God" as part of the theoretical explanation. Hence *any* scientific cosmology must in *some* sense be consistent with the doctrine of creation since it ought not contain within it and proper to it a metascientific counterpart to the concept of God.[46]

On the other hand, if we want to move beyond consistency to consonance, the details of contingency in scientific models of the universe are *essential*. They both prune and fertilize the meaning of the doctrine of creation by providing an interpretative context with empirical pith. Hence by examining in detail the meaning of contingency in scientific cosmology, we may bring new vitality and joy to the root metaphors of this book: "cosmos as creation" and "God as creator."

NOTES

1. Even though he stands outside the public religious circle, Stephen Weinberg closes his recent book on cosmology with a remark that I take as expressing the nihilism so characteristic of our age: "The more the universe

seems comprehensible, the more it also seems pointless." Steven
Weinberg, *The First Three Minutes: A Modern View of the Origin of the
Universe* (New York: Basic Books, 1979), p.154.

2. A. R. Peacocke, *Creation and the World of Science* (Oxford: Clarendon
   Press, 1979).

3. In this short essay I will not examine the implications of quantum physics,
   quantum field theory, or non-linear non-equilibrium thermodynamics,
   fruitful though these areas are, but will restrict my essay to the specialized
   questions arising out of standard Big Bang cosmology and related models of
   the universe. Similarly, I will emphasize the meaning of creation theology
   in some forms of Protestant and Roman Catholic thought but leave aside
   the important critiques of process and deconstructionist theologies. A
   more extended discussion would argue that these other areas serve to
   relate novelty, the emergence of order from chaos, and the relation of
   chance and law to the creation tradition in important and differing ways.

4. Langdon Gilkey, *Maker of Heaven and Earth* (Garden City, N.Y.:
   Doubleday, 1959).

5. Ian G. Barbour, *Issues in Science and Religion* (New York: Harper & Row,
   1966).

6. Peacocke, *Creation and the World of Science.*

7. Philip J. Hefner, "The Creation," in *Christian Dogmatics,* ed. Carl E.
   Braaten and Robert W. Jenson (Philadelphia: Fortress Press, 1984), 2 vols.
   I:265-358.

8. Wolfhart Pannenberg, "The Doctrine of Creation and Modern Science,"
   Zygon 23:1 (March 1988) 3-21, and in altered form appearing in this
   volume.

9. Jürgen Moltmann, *God in Creation: A New Theology of Creation and the
   Spirit of God* (New York: Harper & Row, 1985).

10. Indeed process theologians rely exclusively on the continuous creation
    hermeneutic, finding no further value in maintaining *creatio ex nihilo.*

11. Karl Rahner and Herbert Vorgrimler, *Dictionary of Theology,* 2nd ed.
    (New York: Crossroad, 1981), p. 94.

12. Paul Tillich, *Systematic Theology,* 3 vols. (New York: Harper & Row for the
    University of Chicago Press, 1967), I:196.

13. Gilkey, *Maker of Heaven and Earth,* p. 47.

14. Pannenberg, "The Doctrine of Creation and Modern Science." See my
    response in Robert John Russell, "Contingency in Physics and Cosmology:
    A Critique of the Theology of Wolfhart Pannenberg," *Zygon: Journal of
    Religion and Science* 23:1 (March 1988), pp. 23-43.

15. Charles W. Misner, Kip S. Thorne, and John Archibald Wheeler,
    Gravitation (San Francisco: W. H. Freeman & Co., 1973), p. 5.

16. Ibid., p. 1198.

17. See S. W. Hawking and R. Penrose, "The singularities of gravitational
    collapse and cosmology," Proceedings of the Royal Society of London *A 314*
    (1969), pp. 529-48; and S. W. Hawking and G. F. R. Ellis, *The Large Scale
    Structure of Spacetime* (Cambridge: Cambridge University Press, 1973).

18. For a more extended discussion, see Jastrow's *God and the Astronomers*
    (New York: W. W. Norton & Co., 1978).

19. Pope Pius XII, "Modern Science and the Existence of God," *The Catholic
    Mind,* March 1952, pp. 182-92.

20. Interestingly, an infinitely old universe takes us back to the problem of metaphysical dualism and the early battles fought over *creatio ex nihilo*. If there were a bounce, what has survived from the previous universe? According to many physicists, nothing more structured than fundamental particles could have survived the unbelievable temperatures during a "bounce." Such temperatures would reduce any prior structures—galaxies, planets, civilizations, whatever—to quarks. In this sense even if the laws and elementary matter of our universe are infinitely old, our universe in all its macroscopic features is radically new since $t = 0$!

But what about the laws of physics? Do they govern all universes linked by bounces? Was God forced to work with physical laws as a modern equivalent of the Platonic forms and elementary particles as proto-matter in creating our universe? Or does even the space-time arena, its dimensions and topological structures, and with it the particles and laws, evaporate at each bounce? What about the laws of logic, of which physics is only one form? Perhaps all these get created by a God who transcends all physical "beginnings."

21. I still remember the scathing humor of a physics professor who caricatured theologians as "archers who first shoot their arrows, then paint the target: they can't miss—but then they can't afford to!"

22. Ernan McMullin, "How Should Cosmology Relate to Theology?" in *The Sciences and Theology in the Twentieth Century*, ed. A. R. Peacocke (Notre Dame: University of Notre Dame Press, 1981), pp. 39-52.

23. Is this a legitimate way to interpret physics? Many philosophers have stressed the irreducible role of time in subjectivity, and have been highly critical of any epistemology that rejects temporal passage and the distinction between past and future. Milic Capek, for example, argues that we should temporalize space, not spatialize time, as physicists do when they take space-time to be a four-dimensional space. For a recent discussion see *Physics and the Ultimate Significance of Time*, ed. David R. Griffin (Albany: State University of New York Press, 1986). Actually non-equilibrium thermodynamics and quantum physics offer potentially fertile ways to reconcile subjective and physical time. See for example Ilya Prigogine and Isabelle Stengers, *Order Out of Chaos* (Toronto: Bantam Books, 1984). Since Einsteinian relativity is a classical theory in many senses, it is not surprising that it lends itself to a timeless interpretation. Nevertheless its perspective offers a way to study the question of finitude, and its timeless quality is generally accepted among physicists.

24. Misner et al., *Gravitation*, p. 1198.

25. This is not strictly correct. The Einstein-de Sitter cosmology, with type VIII infinities in time *and* space, can be interpreted as a limiting case of type V for positive lambda for very large "radius" (scale factor) and negligible matter density. For details see Misner, et al., *Gravitation*, chapter 27, especially Box 27.5.

26. A similar though inverted figure could be drawn to suggest the infinities found in these models.

27. Sallie McFague argues that when the "is not" quality of a metaphor is forgotten, the theological result is idolatry. Sallie McFague, *Metaphorical Theology* (Philadelphia: Fortress Press, 1982).

28. Paul Tillich, *Systematic Theology*, I: 196.

29. When thinking about the universe in this way I am reminded of a passage from T. S. Eliot: "What might have been is an abstraction/Remaining a perpetual possibility/Only in a world of speculation./What might have been and what has been/Points to one end, which is always present." T. S. Eliot, "Burnt Norton," in *Four Quartets* (New York: Harcourt, Brace & World, 1943), p. 3.

30. Sir Arthur Eddington and P. A. M. Dirac made the most significant early contributions to this argument, but there were many other persons involved in the "large numbers hypothesis" debate. For a careful history, see John D. Barrow and Frank J. Tipler, *The Anthropic Cosmological Principle* (Oxford: Clarendon Press, 1986), chapter 4.

31. There are several versions of the Anthropic Principle, including so-called Weak and Strong forms. I am using the latter here. For more detailed discussion see Barrow and Tipler, *The Anthropic Cosmological Principle*.

32. B. Carter, "Large Number Coincidences and the Anthropic Principle in Cosmology," in *confrontation of cosmological theories with observation*, ed. M. S. Longair (Dordrecht: Reidel, 1974), pp. 291-98.

33. Freeman J. Dyson, *Disturbing the Universe* (New York: Harper & Row, 1979), p. 250.

34. John Leslie, "Modern Cosmology and the Creation of Life," in *Evolution and Creation*, ed. Ernan McMullin (Notre Dame: University of Notre Dame Press, 1985), pp. 91-120. Clearly Leslie's conclusions are far removed from eighteenth-century deism, and hence ought not to be considered a design argument in the narrow sense.

35. Barrow and Tipler, *The Anthropic Cosmological Principle*.

36. Taking a different tack, some believe that the universe should not be characterized by *any* arbitrary parameters. Ultimately all the laws of physics should be mutually interdeterminate. One sees this, for example, in the hermeneutic of self-consistency used so creatively in the bootstrap theory of particle physics by Geoffrey Chew. From this point of view our universe would be the *only* possible universe, and when a complete scientific cosmology is obtained, all the physical constants will fall out naturally from the theory.

37. James S. Trefil, *The Moment of Creation: Big Bang Physics from Before the First Millisecond to the Present Universe* (New York: Collier Books, 1983), p. 223.

38. Peacocke, *Creation and the World of Science*, p. 105.

39. Thomas F. Torrance, *Space, Time and Incarnation* (New York: Oxford University Press, 1969), p. 66. I am not sure whether Torrance means that all such possible worlds are actual and real, or whether they are only possibilities in the Creator's mind. It would be intriguing to explore this direction further.

40. In many-worlds arguments based on a bounce model of the quantum-gravitational universe, Wheeler suggested that even the laws of physics, as well as the natural constants, get recycled with each bounce. This would conflate levels one and two in Figure 2.

41. Bertrand Russell, "A Free Man's Worship" (1903), in *Mysticism and Logic and Other Essays* (London: Allen & Unwin, 1963 ed.), p. 41.

42. Weinberg, *The First Three Minutes*, p. 154. Cf. footnote 1.

43. Freeman J. Dyson, "Time without End: Physics and Biology in an Open Universe," *Review of Modern Physics* 51 (1979), p. 447 f.

44. Again in this paper I am ignoring quantum-gravitational models and concentrating on standard cosmology.

45. Barrow and Tipler, *The Anthropic Cosmological Principle*, p. 641.

46. Consequently theological programs, such as neoorthodoxy, which separate their domains from science are not so much wrong as inadequate for both dogmatic and apologetic reasons. It would be worth exploring how substantial issues do arise between theism and naturalism or theism and pseudo-science when ultimate categories are introduced into a science-based world view.

The Evolution of
the Created Co-Creator

PHILIP HEFNER

Is the cosmos essentially friend or foe? We ask this question from the human point of view, of course. Given the billions of geological aeons and light-years of astronomical distances that constitute the cosmos in which we wake up and find ourselves, do we find ourselves essentially at home or in a hostile environment? Are the elements out to destroy us or to edify us? The answer the Christian theologian gives is this: the cosmos is a creation, therefore, ultimately it is friend.

Our task in this chapter will be to examine the ways in which the theory of evolution is potentially important to Christian theology. In particular, we will focus on the Christian doctrine of anthropology within the wider *locus* of creation. Just how we should understand the human condition in light of evolutionary development and in light of the Christian belief that the cosmos is a creation will be the guiding question. Toward this end we will first cite the problem: the long evolutionary history of the nonhuman cosmos seems to swallow up any significance for the

Philip Hefner is professor of systematic theology at the Lutheran School of Theology at Chicago and director there of the Center for Religion and Science. This chapter, written for this book, appeared also in *Currents in Theology and Mission*, December 1988, pp. 512-25.

human race; therefore, it seems that the cosmos is not a creation. Yet we want to affirm divine purpose in the evolutionary processes. Following this formulation of the concern, we will identify three different approaches to relating evolutionary concepts to theology: the reforming, the historical, and the apologetic. We will then examine the apologetic approach and identify a number of issues to which Christian theologians should give attention. Turning finally to the reforming approach, we will define the human being as a "created co-creator" and draw out its implications within an evolutionary-conscious understanding of the doctrine of creation. All along we will work with the methodological assumption that theological theories should be commensurate—though not necessarily identical—with scientific theories about the world.

It will be my material contention that the evolving cosmos is an ongoing creation. The complex interaction in the co-evolution of genetic and cultural information, mediated by the human brain and selected by the system of forces that selects all things, can be said to be the means God has chosen to unfold the divine intention and to bring all of nature to a new stage of fulfillment. This entails a corollary understanding: the human being is God's created co-creator, whose purpose is the modifying and enabling of existing systems of nature so that they can participate in God's purposes in the mode of freedom.

Creation and the Theory of Evolution

The concept of evolution has been a difficult one for Christian theologians to handle. Since Charles Darwin formulated it in 1859, many church leaders have rejected it because it seems to leave out any divine role in the ongoing creative process. Numerous theologians have accepted the concept, but even these acceptors have done relatively little toward reformulating Christian doctrine to make it both commensurate with evolutionary theory yet faithful to the biblical tradition. The task of reformulating is one that needs to appear on the theological agenda in the near future.

One sub-item that must appear on this agenda is the

enormous time scale needed for evolutionary development and the question regarding the significance of the human species which this raises. To put it in perspective, we note that the universe most likely came into existence with the Big Bang about 18 billion years ago; the earth's crust congealed about 4 billion years ago; dinosaurs flourished from 180 million to 63 million years ago; our important ancestor *homo erectus* flourished 600,000 to 350,000 years ago. If we were to plot this sequence of events on a calendar with one day equaling 14 million years and one hour equaling a half million years, our natural history would look like this: on January 1 the earth's crust congealed; dinosaurs appeared on December 21; Neanderthal man arrives only at 11:50 P.M. on New Year's Eve. Relative to the overall history of the natural cosmos, the role of the human species is staggering in its minuteness.

Yet we Christians think of ourselves as having been created in the image of God and of our history as the arena of divine providence. So we need to ask in light of evolutionary theory, Does this tiny portion of nature's history detract from the marvel that we attach to human existence? Or does it simply add a dimension of mystery and complexity without fundamentally changing our view? We need to ask further, Why was *homo sapiens* created in this manner? What is the significance of the aeons of nonhuman history? Why did God do it this way? In short, what does evolutionary theory do to Christian anthropology?

Evolutionary Interpretations of Christianity

The above list of questions aimed at reformulating our anthropology represents one way in which evolutionary theory may have an impact on Christian thinking. At the heart of this approach is the task of adapting doctrinal teachings to the evolutionary vision. We will call this the *reforming* approach, because it aims at a reform of Christian theology. Much of the work of Teilhard de Chardin[1] and, more recently, Arthur Peacocke[2] is of this type. This concern will draw our attention in the latter section of the present chapter.

A second and quite different approach, the *historical* approach, tries to show that the Christian faith itself has evolved in the context of its sucessive environments. This type of historical study has been extensive, and its significance is widely recognized. The great nineteenth-century theologians brought this approach to a high point, as the work of F. C. Baur, Albrecht Ritschl, Adolf von Harnack, and Ernst Troeltsch demonstrates. Revisionist accounts from many quarters today still carry on this effort. This will not be a concern of the present study.

The third approach shares much with the second; yet its main thrust is of another type. It seeks to identify just what significance Christian faith itself *has for* the evolutionary process. I call this the *apologetic* approach, because it aims at articulating a proposal that is of interest to Christians and non-Christians alike. Ralph W. Burhoe and especially Gerd Theissen follow the apologetic track.

The third or apologetic approach deserves our initial attention. This is the case not only because of its intrinsic interest, but also because decisions we make here will redound back upon the reforming approach and give direction to doctrinal reformulation. I therefore propose that we take a look at one example of the apologetic type, draw out some of the issues posed, and then return to our task of formulating a Christian anthropology in light of evolutionary theory.

The best example in the current discussion of the apologetic approach is Gerd Theissen's brilliant book of 1984, *Biblical Faith: An Evolutionary Approach*. There are six key arguments in this work. These arguments are not necessarily the ones Theissen himself gives most attention to, but they are the basic ideas that make the book possible.

Theissen's first argument is that the evolving world process (as a whole and in its parts) is caught up in a process of relating to a central reality that our religious traditions call "God." The second argument is that this process of relating to the central reality is today termed *evolution*, which is fundamentally a process of "finding increasingly more adequate structures for adapting" to this ultimate or central reality.[3]

Third, the process of evolution is both biological and cultural. We note that Theissen does not mention the pre-biological. He follows the now familiar insight that the phases of the process of evolution all take the course of producing a multitude of variations, of which one or a few are selected and integrated within systems that are adaptive to the environment. The most important environment for Theissen is the central reality, God.

Fourth, Theissen views the human being as a complex creature who is characterized most importantly as a biological animal that has become a cultural being, and whose most critical challenge is the ongoing task of properly integrating these two "natures," the biological and the cultural. A better way to put it is to say that the human being is a biologically evolved creature who is culturally ambient, and who must continually struggle, if it is to remain a genuinely *human* creature. This struggle consists in modulating its biological equipment and the rationale of that equipment in a way that is consistent with and appropriate to the possibilities of its present and future cultural ambience. Or we could say that *the human being is always struggling to integrate its biological equipment into the cultural configuration that the human has become*. Teilhard painted this struggle vividly in his saying, "Pay attention to what is going on, because we are now leaving the stone age." He meant that we must attend carefully to the danger that exists because we bring stone-age biological drives into a contemporary technological milieu to which our biological equipment is but poorly adapted. Anthony Stevens points to this same issue when he subtitles one of his books, "a natural history of the self."[4] Victor Turner devoted his famed article, "Body, Brain, and Culture" to the same insight.[5] Theissen seems to understand the argument.

Fifth, the key to understanding biblical faith, says Theissen, is to perceive its significance as a phenomenon within the evolutionary process, specifically as it affects human persons in social or cultural evolution. We remember, of course, that these human persons have entered the evolutionary process as creatures who have also evolved biologically. This leads us to the sixth argument: the biblical faith contains a proposal for what is possible within cultural evolution by human creatures who are also biologically evolved. This proposal has both a scientific and a theological rendition:

SCIENTIFIC	THEOLOGICAL
1. Evolution of the cosmos is adapting to a central reality.	1. Evolution of the cosmos transpires within the hands of God and adapts to God.
2. Altruism beyond the kin group is a universal value for humanity.	2. The core of biblical faith is the revelation of the love-principle.
3. The premier possibility opened up for human cultural evolution is that we can diminish "selection." Such diminishment allows the biological components of the human being to be transcended, so that we can be the cultural creatures that we have it in us to be. Behaviors and social forms that inhibit us from becoming such cultural creatures are inadequate.	3. This love-principle is a significant option within human cultural evolution; it is the command of God. Behaviors and social forms that oppose or restrict the practice of universal love for neighbor are contrary to the will of God. God will enable us to practice it. This is the content of the "image of God."

These six arguments rest upon four assumptions, two theological and two scientific. The two theological assumptions are these: (1) the evolution of the cosmos transpires within the will of God and adapts to God, and (2) the central feature of God's will for this cosmic process is expressed in the love-principle. The scientific assumptions are these: (1) we cannot understand the human being unless we recognize that it is a culturally evolving form that entered the cultural evolutionary process as a creature that had already evolved biologically, and (2) the love-principle is significant for interpreting the process of cultural evolution, because of the impact that it has on the biological component of this biological-cultural human being.

Although interesting, none of these four assumptions is in itself startling or original. It is in the conjunction of the four that Theissen's thinking becomes exciting and provocative. Conjoined, the argument takes this useful shape: the evolving world process is actually a process of responding and adapting to God. God has created a process that is woven on the loom of adapting to its creator. This adapting is what constitutes the basic character of the world process.

The purpose of outlining Theissen's thought is to use it as a way of unearthing basic issues for the larger attempt to interpret Christian faith in evolutionary modes of thought. With this in mind, let me raise a number of issues and suggest possible directions for theological reflection if not reform.

Issue 1: Which aspects of evolution are to be considered? Should we consider biological evolution and cultural evolution together? In the past very few have attempted to deal seriously with the interface between biological and cultural evolution. For some, it has been unacceptable even to bring culture within the evolutionary conceptuality; while for others, the interface has been dealt with only simplistically. There is no question, however, in light of current research in the neuro-sciences, anthropology, psychiatry, experimental and developmental psychology, ethology, and related fields, that we have now reached the point where biogenetic and cultural processes must be examined in their interrelatedness if we are to understand cultural phenomena adequately. Perhaps no single text makes this point more clearly than the aforementioned article by Victor Turner, "Body, Brain, and Culture," even though dozens of other scholars have argued for this as well.

The imperative to interrelate cultural with biological evolution does not stem from any reductionistic impulse. Rather, it is a response to the fact that culture has emerged within the realm of biological development. Consequently, the meaning and coherence of the cultural dimension must be consistent and continuous with that of the biological dimension. Just what this consistency and continuity are, precisely, is a matter of dispute—ranging from those sociobiologists who claim that culture is on a rather short genetic leash, to cultural anthropologists and humanities scholars who deny even a long leash between the two. One thing is clear: any future attempts to interpret Christian faith in evolutionary perspective must take account of this relationship between biology and culture, and it must further attempt to sort out the results of the researchers in the field. Among those thinkers, besides Turner, who have made attempts in this area are Ralph W. Burhoe, Donald Campbell, Solomon Katz, and Karl Peters.[6]

Although Theissen's work makes a contribution for its broad treatment of the concept of evolution, I believe it can still be faulted for not being broad enough. What is missing is the cosmic and physical. My point is not that Theissen should account for a greater quantity of data. Rather, what he and we need to recognize is that the bio-cultural continuum is itself a development within the cosmic processes that were unleashed in the singularity that gave birth to the Big Bang. Culture and biology are chapters in the physical story of the cosmos.

What is at issue is whether or not we will treat with consistency and continuity the cosmic-physical processes and the biological-cultural developments. This issue is as intellectually demanding as any that a contemporary theologian might encounter. The difficulty is not so much one of understanding how the animate and the cultural can emerge from the inanimate and impersonal—this question is being addressed by a large number of scientific researchers—but rather the challenge is to ask this question, How can we paint a picture of the meaningfulness of human developments when the canvas for interpretation is the unfolding of cosmic processes over an enormous 18-billion-year span?

Issue 2: The status of the Christian faith. Nearly a century ago, the Yale natural historian Newman Smyth argued that theology could be done in the context of evolution on the grounds that scientific research into the nature of evolution would lead necessarily to the God of the Christian faith. Although that is still the conviction of many Christian adherents, virtually no one today would suggest that a presuppositionless study of evolutionary theory would lead to such a conclusion. The prevailing method today among theologians who take evolution seriously is to assume the actuality of Christian faith as a historical datum. From this assumption we may then ask without apology (a) what difference evolutionary theory makes for Christian faith and (b) what significance might the Christian faith have for the evolution of the universe.

If the givenness of the Christian datum within the evolutionary continuum is our starting point, then the theologian ought not be inhibited from interpreting the Christian faith from the point of its most particular and distinctive identity, namely, Jesus Christ. The evolutionary processes have engendered this distinctive particularity; no apology for this starting point is required. What is required, however, is the strenuous effort of articulating what the continuities are between the evolutionary processes and Jesus Christ, and what the significance of Christ within those processes is.

Issue 3: Evolutionary processes within God's action. Since the time of Charles Darwin there has existed a tradition of theological interpretation that has asserted that "evolution is God's way of doing things." This basic assertion has taken on different meanings depending on the intention of the theologian. One thread of interpretation is the simplistic assertion of Newman Smyth and Asa Gray that evolutionary process is the way God brings spirit to life from matter. Another interpretation is that of Social Darwinism, which adds quite a different nuance to the way God's action is understood. In our own time Arthur Peacocke's image of God as the composer of fugues, the creator of an infinite set of complexities from simple foundations, is yet another variation on this theme.[7] Along with Gerd Theissen, Ralph W. Burhoe adds the emphasis that evolutionary processes are themselves responses to God, and through the processes of selection, divine purposes are achieved.[8]

Now not all thinkers who see evolution as God's tool focus on selection as part of that tool. Still fewer understand adaptation in the selection process as itself a response to God. Evolutionary interpretations that are silent on the role of selection are less credible, in my judgment, because the concept of selection is so significant to evolutionary theory.

Be that as it may, to focus on selection within God's activity is to face directly the issue of theodicy. Why? Because the selection processes go hand-in-hand with the failure and death of living forms, human persons, social institutions, and ideas. There is perhaps no more difficult issue for the theologian than the interpretation of why there is selection and what divine purpose it might serve. Few theologians even attempt to deal with this challenge. The issue of selection raises the same questions as those that are part of the reflection on why God should have created an evolutionary process that responds to God as the selecting environment.

In the context of thinking about theodicy, John Hick rightly raises the question of freedom in relation to the selection process. For freedom to be genuine, he argues, the creation could not be fashioned initially in a fully free state; rather, it must become free. In order to become free, the initial conditions of any individual must be at an epistemic distance from the goal that is to be attained.[9] Furthermore, the goal must be worthwhile, not on extrinsic or utilitarian grounds, but rather it must have intrinsic worth, with no sure extrinsic profit. The evolutionary process makes freedom possible, provided that evil and misfortune fall haphazardly and randomly upon the world, so that no free behavior can be certain to avoid evil. The free choice must, on the contrary, be chosen for its intrinsic worth alone.

This kind of fundamental reflection is required by today's theologians if an evolutionary interpretation of the Christian faith is to be pursued adequately. The question of freedom is of particular significance, because I believe a good case ought to be made for interpreting the entire physical and biological nonhuman prehistory as the instrumentality employed by God to introduce freedom into the cosmos and set up the introduction of the human being as the created co-creator.

Issue 4: The human being as a two-natured creature. Can we through culture transcend our biological foundation without eroding it? This is a double challenge. On the one hand, will the biological dimension allow itself to participate in the sort of transcendence that the cultural dimension represents? On the other hand, can culture fashion a lifeway that can actualize the possibilities that culture can attain while at the same time doing so in a way that represents the genuine destiny of the biological processes? Or, to put it another way, Can culture open up genuine possibilities that are appropriate to both the biological and the cultural dimensions without either destroying the biological or betraying the cultural?

It is in the cultural sphere we know as ethics and morality where the issue arises. H. Kummer, working with the definition of morality as the "absence of selfish opportunism," argues that there is no analog to morality among animals, even at the higher primate level.[10] Selfish opportunism reigns in the nonhuman animal kingdom. Kummer believes it is the evolution of human cognitive abilities—especially self-consciousness and decision-making—which makes morality both possible and necessary. The purpose of morality is to enhance cooperation, thereby reducing the dangers of species self-annihilation through competition. If Kummer is correct, then two things become significant. First, the cultural configurations of the human race make it possible to destroy itself. Second, the cultural phenomenon of morality may itself be an adaptive process belonging to the long history of evolutionary selection. In either case, the cultural production of altruistic moral codes represents a going beyond our biological determinants.

The transcending of the biological has been a topic in several discussions in recent years. The issue is altruism: Is the love-principle anti-evolutionary because, as self-sacrificing, it tends toward self-elimination rather than self-selection?[11] Richard Dawkins, in his book *The Selfish Gene,* argues that culture must oppose the "selfishness" of the genes if love and other basic human values are to succeed; because the genes act in no other way than to work for their own literal survival.[12] In a similar fashion Theissen speaks of cultural evolution—and particularly the Christian faith within culture—as "anti-selection." Now this position has been criticized in part. Yet a truth remains: if altruism in culture really does oppose the genes, it will be signing culture's death warrant, since genetic evolution is the host in this symbiosis. Without the biological host, culture cannot enjoy the party.

Despite the possible inadequacy of "anti-selection" rhetoric, the intention of Dawkins and Theissen is clear and significant. They are asking us to face the fact that culture enables the biological host to surmount or even alter patterns of behavior which might otherwise seem inevitable. Genetic evolution, for example, limits the range of altruism to the kin-group; whereas Christian faith enables the human creature to extend the principle of altruism beyond the kin-group. The biological component of a human being faces the developmental challenge to sculpt itself in ways that surmount some of the basic drives or behaviors that are wholly undesirable in a human community.[13] It is no mean developmental task for culture to enable such surmounting without destroying the biological ladder by which it has climbed to this position.

Once again, freedom enters into the discussion. Human agency becomes a factor in evolution proper. The human agent, though certainly conditioned by its genetic and environmental host, enjoys a certain measure of freedom. This freedom is concomitant with the self-consciousness and decision-making capacities endemic to cultural life.

The appearance of ethics and morality reminds us of our biological dependence and our cultural freedom. Although we cannot go to the party unless invited by the host, once we are there, we have sufficient freedom to alter the menu, determine which games are played, make it joyful or boring, and even to leave early. What theologians need to do, I think, is negotiate the complexities of the genes-culture interface and relate that interface to the physical cosmos as well.

Issue 5: How should we understand divine revelation? On the basis of the above, we should be able to say that our creator God has mandated that we should come to know life in a two-natured way: biological and cultural. Therefore, it seems to me that we should also be able to say the following: the task of properly integrating the two natures is God's way of sculpting the means by which we attain and exercise our humanity and also the path by which we enter into relationship with God. The divinely intended fulfillment of human destiny will include the proper integration of our biological and cultural natures.

If this is the set of conditions in which God has created us, then it should not surprise us that the good God bestows gifts that are relevant to the task that is ours by virtue of our creation. God's revelation, consequently, cannot but be a cultural evolutionary possibility for the carrying out of our humanity in ways appropriate to the two-natured creatures that we are. If the heart of our Christian revelation is that of unqualified love for all creatures as the nature and will of God, then that love-principle must be seen as a cultural evolutionary proposal for the well-being of the creation in general and for us humans in particular. It belongs to our process of becoming fully human. It is not helpful to think of the revelation as some initially abstract and unrelated reality that only secondarily is a possibility of cultural evolution. That could be true only if we were created initially in the abstract and only secondarily as the two-natured creatures that we have described. We were created in no other way than as such bio-cultural creatures, and God's revelation has neither reality nor force apart from its significance as a possibility for creatures such as we are.

Issue 6: The significance of Christian faith. I contend that the Christian faith, if it is to be interpreted adequately in an evolutionary framework must be related to the sorts of issues that have figured in the discussion to this point. It must be related to all the phases of evolution and to the processes of selection. We need to ask just what is it that the historic

Christian faith contributes to the cultural evolutionary process.

More than simply placing the Christian faith in the evolutionary context is called for. We need to speak theologically to the question of God's will for the destiny of the processes themselves. The majority of interpreters who have tackled this issue in recent decades have focused on something to do with the love-principle, with altruism, with the freedom to cross boundaries and identify with outsiders. We need to show that such things as the love-principle are not essentially anti-evolutionary but rather intrinsic to the broader evolutionary purpose. To do so means, among other things, bringing the Christian doctrine of eschatology to bear, since we cannot speak of the destiny of the world without speaking about its future and its eventual culmination.

Teilhard de Chardin, among preciously few others, understood the cultural evolutionary significance of Christianity to be the embodiment of the love for the world that can motivate acts that would actualize human solidarity in tandem with enhanced individualization. This individualization-within-solidarity is what he termed "building the earth," and he considered it to be the current imperative required by the trajectory of evolution in which we exist.[14]

Ralph Burhoe interprets Christianity (and by extension he would apply this interpretation to other religions as well) as a body of well-winnowed wisdom (Donald Campbell's term) which has emerged within the evolutionary process precisely because it has been selected. Hence, it has served the survival value of the process in which it has appeared.[15] This large packet of cultural information cannot be identified with only a single message, since its mores and rituals pertain to many aspects of life. However, Burhoe gives special attention to the love-principle, which he is inclined to speak of as "trans-kin altruism." This altruism has not only been instrumental in enabling the higher primates to become human beings, but it has also played a key role in subsequent developments. Today the love-principle is, in Burhoe's opinion, the chief imperative for the human community if it is to avoid destroying itself.

Gerd Theissen also emphasizes the love-principle as the

force that enables human beings to transcend and yet fulfill the biological dimension of existence. The biological dimension manifests itself as *sarkic* (fleshly) behavior, which seems to be explicitly biological; but it also manifests itself as deadening "law" in the cultural sphere, as rigid "tradition" at the level of cognitive systems. Christ's love-principle enables persons to dare to transcend flesh, law, and tradition. At this point, Theissen brings to bear his concept of evolution as variability, selection, and adaptation. All the variable attempts that arise in the process are essential for satisfactory adaptation, since a large number of variants is desirable so that the best options can be winnowed by the selection process. Even the abortive variations are therefore integral to the process. Further, each of the variable attempts is equidistant from the center of the process and whatever intentionality it has. Theologically, this train of thinking is equivalent to a concept of justification and grace. God requires no set pattern of successful adaptation. Rather God requires an earnest and responsible life of attempting to adapt to the divine reality and will, from which attempts the most adequate can be selected. All such attempts are equidistant from the center of God's will and grace.

The Created Co-Creator

What we have been looking at is the broad range of issues that we must confront if we are to follow the apologetic approach, the approach that seeks to identify the significance the Christian faith has for the evolutionary process. Now let us turn back to the Christian doctrine of anthropology, thinking it through with an eye to the reforming approach and what we have learned from evolutionary concepts. Granting a degree of consonance between evolutionary science and constructive theology, what can we say about the human condition?

I recommend that we think of the human being as the *created co-creator*. This term does a number of things. Because we are *created*, we are reminded that we are dependent creatures. We depend for our very existence on our cosmic and biological prehistory; we depend on the creative grace of God. Yet, we are also *creators*, using our cultural freedom and power to alter the course of historical events and perhaps even evolutionary events. We participate with God in the ongoing creative process. In addition, the term "created co-creator" connotes the fact that we have a destiny. We have a future toward which we are being drawn by God's will. Only when we understand what this destiny is will we be able to measure and evaluate the direction we take in our creative activity. To unearth the significance of this understanding of the human condition, let us look at the idea of the created co-creator in light of five classical Christian doctrines.

Doctrine 1: Creation Out of Nothing

Fundamental to both the Jewish and Christian view of the world is the doctrine of creation out of nothing, *creatio ex nihilo*. This affirms that God is the source of all that is. The nub of *creatio ex nihilo* is this: the only relationship between the world and God that is consistent with what Christians and Jews believe about God is one in which the universe and our planet within it are totally dependent upon God for its origin and perseverance.

The doctrine of *creatio ex nihilo* is not so much a material concept as it is a methodological strategy. The point of *ex nihilo* is not specifically aimed at identifying the lack of preexisting materials from which he constructed the world. It does not assert that God created all things out of the prior reality called "nothing," "nonbeing," what the Greeks dubbed οὔκ ὄν. The doctrine has less to do with origins than it does with dependence. Rather, as a methodological strategy, it insists that everything that is depends for its being on God the creator.

On the basis of this assertion of the total dependence of all things on the creator God, I raise as an additional axiom that there is a correlation between the nature of the world and the nature of the God who created the world.[16] As a negative correlation it affirms that if God is the creator out of nothing, then this world is totally and completely a creature. When Christian witnesses take this axiom seriously, its proclamation demands attention. What it says makes a difference. It affirms, among other things, that our cosmos is a creation.

We human beings, then, are first and foremost creatures. We are caused. We are created. We are not self-generating. This is obvious whether one reads Genesis 2–3 to see that we have sprung from God and dust, or when one looks through evolutionary glasses and reviews the long prehistory about the emergence of life in planet Earth's primordial soup. We have come from a source well beyond ourselves.

We humans, then, can claim no arrogant credit for being co-creators. We have been created *as* co-creators. Put in scientific terms, we did not evolve ourselves to this point; rather, the evolutionary process—under God's rule, I am arguing—evolved us as co-creators. We could not even choose to be created as non-creators. God chose. That we exist as created co-creators is God's decision, not ours.

Doctrine 2: Continuing Creation

Creation for Christian theology is by no means limited to protology. It is not limited by what happened at the beginning when time was first created. Creation also refers to God's ongoing sustaining of the world. Every moment of the world's existence depends on the ongoing grace of God.

This assertion of continuing creation, when coupled with the creation-out-of-nothing concept, makes a powerful statement about the nonhuman creation as a trustworthy environment for the human. It asserts that the world about us is not antithetical to our human destiny and God's will; but rather it is a fundamentally friendly home for us. The ecosystem is benevolent and reliable. It cannot be otherwise if it has proceeded originally from God's creative intention and continues to be sustained by the will of God.[17]

If we invoke our correlation axiom at this point, we get a positive correlation: God creates and so do we. We are active participants in the ongoing divine work. We make decisions and take actions that determine in part the course of events. Events bring new things. The human race is daily inventing new things that hitherto never existed. It is a dependent co-creation, to be sure; yet there is a genuine advance due to the contributions of human ingenuity and energy.

And, if evolutionary advance is influenced by our adaptation to God, then altruism may eventually lead to a qualitatively new reality. As co-creators with God, the dramatic possibility is opening up that the love-principle might actually introduce into bio-cultural evolution a new selection principle, a principle that goes beyond the previous gene selfishness.

Doctrine 3: The Imago Dei

A third and important component in theology's understanding of the world's status is the teaching concerning the *imago dei,* the image of God in the human race. Although the term has a long history and is almost universally attested in the theological tradition, there is only modest agreement regarding its exact meaning. At least two distinct traditions of interpretation can be identified: the common characteristic tradition and the relationship tradition. The first tries to identify specific human characteristics that are Godlike: love, uprightness, the capacity for dominion over the animals, and so forth. The second, the relationship perspective, suggests that the *imago dei* refers to the basic structure of the human being that enables communication between humans and God. Augustine gave voice to this second strand with his oft-quoted prayer: "O God, Thou hast created me for Thyself, and my heart is restless until it find its rest in Thee."[18] Of these two traditions, my inclination is to side with those who hold that the *imago dei* refers to our relationship with God.

I suggest that we identify our co-creatorhood with the image of God. We humans have certain characteristics that constitute the *imago dei* in us—we are able to make self-conscious and self-critical decisions, we are able to act on those decisions, and we are able to take responsibility for them. The human race can be dubbed *homo faber,* as our great technological achievements testify. We have altered the face of the earth and even dented the facade of outer space. In addition, we have moral capacity. We can look at what we have done and evaluate it. We can ask about its purpose and decide to redirect our decision-making and action-taking. God creates. So do we.

Now it may appear that I am identifying with the common characteristics tradition. But the relational perspective is what I really have in mind. It is the *co* in *co-creator* that I wish to emphasize. It is because we are grounded in a prior relationship with God who is bearing us along according to his will for the destiny of the cosmos that we find our creative characteristics significant. We are participants in a much larger ongoing creative process. Without such grounding, these characteristic abilities would mean little.

Doctrine 4: Christology

Through adaptive and creative work in culture, the human being represents a proposal for the further evolution of the created world. We humans have the potential to actualize a new phase of evolution. This is one of the implications of the doctrine of the image of God in us. But something else needs to be added here, namely, that in the New Testament the phrase "image of God" refers to Jesus Christ. Jesus Christ is the New Adam, the prototype of the true *humanum*. We fulfill the image of God insofar as we participate in Christ's new nature.

In Jesus Christ we find the power that enables us to participate in the purposes of God. Jesus, the second Adam, embodies anticipatorily what the first Adam can become. Jesus is that for which the creation of the first Adam was intended. Whereas the first Adam is a symbol of the essential humanity that belongs to every member of the species, the second Adam speaks of what humanity may yet become.

Jesus Christ becomes the central event for understanding what it means for humans to be God's proposal for the future of the evolutionary process. In freedom—a freedom that has been bequeathed to our race from the aeons of previous physical and biological and cultural development—we have the option to live now according to what has been set forth by Jesus as

God's ultimate purpose: the renewal and perfection of all creation.

We can think of the Christ-event as an act of God to which we should adapt and of our adaptation itself as having an impact on the future of evolution. Gerd Theissen said that we encounter "the central reality," God, on all levels of evolution.[19] In his life, death, and teachings, Jesus offers us the possibilities for raising human living to a higher plane, one which will reveal new ways of adapting to the reality system of nature and of God. Jesus' proposal for the love-principle—a universal love that crosses boundaries, including the boundaries of kinship—is a new way of life that stretches and bends the requirements of adaptation in novel ways. This proposal for trans-kin altruism is scandalous to many, because it appears to be a formula for maladaptation if not extinction. Yet, theologically, we want to say that the cross and resurrection represent the divinely willed direction for future cultural evolution.

Doctrine 5: The Eschatological Destiny of the Creation

The question of ultimate destiny is central to the assessment of the world and of the human place in it, because destiny suggests that there is a basic purpose or meaning inherent in existence as creation. If this is so, then the condition of the world at any moment can be judged by comparing its trajectory with its destiny.

What is the intention of God toward the world? I believe Christian theology is clear on this point: God intends to perfect or fulfill the creation. This is based upon two elements within the revelation, God's promises and God's faithfulness. God is faithful. God is not a deceiver. And, furthermore, God makes promises. Therefore, we can expect God to keep the promises he has made. Time and again this has been asserted in the Jewish and Christian interpretation of historical events. It is equally applicable to the history of nature, to cosmic history. Indeed, with our knowledge that humans are a part of the ecosystem and its evolution and not separate from it, if

God is faithful in any portion of the world, such as human affairs, then God must be faithful in the whole, since the world is a seamless robe.

What this means for cosmic evolution seems to be this: the material order carries out its career from origin to end as God's creative process. This speaks to our earlier question as to the relationship between the 18-billion-year prehistory and the place the present human race has in this larger scheme. All must be conceived as somehow belonging together as part of God's grand program for the created world.

What this means for us humans seems to be this: our created status is thoroughly eschatological; that is, it is an *unleashing*, not a full-blown given that has simply to be reiterated and replicated throughout time. Human nature was not defined and fixed at some point of origin in the past. Whatever we were in the primordial past, we are not that now. Nor will we be the same in the future. Our essence is yet to be determined. Our nature is dynamic. And the dynamism comes from the eschatological future. The essential *humanum* that is emerging is being continually called by its destiny, and our ability to participate as an ordained co-creator is the result of the creative thrust of God. That thrust consists of sharing as a free, self-conscious creature in shaping the passage forward toward God's own *telos* or purpose which will appear in its fullness at the consummation, at the final perfection of the whole cosmic history of the creation.

Conclusion

Is nature friend or foe? Friend, we can say theologically. Nature in its entirety—from its original singularity 18 billion years ago, through the Big Bang, through the formation of planet earth, through the appearance of primordial soup and the flourishing of animate life, through the long genetic history of biological development, through the appearance of human culture, through the history of the Hebrew and Christian religions, and through chapters in our future story that have yet to be written—is being guided by the eschatological purpose of the one God who is the creator of all things. And this purpose is to perfect all that constitutes the creation, human beings included. More than that, we humans created in the image of God are participants and co-creators in the ongoing work of God's creative activity. We are being drawn toward a shared destiny that will ultimately determine what it means to be a true human being.

NOTES

1. Pierre Teilhard de Chardin, *The Phenomenon of Man* (New York: Harper & Row, 1959).
2. Arthur Peacocke, *Creation and the World of Science* (Oxford: Clarendon Press, 1979) and *God and the New Biology* (New York: Harper & Row, 1986).
3. Gerd Theissen, *Biblical Faith: An Evolutionary Approach* (Philadelphia: Fortress, 1985), pp. 23, 25.
4. Anthony Stevens, *Archetypes: A Natural History of the Self* (New York: Morrow, 1982).
5. Victor Turner, "Body, Brain, and Culture," *Zygon* 18:3 (September 1983), pp. 221-45.
6. See "Religion's Role in the Context of Genetic and Cultural Evolution: Campbell's Hypotheses and Some Evaluative Responses," ed. Ralph W. Burhoe in *Zygon* 11:3 (September 1976), pp. 115-303.
7. Peacocke, *Creation and the World of Science*, pp. 105-6; and "Theology and Science Today," chapter 1 of the present volume.
8. Ralph W. Burhoe, *Toward a Scientific Theology* (Belfast, Dublin, and Ottawa: Christian Journals, 1981).
9. John Hick, *Evil and the God of Love* (New York: Harper & Row, rev. ed., 1978), pp. 280 ff; and "An Irenaean Theodicy" in *Encountering Evil*, ed. Stephen Davis (Atlanta: John Knox Press, 1981), pp. 69-100.
10. H. Kummer, "Analogs of Morality Among Nonhuman Creatures," in *Morality as a Biological Phenomenon*, ed. Gunter Stent (Berkeley: University of California Press, 1980), pp. 33-42.
11. E. O. Wilson has said altruism is the "central theoretical problem of sociobiology." *Sociobiology: The New Synthesis* (Cambridge, Mass.: Harvard University Press, 1975), p. 46. John Maynard Smith poses the issue by defining altruism as "a trait which, in some cases, lowers the fitness of the individual displaying it, but increases the fitness of some other members of the same species." "The Evolution of Social Behavior—A Classification of Models," in *Current Problems in Sociobiology*, ed. King's College Sociobiology Group (Cambridge: Cambridge University Press, 1982), p. 43.
12. Richard Dawkins, *The Selfish Gene* (Oxford: Oxford University Press, 1976).

13. See my discussion in "Sociobiology, Ethics, and Theology," *Zygon* 19:2 (June 1984), pp. 185-207; and "Survival as a Human Value," *Zygon* 15:2 (June 1980), pp. 203-12.
14. Teilhard de Chardin, *The Phenomenon of Man.*
15. Burhoe, *Toward a Scientific Theology.*
16. See my "Fourth Locus: The Creation," in *Christian Dogmatics,* 2 vols., ed. Carl E. Braaten and Robert E. Jenson (Philadelphia: Fortress Press, 1984), I:298, 310.
17. Cf. Hefner, "Sociobiology, Ethics, and Theology," p. 191; cf. also "Creation Viewed by Science, Affirmed by Faith," in *Cry of the Environment,* ed. Philip N. Joranson and Ken Butigan (Sante Fe: Bear & Co., 1984), pp. 199 ff.
18. Augustine, *Confessions,* 1:1.
19. Theissen, *Biblical Faith,* p. 114.

SEVEN

Does Prayer Make a Difference?

Nancey C. Murphy

And [Jesus] said to them, "Which of you who has a friend
will go to him at midnight and say to him, 'Friend, lend
me three loaves; for a friend of mine has arrived on a
journey, and I have nothing to set before him'; and he will
answer from within, 'Do not bother me; the door is now
shut, and my children are with me in bed; I cannot get up
and give you anything'? I tell you, though he will not get
up and give him anything because he is his friend, yet
because of his importunity he will rise and give him
whatever he needs. And I tell you, Ask, and it will be
given you; seek, and you will find; knock, and it will be
opened to you. For every one who asks receives, and he
who seeks finds, and to him who knocks it will be opened"
(Luke 11:5-10).

Christians (and perhaps other believers as well) have been
commanded to pray for what they need. The above parable not

Professor Murphy teaches on the faculty at Whittier College and serves on the
board of trustees for the Center for theology and the Natural Sciences in
Berkeley. Her work focuses on philosophy of science and its value for Christian
theology.

only speaks of the necessity and efficacy of prayer, but suggests that God, like the neighbor next door, is open to having his mind *changed* by a friend's plea on behalf of self or others.

In some churches, however, most notably those with a highly educated population, there is little enthusiasm for petitionary or intercessory prayer. Well might this be the case, for it is not clear that Christian belief still supports such a practice. Prayer for recovery of the sick, for jobs for the unemployed, for favorable weather in agricultural areas, has become an anomalous practice for many. In this essay we explore two sorts of reasons for such a development. The first is philosophical; the second is scientific—a consequence of the scientific world view developed in the early modern period. However, we shall see that recent changes in both philosophy and science have defused both sorts of objections to prayer. First, however, let us see in what sense petitionary and intercessory prayer have become "anomalous practices."

Petitionary Prayer as an Anomalous Practice

Petitionary prayer and intercessory prayer are requests—requests of God for favors for ourselves and others, respectively. However, the linguistic practice of making a request requires that certain conditions be met. Alice asks Bob to close the door but, when he responds, complains that she didn't want it closed. A request when one doesn't want what one asks for is a speech act that has misfired; it is defective. Similarly, suppose Bob is in a body cast and cannot move. Again the request misfires, since Alice knows that Bob cannot possibly comply with her wishes. Hence, happy requesting requires that the one making the request have some reasonable expectation that the one addressed will be able to do as asked. Finally, consider the case where Bob is already in the process of closing the door. Again, we have an unhappy speech act, and we may conclude that requesting requires that the thing requested not be expected to come about in the ordinary course of events without the request being made.[1]

Let us now apply these conditions to prayer. The first condition discussed above is usually fulfilled in our requests to

God; we usually do in fact want the things for which we pray. But what about the second and third? For reasons to be examined more carefully below, many contemporary Christians have come to doubt either the efficacy of prayer or its necessity. Their arguments might go something like this: "The weather is determined by the laws of nature, which God set up in the beginning when the world was created. If God changed the course of those processes he would be violating his own laws, which would be inconsistent. So, either it's going to rain tomorrow or it's not (the person will get well or die), and in either case that is God's will." On the other hand: "God knows all of our needs before we ask. If we needed rain then God would give it to us even if we didn't pray."

Each of these attitudes is such that a person who holds it, yet continues to offer petitionary prayers, is only going through the motions. Such prayer is an empty act, like asking Bob to close the door when he can't, or while he is already doing so. Without the conviction that prayer makes a difference in the world, it is an anomalous linguistic practice.

Science, Causation, and God's Action

Let us look now at how the objections to prayer noted above have arisen. There is a line of thought regarding God's action in the world that goes something like this: "In earlier days people distinguished between events that were acts of God (for example, the plagues of Egypt) and events that were not. Then, as faith and understanding deepened, it was recognized that if there is a God at all, God must be responsible for *everything* that happens." So, three millennia after the plagues, H. R. Niebuhr could base his ethics on the motto: God is acting in all actions upon you; so respond to all actions upon you as response to his actions.[2] "Meanwhile," so the story goes, "the concept of a natural event was developed, along with the notion of a nexus of natural causes."

The main point to stress in this account is that recognition of God's involvement in the whole of reality is seen as a later development that improves upon and hence *replaces* the view that God intervenes in the world's affairs.

The Enlightenment philosopher Baruch de Spinoza (1632–1677) was one of the first to argue against God's intervention in the processes of nature. "Whatever comes to pass," he said, "comes to pass according to laws and rules which involve eternal necessity and truth."[3] Spinoza based this view on results in physics that suggested to him and many others that all natural phenomena could be explained on the basis of precise mathematical laws. The laws themselves were seen to be fixed and immutable.

Given a view of nature as entirely law-governed, there were three possibilities regarding God's role. One, of course, was to conclude that there was no God—God had become an unnecessary hypothesis. A second possibility was that God had created the world in the beginning, including the laws that were to govern its motion, but thereafter ceased to be involved with it—a position known as deism. The third possibility was to argue that each event is both a product of natural law and of God's continuing, but regular and consistent, involvement. This was the view that Spinoza attempted to develop, in fact claiming that "nature" and "God" were really only two names for the same thing. Since the laws of nature were the direct expression of God's will, any apparent intervention by God in particular events would be a contradiction of his own decrees and therefore absurd. Enlightened piety, consequently, seeks God in the fixed and wisely ordained order of nature, not in irregular miracles and mysteries.

Few have been tempted by Spinoza's pantheism, but many have attempted to explain how an event could be caused by other (antecedent) natural events and at the same time be caused by God. The usual move is to distinguish between ordinary causes on the one hand and God's creating and sustaining acts on the other. Thus the whole network of created causes and interactions is constituted and supported by the action of God, which is not itself a part of this network, but the ever-present source of its existence and functioning. Notice how such a theory makes it conceptually problematic to attribute any particular event to God's action. No event can be God's act any more than another. Thus it makes no sense to ask whether a healing, say, is to be attributed to God or to the doctor. The answer, if the question be raised, must be, "Both, of course."

However, the attempt to see God and natural events as constant co-causes of all that happens too easily becomes an opposition. God's contribution must either be a rubber-stamp approval of whatever will happen naturally, or else God must intervene. But interventionism is ruled out as unscientific and un-Enlightened, so the world must roll along its determined or statistically regular course—with God's approval. And it becomes difficult to see what role prayer could possibly have in the course of events—except perhaps in cases where prayer leads to an attitudinal change in the one who prays or is prayed for, which may in turn have other effects, such as on the course of an illness.

Even apart from the difficulties created for Christians whose Lord and liturgies require prayer, there is a new conceptual problem created by the foregoing rejection of the efficacy of prayer and of God's involvement in particular events, namely, that there can no longer be any *evidence* for God's dominion over the whole of reality or for God's providence in our lives. As suggested above, modern reasoning takes the theory of God as the universal and ultimate cause of all things as a *replacement* for the view that recognizes particular historical events as acts of God. The problem arises as follows: God's universal causality must either be a philosophical or theological doctrine with *no* evidence on its behalf, or else it must be a *theory* to explain the observed instances of God's action. In the latter case, it answers the question, What relationship to the world must God have in order that he be able to perform these mighty acts? As a matter of fact, this was apparently the order of development in Hebrew thought. First came the recognition of the mighty acts of God performed on behalf of Israel at the time of the Exodus. Only later, especially when faced with claims made on behalf of the gods of other nations, were the creation stories composed to attest to *this* God's dominion over *all* things.

So, to accept the theory of God's universal causality while rejecting the possibility of recognizing particular events as acts of God is to deny the very evidence upon which the theory is based. It is to use the theory to *explain away* its only available support.

Israel and the early Christians were able to recognize both God's lordship over the whole of reality and God's involvement in particular events. The Hebrew creation stories and the christological understanding of creation in the New Testament attest to the universal dominion of God. Yet, this same Jesus who was proclaimed as the one through whom all things were made is also represented in the Gospels as teaching his disciples to pray for their daily bread.

Two things have intervened in our history to drive a wedge between God's dominion and action in the world. One was the development from science of a determinist and reductionist view of natural processes. The second intervening factor was the development of theories of causation with universal scope. We must now examine each of these developments and see whether more recent work in both philosophy and science offers hope for rehabilitating the practice of petitionary prayer.

An Alternative View of Causes

Philosophical doctrines come and go. Recently many philosophers have become skeptical of all general philosophical theories, including universal theories of causation. These philosophers see their task not as system-building but as therapy[4]—to free us from confusions created by the misuse of language. While it may not be the case that all philosophical problems are linguistic, I believe that the dilemma that faces moderns when thinking about petitionary prayer is just such a puzzle. It results from accepting a general theory about the meaning of the word "cause" while ignoring the way the word actually functions in discourse.

In philosophical theories of causation associated with the view of events as products of natural laws, a cause is defined in terms of regularity. If Bs are regularly preceded by As then As cause Bs. But notice how this conflicts with ordinary usage. If we ask about the cause of an ink stain on the rug we are not at all put off by the fact that there are no laws regarding events regularly preceding the appearance of ink stains. When we ask about the cause of a death, we are not swayed by the observation that death is regularly preceded only by life.

In everyday questions about causes, we recognize that there are a vast number of antecedent conditions without which the event in question could not have happened. In fact, each event represents the intersection of numerous *chains* of antecedents. To decide which of these many conditions to honor with the title "cause," one must consider the context. In the case of the ink stain, the answer that the cause was the bottle's turning over would be taken as an evasion rather than a serious answer. Ordinarily such a question calls for information about *who* was responsible and *how* it happened—accidentally or maliciously. This sort of answer is wanted because it is relevant for future action. Should the child be punished? Should the ink be kept in a more out-of-the-way location?

So, to sum up, we might say that to ask for the cause of an event is ordinarily to request information about one *relevant* condition among the many, relevancy being determined by context. Notice that this is not a metaphysical theory about the nature of causation, but rather a generalization about how we usually talk about causes.[5]

Now consider two stories: Alice and her husband are trying to conceive a child. For years they go from one specialist to another for tests and treatments. Then one day Alice joins a Christian community and requests prayer that she conceive. Six weeks later it is confirmed that she is pregnant, about six weeks along.

Barbara and her husband also want a child. Barbara is a long-time member of Alice's new-found community, which prays regularly that Barbara conceive, while she, too, visits all the local doctors. At last, Barbara visits a new specialist who recommends yet another treatment, and soon after she conceives.

If Alice has not been unduly influenced by troublesome philosophical theories, she will attribute her pregnancy to prayer and thank God for giving her a child. *And is she not entirely justified in so doing—it being our ordinary practice to attribute causal efficacy to that one variable that makes a practical difference?* Notice that it was the practice of petitionary prayer that created a context in which God could be recognized as the relevant factor here.

Now, what of Barbara? No one would hesitate to attribute her pregnancy to the new treatment. But what if besides thanking the doctor, she also thanks the community for their prayers and thanks God for giving her a child? She has no *immediate* reason for asserting that God is the cause of her pregnancy. We might say that she thanks God because she has a *theory* regarding God's dominion over the natural world and his provident love for his creatures. Furthermore, it is cases like Alice's that provide the *evidence* for theories such as Barbara's. If there were no particular cases where we were justified in naming God the cause of an event, what empirical grounds could we have for believing in God's providence and dominion at all? If there were no cases where God evidently responds to our prayers, what empirical evidence could we have for trusting in the efficacy of prayer? Prayer itself provides the setting wherein God's activity can (perhaps only occasionally) be glimpsed.

Petitionary prayer, as we saw above, is a defective linguistic practice apart from the expectation that God will answer prayers. Correlatively, the belief that God is causally involved in the world is a defective theory—that is, unsupported by evidence—apart from the context of the praying, expectant church. Rightly understood, petitionary prayer and belief in God's universal dominion are not inimical but mutually supportive.

An Alternative View of Science and Its Laws

In part we are freed from a view of the universe as causally determined by a different philosophical analysis of causation itself. If we reject the view that causation implies regularity, we are no longer forced to conclude that, if all events are caused, then they must be the result of invariable natural laws.

However, the move away from a determinist view of the universe has been motivated as well by changes in science.

From the earliest days of modern science, and up to at least the middle of this century, an influential view has involved a hierarchical ordering of the various sciences in such a way that the components of entities studied at one level become the subject matter for the next lower science. That is, chemistry is higher than physics since the components of chemicals, the atomic particles, are the province of physics. Then, moving upward, come organic chemistry, biology, and even, perhaps, psychology and sociology. It was long assumed that with the advance of science the laws of each level could be explained on the basis of (reduction to) the laws of the next level down. The assumption lurking behind this hope was that the laws of the most elementary bits of the world (physics) in effect govern the behavior of virtually all events, including human thought.

This reductionistic and deterministic view of the universe has long troubled theologians, who saw it as a denial of human freedom. It provides as well a more striking version of the problem that is the central concern of this essay, namely, how can prayer be efficacious if the world is governed by natural laws.

Fortunately for the theologian and for the would-be intercessor, science itself has led to a rejection of this reductionist view of the natural world—it has turned out not to be adequate for accounting for the phenomena. Entities at one level cannot be explained solely in terms of constituent parts; rather one must take account of their environments—the higher-level systems of which they are a part. We might say that causal influence moves down the hierarchy as well as up.

As previous essays in this volume attest, the natural world is now viewed as open, dynamic, contingent. Arthur Peacocke's suggestion that theology be viewed as the highest science in the hierarchy provides an appealing view of the relationship between God and the world. God is the all-encompassing "environment" for the universe, whose plans and actions can influence all else without necessarily violating constraints placed on events by the laws of lower levels.[6]

To see how this may be possible, consider a very homely example involving human rather than divine agency. A wagon placed on an incline will roll downhill if not constrained. This is all that can happen when the laws of physics are considered in isolation from those of the higher levels of complexity. But if a child decides to do so (an event at the mental or psychological level), she or he can pull the wagon uphill—a *violation* of the law of gravity as it would operate without the influence of the higher levels, but obviously *not* a violation of any physical laws if we consider the entire system. The laws of physics put genuine constraints on what the child can do—for example, a fifty-pound child cannot pull a two-hundred-pound wagon uphill. But these constraints merely define broad limits. Within those limits the child is free to bring about a number of possible outcomes not predictable on the basis of physics alone.[7]

Likewise, Christian tradition teaches that God is personal and free. Just as a mother can affect her child in numerous ways—physically, by direct force; chemically, by what she eats during pregnancy; psychologically, by persuasion or example—so God must be able to affect the world in a number of ways, at each of the levels of the hierarchy of being.

Conclusion

In the determinist world of early modern science God's ongoing action in the world became problematic. Doctrines of creation therefore focused on *creatio ex nihilo*—God's mighty act in the beginning. Deism, which eliminated God's continuing creative or providential action, always threatened. We are still feeling the effects of such thinking in churches today, expressed as a lack of confidence in the importance of petitionary prayer.

We have seen, though, that changes in philosophical approaches in understanding causation, and changes in science itself, have in effect removed the major obstacles to belief in God's continuing action in the world. At the same time, these changes free us to pray expectantly. As a father is moved to act by the pleas of his children, Jesus tells us, so too is God moved to act by the pleas of his friends.

Why doesn't God simply do all the good we can think to ask of him? Apparently a great measure of the good in God's kingdom is our opportunity to participate in his work. P. T. Forsyth, a Scottish theologian writing early in this century, suggested that it is God's *intention* that we should change his will by prayer. "It is His will—His will of Grace—that prayer should prevail with Him and *extract* blessings."[8] And in the process we become co-creators in the drama of God's continuing creation.

NOTES

1. For an enlightening account of conditions for successful use of religious language see James W. McClendon, Jr., and James M. Smith, *Understanding Religious Convictions* (Notre Dame: University of Notre Dame Press, 1975). McClendon and Smith's analysis draws heavily from the work of J. L. Austin. See his *How to Do Things with Words* (Oxford: Clarendon Press, 1962), originally his William James Lectures, delivered at Harvard, 1955.
2. H. R. Niebuhr, *The Responsible Self* (New York: Harper & Row, 1963), p. 126.
3. Spinoza, *Tractatus theologico-politicus*, trans. R. H. M. Elwes, 2 vols., rev. ed. (London: Bohn's Philosophical Library, 1900), p. 83.
4. This is Ludwig Wittgenstein's term.
5. For a more detailed account see Joel Feinberg, *Doing and Deserving* (Princeton: Princeton University Press, 1970), pp. 142-48.
6. See Peacocke, *Intimations of Reality* (Notre Dame: University of Notre Dame Press, 1984), pp. 36-37.
7. One might object that the laws of physics are nonetheless determinative of the outcome, since they govern the activity of the brain upon which thought depends. Therefore they indirectly determine the uphill movement of the wagon. However, I would respond that in the absence of any evidence for such mental determinism, this objection simply begs the question.
8. P. T. Forsyth, *The Soul of Prayer*, 3rd impression (London: Independent Press, 1954), p. 90.

EIGHT

Scientific Creationism and Biblical Theology

ROGER E. TIMM

The Current Creationist Controversy

The Scopes "monkey trial" settled the issue once and for all, or so most Americans thought, until five or ten years ago. The 1925 trial of John Thomas Scopes for violating the Tennessee state law prohibiting the teaching of evolution in public schools is remembered in the American consciousness as the classic confrontation between Clarence Darrow and William Jennings Bryan, in which a belief in the literal truth of the creation account in Genesis 1 was held up to be untenable for thinking people. It turns out that this little segment of American mythology is not true. On the one hand, the trial was not in fact a victory for the supporters of the teaching of evolution, since Scopes was found guilty, and the law under which he was convicted was not declared unconstitutional until 1968. On the

Roger E. Timm is assistant professor of religion, Muhlenberg College, Allentown, Pennsylvania. This chapter is a revision of his article, "Let's Not Miss the Theology of the Creation Accounts," *Currents in Theology and Mission*, April 1986, pp. 97-105.

other hand, belief in the literal truth of the creation account continues to be held widely and firmly in our country.

Commitment to the literal truth of the Genesis creation account—a position typically referred to as creationism—has been demonstrated in the past few years by a number of political moves taken in an attempt to ensure that the creationist point of view receives a hearing in the public school system. Although laws prohibiting the teaching of evolution, as well as laws requiring the teaching of the biblical view of creation, have been declared unconstitutional by the United States Supreme Court, contemporary creationists have employed several other tactics to achieve their goal.[1] They have argued, for example, that the theory of evolution is a tenet of secular humanism and as such is a part of a religious system. The exclusive teaching of the evolutionary theory of the origins of the universe in the public school system is, from this point of view, the establishment of a particular religion. Or, conversely, this situation constitutes a limitation of the free exercise of the religion of those public school students who are creationists. In other words, the teaching of the theory of evolution in public schools is a violation of the freedom of religion guaranteed in the First Amendment to the United States Constitution. Such was the case made by Kelly Segraves in California. In March of 1981 a state judge in California ruled that the religious rights of Kelly Segraves' child were not violated, but the judge did order the California Board of Education to instruct teachers in California public schools not to be dogmatic in their presentation of the evolutionary theory of human origins. In a sense both sides won a partial victory in this case: The schools may continue to teach the theory of evolution, but the children of creationists are protected from dogmatic presentations of that theory.[2]

A second tactic employed by creationists has been to attempt to enact state legislation requiring the balanced treatment of evolution and "scientific creationism" in public schools. Creationists recognize that it is unconstitutional to require the teaching of the biblical view of creation in public schools. They believe, however, that a creationist viewpoint can be extracted from the biblical context and taught free of any religious trappings. This view is called "scientific creationism" or "creation science." Although the understanding of scientific creationism varies from author to author, in general creation science entails belief in (1) the creation of humans and the universe out of nothing, (2) the insufficiency of mutation and natural selection to explain the process of evolution, (3) the stability of originally created kinds and the impossibility of evolution from one such kind to another, (4) a distinct ancestry for humans and apes, (5) the explanation of certain geological phenomena by catastrophism (e.g., by a worldwide flood), and (6) the relatively recent formation of the earth (i.e., six to ten thousand years ago).[3]

Although attempts have been made in a number of states to pass legislation requiring the balanced treatment of scientific creationism and evolution, creationists have been successful only in Arkansas and Louisiana. In March of 1981 the Arkansas state legislature passed Public Act 590 requiring the "balanced treatment of creation-science and evolution-science in public schools" via lectures, textbooks, library materials, or educational programs that "deal in any way with the subject of the origin of man, life, the earth, or the universe."[4] The American Civil Liberties Union, supported by a broad coalition of religious leaders and scientists, filed a federal lawsuit against this act, and on January 5, 1982, United States District Court Judge William Overton declared the law unconstitutional since it violated the constitutional safeguards against the establishment of religion. In effect Judge Overton ruled that "scientific creationism" is as religious as "biblical creationism" and that creationism, at least as presented in the Arkansas case, cannot be presented in a way that removes it from its foundation in the biblical view of creation. "Scientific creationism" is in its essence, the judge argued, a religious position, not a scientific one.[5]

On July 20, 1981, the Louisiana state legislature passed a bill similar to the Arkansas law, the "Balanced Treatment for Creation-Science and Evolution-Science in Public School Instruction" Act (or the "Creationism Act"). In late 1982

Federal District Judge Adrian Duplantier ruled that the Louisiana state constitution did not allow the legislature to set such curricular standards, but later still the state supreme court disagreed. The case returned to Judge Duplantier's court, and on January 10, 1985, he ruled that "creation science" as defined in the Creationism Act is religious and that teaching it in public schools violates the U. S. Constitution, a ruling upheld by the Fifth U. S. Circuit Court of Appeals meeting *en banc* in December 1985.[6]

The case was appealed to the U. S. Supreme Court, and on June 19, 1987, in a 7-2 vote the Supreme Court upheld the decision of the lower courts. Justice William J. Brennan, Jr., delivering the opinion of the majority of the Court, argued that the Creationism Act lacks any clear secular purpose and that this Act, though it refers to *scientific* creationism, in fact advances the religious views of a particular set of those people who affirm that God created the world. Citing Judge Overton's decision in the Arkansas case favorably several times, Justice Brennan argued that therefore the Creationism Act violates the First Amendment's provision against the establishment of religion. Justice Antonin Scalia, in a dissent joined by Chief Justice William H. Rehnquist, argued that the Creationism Act does have a legitimate secular purpose: protecting the academic freedom of students, i.e., their right to freedom from indoctrination. The majority opinion rejected this argument, suggesting that the Act constricts and limits academic freedom by placing limits on what may be taught in the classroom.[7] With this Supreme Court decision the second tactic of contemporary creationists—seeking balanced treatment of evolution and creation science—has been frustrated.

A third tactic used by creationists has been to attempt to influence the materials included in science textbooks. The Texas Board of Education, for example, had adopted a rule requiring that science textbooks describe the theory of evolution as only one of several theories of origin. Since all textbooks used in public schools in Texas must meet the criteria of the state's Board of Education, this rule had a tremendous effect on textbook publishers, for not only is the state of Texas a huge market itself, but also, due to the prohibitive cost of publishing separate editions, publishers produce textbooks for the entire country that meet the Texas standards. Therefore in the past several years the amount of space given to the discussion of evolution in science textbooks has decreased. This situation has changed, however, for in March of 1984 Texas Attorney-General Jim Mattox ruled that the anti-evolution textbook standards of the state Board of Education were unconstitutional, and therefore in June, 1984, the Board of Education finally and officially repealed them, insisting though that textbooks must be clear about what statements are factual and which ones are theoretical. A backlash has set in, especially in California, where in the fall of 1985 the state's Curriculum Development Commission rejected more than twenty science textbooks for omitting or minimizing information on the theory of evolution.[8]

None of the recent tactics used by creationists to introduce creationism into the science curricula of public schools in the United States has been successful. Nevertheless, the debate between supporters of scientific creationism and evolution does raise some important issues. On the one hand, I believe that the creationists have some valid, or at least understandable, concerns. On the other hand, I think that they simply miss the point of the biblical creation accounts.

Creationists' Valid Concerns

Creationists often refer to evolution as "only a theory," attempting to denigrate evolution but also displaying an ignorance of the meaning and role of theories in science. On the other side of the issue, some scientists tend to characterize the creationist-evolution debate as a controversy between fact and faith, a view that is likewise not accurate.[9] The theory of evolution is indeed a theory, not a fact. A theory is a proposal for explaining or interpreting a set of observations. Theories by their nature, then, involve human interpretation and the placing of observational evidence in an explanatory framework. Yet theories are more certain than mere hypotheses; a proposal merits the name "theory" only after substantial confirmation and corroboration by empirical data.[10] The theory of evolution happens to be a theory that has been confirmed by an overwhelming body of data and that plays a fundamental role in all of science, especially the biological sciences.[11] But a theory it remains, and the nature of science being what it is, theories are always open to amendment or rejection if there is sufficient data to warrant it. It is misleading, therefore, to refer to the theory of evolution as "only a theory," for it can be nothing else but what it is—a theory—but it also happens to be a theory that has been substantially corroborated and that enjoys a high degree of confidence in the scientific community. Yet it is also misleading to suggest that it is fact as opposed to faith. It is not fact; it is an interpretation and explanation of facts—one that perhaps seems to be quite reliable but one, nonetheless, that remains open to modification, should the evidence suggest it.

Another valid, or at least understandable, concern that has prompted much of the intensity behind the creationist campaign is a fear on the part of many evangelical Christians that the theory of evolution is undermining belief in the Bible, human dignity, and standards of morality.[12] Creationists tend to hold the view that the Bible is inerrant and literally true; if the theory of evolution is true, the Bible must be false. Furthermore, if humans are descended from apes, creationists believe that humans would not have the special dignity given to them in the Bible. If life is simply an evolutionary struggle of the fittest to survive, then basic principles of ethics seem to be undermined. I do not believe that these fears are well-grounded, but it is easy to understand that if someone holds the beliefs that many creationists do, then they would indeed see the theory of evolution as a fearsome enemy.

Finally, in spite of the California court's decision in the Segraves' case, I wonder if there are not indeed serious questions of the religious rights of creationists involved here.[13] I agree that it is unconstitutional for the teaching of creation science to be mandated along with the teaching of evolution. Yet may it not be the case that the right of the children of creationists to believe in a literal interpretation of the Genesis 1 creation account is being jeopardized by the teaching of evolution? Do they have a right to an education that does not challenge the truth of one of their firmly and sincerely held religious beliefs? Shall we allow released time for creationists to offer creation science courses? A more serious suggestion is to provide for teaching about religion in the social science curricula of public schools. There a variety of religious views of the origins of the universe could be discussed, including those of the creationists.

Huston Smith writes in a similar vein in his article, "Evolution and Evolutionism." There he agrees with using the term "evolution" in a descriptive sense to refer to a variety of already-observed data, but he warns against overextending the use of the theory of evolution as an explanation of the meaning of life, especially if it means adopting an entirely naturalistic understanding of life. This view he calls "evolutionism" and argues that evolutionism is not properly taught in public schools.[14]

The Theology of the Creation Accounts

The creationist position, then, does raise some valid or legitimate concerns, but my main interest is in discussing how I believe it misses the main points of the biblical creation accounts: *by focusing on the issue of their supposed literal truth, the creationists tend to overlook the theological message of the creation accounts.*

I have found that the theological message of the biblical creation accounts becomes clearer when it is compared with other creation accounts from neighboring cultures. In ancient Mesopotamia, for example, the epic *Enuma Elish* describes the origin of the gods as the result of sexual generation that began with the first gods, Apsu and Tiamat. The earth was formed when there was warfare among the gods, and the god Marduk killed the goddess Tiamat, cut her into pieces, and formed the earth from pieces of the slain goddess. Sometime later humans were created to provide the gods with slave labor to relieve them from their work and give them leisure. A similar scenario is portrayed in the Greek myths. In Hesiod's *Theogony* the gods are created by sexual generation, and a succession of gods maintain power over the other gods by violent means. The god Kronos gains power over his father Ouranos by castrating him. Zeus finally becomes king of the gods by tricking and overpowering his father, Kronos. In Hesiod's *Works and Days*, Pandora, the first woman, is created by the gods to trick and deceive man in order to punish Prometheus for tricking the gods and stealing fire from them.[15]

The rather sharp differences between these two creation narratives and the Genesis accounts seem clearly to suggest that some of the main theological points of the Bible are to emphasize that (1) God is one and separate from nature, rather than a system of many gods often identified with some aspect of nature; (2) the earth was created good by a loving and gracious God, rather than formed out of bloody and violent conflict among the gods; and (3) humans were created as the crown of creation and intended to live in relationship with God, rather than being created out of spite or to serve as slaves for the gods.[16]

This comparison of other creation accounts with those of Genesis suggests in outline form the theological message to be found in the biblical view of creation. In the following paragraphs I want to unpack this message in greater detail by examining some of the features of several of the biblical descriptions of God's creative activity both in Genesis 1 and 2 and in other passages in Scripture. While creationists tend to view Genesis 1 and 2 as two parts of the same creation story, most biblical scholars see them as two separate and parallel accounts of creation, each with its own distinctive theological emphasis. If this latter position is true, viewing Genesis 1 and 2 as one account risks missing some of the real theological meat of these chapters.

Of course, both chapters do share some quite important views—that God is one, that the creation is good, that humans were created for relationship with God and one another. It is in Genesis 1, however, that humans are said to be created in the image of God and where they are told to subdue the earth and have dominion over every living thing. What it means to be created "in the image of God" has been the subject of much speculation and debate for centuries. I think the most helpful way of interpreting the image of God is to understand it as referring to humans as God's representatives in the world.[17] Humans stand in the place of God—are the image of God—in the world God has given us to subdue and have dominion over. Being created in the image of God gives us both privileges and responsibilities in the world God has created.

"Subdue the earth and have dominion over it." These have been troublesome words, for they have on occasion been used to justify abuses of both our living and non-living environment. Later I will discuss the recent debate over the meaning of "dominion," but suffice it to say here that the Hebrew word that is translated by "have dominion" does not imply a rule that exploits and abuses. Rather it is used to describe the kind of rule that a responsible and caring king exercises over his people.[18] Genesis 1, then, does not sanction abuse of the environment but calls us to responsible and caring stewardship of the earth and its resources.

This view of our human relationship with the earth is expressed more clearly and graphically in the creation account in Genesis 2. Adam and Eve are placed in the Garden of Eden to till it and to keep it. The human relationship with the earth is described by analogy with the gardener or farmer who carefully tends the earth so that it thrives and flourishes. Farmers who abuse their land or livestock will not long be successful farmers; farmers recognize that their livelihood depends on their treating their land and animals with care and respect. Such is the relationship with the rest of the created world envisioned in Genesis 2.

By focusing their attention on the literal truth of Genesis 1 and 2, creationists miss the rich creation theology scattered throughout the rest of the Bible. Psalm 104, for example, describes the creative activity of God in poetry and uses a piece of Ancient Near Eastern mythology to do it: in the Near East the act of creation was often depicted as the slaying of a primordial sea monster (as in the case of Tiamat, who was pictured as a monster); in Psalm 104 God is described as having tamed—not killed—Leviathan, the sea monster, and as having placed it in the sea as a kind of domesticated reptilian pet. The dramatic poetry of Job 38 to 41 uses creation imagery to emphasize the transcendent power, majesty, and wisdom of God—a power and wisdom beyond the full comprehension of humans. Bernhard Anderson has argued that there are at least four levels of creation theology in the Hebrew Scriptures, each reflecting different historical and theological circumstances among the people of Israel: the pre-monarchic (creation as creation of human community in the Exodus—Exodus 15), the monarchic (creation as creation of social order—Genesis 2), Wisdom (creation as expression of God's Wisdom—Psalm 104; Job 38–41), and the Priestly (creation as the origination of a series of covenants—Genesis 1).[19]

So far I have dealt with biblical passages focusing on God's creative activity at the beginning of time. I also want to consider one passage that looks to the present and future and that connects God's creative activity with God's redeeming and liberating activity.

> For the creation waits with eager longing for the revealing of the [children] of God . . . because the creation itself will be set free from its bondage to decay and obtain the glorious liberty of the children of God. We know that the whole creation has been groaning in travail together until now; and not only the creation, but we ourselves, who have the first fruits of the Spirit, groan inwardly as we wait for adoption as [children], the redemption of our bodies. (Rom. 8:19-23)

Notice how Paul ties all of creation into God's liberating activity—not just humans, not just the spiritual dimension, but all of creation. We cannot be sure just how metaphorically Paul is writing here, but he may well be countering two views that were and still are quite common among Christians: one so emphasizes the spiritual dimension of Christian faith that it downplays or even denigrates the physical, and a second sees God's salvation as basically an other-worldly affair that will come with apocalyptic fireworks at the end of time. In opposition to these views Paul seems to be arguing that God's salvation includes the physical and the fleshly, not just the spiritual, and that we are bound up with all of creation in God's saving process right here and now, even if full salvation may lie off in the future. Moreover, these words from Paul undercut any view of God's redemption that would separate humans from the rest of God's creation.[20]

What seems almost tragic to me is that many creationists miss the theological messages of these rich biblical creation materials. In what follows I would like to flesh out what theological messages for today are implied by the various biblical passages I have discussed. When the creation accounts were written, one of the main points was to assert the oneness and transcendent power of the God of Israel over against the polytheistic religious systems of Israel's neighbors. That message is perhaps of less relevance for us than it was then, although we may need to be reminded of it as we worship at the various shrines of the gods of success, money, and upward mobility. The biblical creation accounts also portray God as essentially a good and caring God—with, of course, demanding expectations of his human creatures—over against the view of God as arbitrary, vindictive, and violent in other contemporaneous creation accounts. This message too is less relevant for us, although there are people for whom God continues to be a harsh and vindictive force who need to hear this message of creation.

Genesis 1 especially emphasizes the message of the goodness of God's creation. True, the story of the fall into sin that follows the second Genesis creation account must balance this view, but nonetheless Genesis 1 portrays God as pronouncing the creation as good and thus counters all those who would reject this physical world as essentially evil. Perhaps this likewise seems to be an ancient point, but there are many today who believe that the Bible requires the rejection of some aspect of God's creation, whether drinking or dancing or music, whether the human intellect or sexuality.

Creation Theology and the Environment

Of special importance to us today is what the creation materials of the Bible have to say to us about the status and responsibilities of humans. Clearly both Genesis 1 and 2 give humans special status—Genesis 1 by describing humans as created in the image of God, and Genesis 2 by giving Adam and Eve control over the garden and the animals. It needs to be said today, however, that this special relationship humans have with God does not give humans *carte blanche* to do what they please with the earth. The creation account in Genesis 2 puts limits on what Adam and Eve can do, and, if what I said above is correct, the description of humans as created in the image of God in Genesis 1 places upon humans the responsibility of representing God and God's values on the earth, not treating earth solely according to human purposes. The creation accounts, therefore, clearly imply that humans have the responsibility of carefully and respectfully tending the earth and seeing that it thrives and flourishes. Moreover, implicit in the Genesis accounts and explicit in the passage from Romans is the belief that humans are not separate from the rest of creation but were created in a relationship of interdependence with the rest of God's created order. Humans are *in continuity with* the rest of creation, even as they have *responsibility* for it.

This perspective has definite applications to our present situation. During the past twenty years a controversy has centered around the proper interpretation of the mandate in Genesis 1 for humans to "have dominion" over the earth. In 1967, UCLA medieval historian Lynn White argued in his classic essay, "The Historical Roots of the Ecologic Crisis," that these words, in Western Christianity at least, have been used to sanction the exploitation of the earth and its resources for human purposes with little regard for the consequences for the environment.[21] While the details of White's argument have been subjected to some well-deserved criticism,[22] his critics often failed to notice that White was not arguing that "dominion" *ought* to be interpreted to allow abuse of the environment, only that sometimes in Latin Christianity it *has* been interpreted that way. White and his critics both tend to agree that in Genesis "dominion" does not refer to tyrannical and abusive rule but to responsible and caring oversight. The biblical creation accounts do not sanction the exploitation of the earth for any and all human purposes; rather they remind us that we are to treasure the earth's resources that have been entrusted to us. Our overconsumption and our depletion of natural resources, our pollution of earth, air, and water are all violations of this responsibility to care for the earth. It would be easy to multiply examples of current issues to which this biblical concern applies; let me suggest just a few.

We continue to build housing developments and office complexes, taking more farmland out of production. Is this the best way to care for the earth? The farms that remain use increasing amounts of chemical fertilizers, whose residue can threaten the potability of nearby water sources. Is this a necessary by-product of modern agriculture, or is there a more responsible way to care for the earth? Acid rain and its effects are an international problem; are the causes of this problem due to failure to take responsibility for the earth seriously? A German theologian, Gerhard Liedtke, has argued that nuclear energy violates the biblical perspectives on caring for the environment.[23] This issue is controversial, of course, but it does concern me that the United States has developed no comprehensive plan for handling the nuclear waste from these power plants. I was also quite surprised recently when I was told by an employee of a power company that nuclear power plants have a usable life of about twenty-five years or so, after which they must be abandoned because they may no longer be safe for operation. What shall we do with these abandoned radioactive hulks of power plants that soon shall begin to dot our horizon?

The biblical creation materials suggest that all of creation, living and non-living, participates in God's eternal plan and therefore merits appropriate care and attention from the humans who are commissioned to tend it, while all of God's creation, human and nonhuman alike, is bound up in solidarity, awaiting the fulfillment of God's promise of final liberation.

This perspective clearly challenges the traditional dichotomy that has been drawn between the human and the nonhuman by theologians, philosophers, and scientists alike. The continuity of all life-forms that is implied by the theory of evolution is ironically supported here by this biblical creation perspective. What does this suggest about animal rights? May we legitimately and morally experiment on animals? The benefits of such research for both humans and animals probably weigh in favor of such experimentation, but clearly creation theology mandates a use of animals that is as gentle and respectful and humane as possible. Finally, do animals or even trees have legal standing?[24] I don't know if they have legal standing, but they do have theological standing and a theological right to expect humans to care for and preserve them. In other words, the biblical creation accounts suggest an ethic for environmental and ecological issues that is based on the intrinsic value and the rights given by God to all of creation, human and nonhuman alike, rather than an ethic that values the nonhuman solely because of its value or usefulness to humans for their science, health, leisure, or aesthetic delight.[25]

Conclusion

In current usage "creationist" often is meant to refer to those who believe in the literal truth of the Genesis creation accounts, whether in the form of "biblical" or "scientific" creationism. The intent of my argument here is to reclaim the title "creationist" for those who willingly confess that God is creator but who do not necessarily interpret the Genesis creation accounts literally. My claim is that being a creationist means affirming the theological implications of the biblical creation accounts. A creationist by this standard is someone who believes in a creator who is one, good, and caring, who created the world good, and who has given humans responsibility for caring for God's creation and for living in harmony with it. Such a creationist does not necessarily insist that the world was created in six days six to ten thousand years ago.

Perhaps a new label is required. In addition to "biblical creationists" and "scientific creationists" let there be "evolutionary creationists." An evolutionary creationist is someone who fails to see why evolutionary theory and biblical creation faith are necessarily incompatible. The definition of scientific creationism, which I outlined at the outset, consists largely in rejecting various aspects of evolutionary theory. While it is beyond the scope of this chapter and my expertise to defend evolutionary theory, I think it is fair to say that evolutionary theory is widely accepted in the natural sciences as a well-confirmed theory—although any careful scientist will acknowledge that the theory is open to change, revision, or abandonment should the evidence warrant it. The evolutionary creationist is open to accepting the position of the scientific community—not always uncritically, however—and does not see a need to join the scientific creationist in rejecting evolutionary theory. The focus of interest for the evolutionary creationist is the theological import of the biblical creation accounts, which simply does not conflict with evolutionary theory, for it deals with a different level of concern.[26] The evolutionary creationist affirms that God is the creator and all that that affirmation implies; if evolution be the process by which the world has developed, then evolution is the method by which God has chosen to create the world.

Finally, I believe that supporters of evolutionary theory and of creationism—whether biblical, scientific, or evolutionary—have much of value to learn from a careful exploration of the theological messages of the biblical creation accounts. I have outlined a number of these messages, but in particular I think we need to pay attention to what the creation accounts tell us about human responsibility and about the participation of all creation in God's plan for the world. From the atmosphere to the ocean, from the forests to the streams, the message in the late twentieth century is all too clear: if we humans do not face up to our responsibility to care for the earth, our planet will face serious environmental crises. Only with significant negative consequences for the quality of our lives can we ignore our responsibility for the earth and our interdependence with the rest of God's creation. What is sadly unfortunate, then, about the recent evolution-creationism debate is that it has diverted attention away from the messages of biblical creation theology that are most crucial for us in the contemporary world. Here lies the challenge for evolutionary creationists: to reclaim biblical creation theology and to proclaim its significance for vital human and environmental issues today.

NOTES

1. Gerald Skoog, "The Textbook Battle over Creationism," *The Christian Century* 97 (10/5/80), pp. 974-75.
2. William J. Broad, "Creationists Limit Scope of Evolution Case," *Science* 211 (3/20/81), 1331-32; and Kenneth M. Pierce et al., "Putting Darwin Back in the Dock," *Time*, vol. 117: 11 (3/16/81), pp. 80-82.
3. William R. Overton, "Creationism in Schools: The Decision in McLean Versus the Arkansas Board of Education," *Science* 215 (2/19/82), 937; also Skoog, p. 975.
4. Madelynne Reuter, "ACLU Challenges Arkansas Act on 'Creationism' in Schools," *Publisher's Weekly*, vol. 219 (6/12/81), p. 16.
5. Overton, "Creationism in Schools," pp. 934-43.
6. Randy Frame, "Once Again, Creationism Goes on Trial," *Christianity Today*, vol. 27, 18 (11/25/83), p. 34; Roger Lewin, "ACLU 2, Creationists O," *Science* 218 (12/10/82), p. 1099; and the *New York Times*, 11/4/82, p. 16; 11/23/82, p. 23; and 1/11/85, I, p. 8; and Frederick Edwords, "Nails in the Coffin," *The Humanist*, vol. 45: 5 (September–October 1985), p. 31; and "Seeing the Light," *The Humanist*, vol. 46: 2 (March–April 1986), p. 33.
7. *Edwards, Governor of Louisiana et al. v. Aquillard et al.*, U. S. Supreme Court, No. 85-1513. Cf. the *New York Times*, 6/20/87, pp. 1 and 6-7.
8. For thorough background on the creationist conflict and its effect on textbooks see Dorothy Nelkin, *The Creation Controversy: Science or Scripture in the Schools* (New York: W. W. Norton and Co., 1982). For other comments on the textbook issue see Frederick Edwords, "The 'Textbook Censorship," *The Humanist*, vol. 43: 4 (July–August, 1983), p. 35; and "A Trend Reversed," *The Humanist*, vol. 45: 6 (November–December 1985), p. 34; Wayne A. Moyer, "Young Earth Creationism and Biology Textbooks," *BioScience*, vol. 33: 2 (February 1983), pp. 113-14; and Pierce et al., pp. 80-81. For the recent repealing of the Texas textbook criteria see Judith Wortman, "Texas Changes Evolution Rule," *BioScience*, vol. 23: 7 (July–August 1984), p. 414; and the *New York Times*, 4/14/84, Section 1, p. 10; 4/15/84, Section 1, p. 1; and 6/3/84, Section 1, p. 36.
9. See Isaac Asimov, "The 'Threat' of Creationism," *New York Times Magazine*, 6/14/81, p. 92; Isaac Asimov and Duane Gish, "The Genesis War," *Science Digest* 89 (October 1981), 87; Langdon Gilkey, "Creationism: The Roots of Conflict," in *Is God a Creationist? The Religious Case Against Creation-Science*, ed. Roland Mushat Frye (New York: Charles Scribner's Sons, 1983), pp. 56-67; Philip Kitcher, *Abusing Science: The*

Case Against Creationism (Cambridge, Mass.: The MIT Press, 1982), pp. 30-32; Nelkin, *The Creation Controversy*, pp. 192-94; and Ronald L. Numbers, "Creationism in 20th Century America," *Science* 218 (11/5/82), p. 539.

10. National Academy of Sciences, *Science and Creationism: A View from the National Academy of Sciences* (Washington, D. C.: National Academy Press, 1984), pp. 8-11. See also Ian G. Barbour, *Issues in Science and Religion* (New York: Harper & Row, 1971), pp. 138-48; and *Myths, Models, and Paradigms* (New York: Harper & Row, 1974), pp. 30-38.

11. See Kitcher, *Abusing Science*, pp. 50-54.

12. Kitcher, *Abusing Science*, pp. 186-202; Nelkin, *The Creation Controversy*, pp. 165-79 and 192-93; Edwin A. Olson, "Hidden Agenda Behind the Evolution/Creationist Debate," *Christianity Today*, vol. 26:8 (4/23/82), p.30 (also included in Frye, *Is God a Creationist?* pp. 40-41); and Huston Smith, "Evolution and Evolutionism," *The Christian Century*, vol. 99:23 (7/7-14/82), p. 755.

13. Huston Smith shares a similar concern. See Smith, "Evolution and Evolutionism," pp. 755-56.

14. Ibid.

15. The edition of these myths that I have used is Joan O'Brien and Wilfred Major, *In the Beginning: Creation Myths from Ancient Mesopotamia, Israel and Greece* (Chico, Calif.: Scholars Press, 1982). The Mesopotamian and Greek creation narratives, as well as those from Genesis, are printed on pp. 9-121.

16. See Bernhard W. Anderson, "The Earth Is the Lord's: An Essay on the Biblical Doctrine of Creation," in Frye, *Is God a Creationist?* pp. 176-96; Conrad Hyers, "Biblical Literalism: Constricting the Cosmic Dance," *The Christian Century*, vol. 99:25 (8/4-11/82), pp. 823-27 (also included in Frye, *Is God a Creationist?* pp. 95-104); as well as his *The Meaning of Creation: Genesis and Modern Science* (Atlanta: John Knox Press, 1984); Claus Westermann, *Creation*, trans. John J. Scullion (Philadelphia: Fortress Press, 1974); and Norman Young, *Creator, Creation and Faith* (Philadelphia: The Westminster Press, 1976).

17. Anderson, "The Earth Is the Lord's," p. 191; N. W. Porteous, "Image of God," *The Interpreter's Dictionary of the Bible*, vol. 2, ed. George A. Buttrick (Nashville: Abingdon Press, 1962), pp. 682-85; and Westermann, *Creation*, pp. 55-60.

18. James Limburg, "What Does It Mean to 'Have Dominion over the Earth'?" *Dialog* 10 (1971), pp. 222-23.

19. Bernhard W. Anderson "Introduction: Mythopoeic and Theological Dimensions of Biblical Creation Faith," in *Creation in the Old Testament*, ed. Bernhard W. Anderson (Philadelphia: Fortress Press, 1984), pp. 1-24.

20. For a helpful and thorough treatment of this passage see Walther Bindemann, *Die Hoffnung der Schoepfung* (Neukirchen-Vluyn: Neukirchener Verlag, 1983).

21. Lynn White, Jr., "The Historical Roots of Our Ecologic Crisis," *Science* 155 (3/10/67), pp. 1203-7.

22. See, for example, Wendell Berry, "The Gift of Good Land," *Sierra* 64 (November–December 1979), pp. 20-26; Thomas Sieger Derr, "Religion's Responsibility for the Ecological Crisis: An Argument Run Amok," *Worldview* 18 (January 1975), pp. 39-45; Limburg, "What Does It Mean to

Have 'Dominion over the Earth'?" pp. 221-23; and Ted Peters, *Futures—Human and Divine* (Atlanta: John Knox Press, 1978), pp. 140-44.

23. See Gerhard Liedtke, *Im Bauch des Fisches* (Stuttgart: Kreuz Verlag, 1979).

24. For what has become the classical discussion of this question, see Christopher D. Stone, *Should Trees Have Standing: Toward Legal Rights for Natural Objects* (Los Altos, Calif.: William Kaufmann, 1974).

25. See the discussion of "an ethic of life" in chapter 5 of Charles Birch and John B. Cobb, Jr., *The Liberation of Life: From the Cell to the Community* (Cambridge, England: Cambridge University Press, 1981), especially pp. 150-51.

26. I admit that this statement is somewhat glib. If evolutionary theory is understood to imply a totally naturalistic explanation of origins, then even an evolutionary creationist is challenged with issues about the nature and existence of God and the relative roles of purpose, chance, and randomness in the evolutionary process. All that I want to claim here is that an evolutionary creationist believes (1) that the challenge of such issues is not insuperable and (2) that evolutionary theory deals with the level of scientific explanation and the biblical creation accounts with matters of religious faith and values, two different, although not totally separate, areas of discourse.

NINE

The Future of the Cosmos and the Renewal of the Church's Life with Nature

H. PAUL SANTMIRE

We are now living in the dawn of the future life; for we are beginning to regain a knowledge of the creation, a knowledge forfeited by the fall of Adam. Now we have a correct view of the creatures, more so, I suppose, than they have in the papacy. Erasmus does not concern himself with this; it interests him little how the fetus is made and formed and developed in the womb . . . , but by God's mercy we can begin to recognize His wonderful works and wonders also in the flowers when we ponder his might and goodness.

—Martin Luther, *Table Talk*

Now if I believe in God's Son and bear in mind that he became man, all creatures will appear a hundred times more beautiful to me than before. Then I will properly appreciate the sun, the moon, the stars, trees, apples, and pears, as I reflect that he is Lord over all and the center of things.

—Martin Luther, *The Gospel According to St. John*

The threat of mass catastrophe is now a commonplace of the popular mind. With the passing of each day, we are becoming

H. Paul Santmire is pastor of Grace Lutheran Church in Hartford, Connecticut. This chapter appeared originally in *Word and World*, fall 1984, pp. 410-21.

more and more familiar with scenarios of global thermonuclear death and devastation, planetary ecological collapse, toxic pollution of our environment, vast blights of deforestation and soil erosion, constant economic crisis for the great majority of the earth's peoples, and rampant starvation in some regions around the world, all punctuated by the threats of nuclear accidents or terrorism and stories of increasingly capricious patterns of global weather. Hovering in our consciousness, as well, is the vague but dismal image of the end of cosmic history itself, ignominiously, eons from now, through some kind of universal "heat death." It is existentially thinkable today, perhaps as never before, that the final word being written across the pages of the whole human drama, and across the chapters of the cosmos itself, is *finis*, termination, death, once and for all, and not some placid passing, but a death with terror, torment, and excruciating moments of pain. These are apocalyptic times indeed. And the dark clouds of a future which is *no future* often flood backward, as it were, into the present, producing a deep-seated and widespread spiritual anomie.

Witness the oft-reported dreams of children today around the world: visions of nuclear winter dance in their heads. Adolescents, likewise, are stricken in large numbers with a "heavy metal" rock music, which is sometimes directly inspired by the apocalyptic visions of world judgment depicted in the book of Revelation and which borders at some points on self-conscious nihilism. Films popular with "mature audiences" often betray a similar spirit of terror before the future and alienation from the present. They are full of images of cosmic horrors, as in *Jaws*, or feature numerous vengeful images of insects or rats or even machines taking over the world, frequently in the aftermath of nuclear catastrophe. To be sure, a Luke Skywalker may somehow manage to triumph over the forces of cosmic evil in a *Star Wars* epic, and audiences may take delight in the sight of cuddly little bear-like creatures, reminiscent of the best of Disney, coming to save the day for the forces of good in the same story. But one can wonder whether that narrative represents anything more than a temporary reprieve, a romantic retreat, from the otherwise daily fears and horrors fixed deeply in our minds from the images generated by narratives such as *The Day After*.

This poses a new kind of challenge for the church and its theologians. Does the church have access to a theological vision that is commensurate with the cosmic despair and the spiritual anomie that characterizes so much of our culture today?

It appears that the theology in which recent generations of church leaders, above all parish pastors, have been trained is no longer fully able to serve the life of the church, precisely because the church lives in a culture in which the thought of mass catastrophe and the despair that goes with that thought are increasingly commonplace. Until very recently, the theology taught in our seminaries, by and large, focused mainly on the "inner agenda" of guilt. This theology took "justification by faith" not only as the central hermeneutical and normative doctrine, by which the church stands or falls, but also as the church's chief substantive teaching as well. This meant that *the content* of the gospel proclaimed was essentially "the forgiveness of sins."

But we live in a world in which an "outer agenda"—is there any meaning, is there any reason to look forward to tomorrow, will there ever be any end to the pain and anguish of this world, is there any reason to go on living?—has come more and more to the fore. This means that our church leaders today, who seem to be relatively well-equipped to proclaim the gospel of God's liberating grace to individuals burdened with guilt, are often, so it would appear, strikingly ill-equipped to proclaim that same gospel to people who are depressed and immobilized by a world that seems to be going to hell at every turn.

Enter the theology of hope. In this time of increasing despair about the future of our species, and the future of the cosmos as a whole, the church needs a theological vision of the future that is larger and deeper than the hopelessness of our souls. The theology of hope has helped make just such a vision possible.[1] Still, notwithstanding many suggestive motifs, no single theologian has yet explored the implications of the theology of hope substantively for "the theology of the earth," that is, the biophysical world, the cosmos, or nature. Thus far protagonists of this school of theology have mainly focused their efforts on the theology of human history, in particular the theology of human liberation.[2] They have been relatively silent about the whole creation's groaning in travail. This is an area in the theology of hope that surely needs to be developed, in a way that is consistent with its overall principles, to the end that the life of the church might be more fully served in these apocalyptic times.[3]

What can a theology of hope tell us, then, about the future of the cosmos, and how might this theology help the church renew its life with nature in this era of growing cosmic alienation?

The Paradigm of Hope

To begin to answer this question, I want to highlight three texts, which I believe can be, and perhaps should be, as charged for us today as the famous justification-by-faith texts of Romans and Galatians were for Luther in his day. The first depicts the cosmic scope of God's gracious lordship, as God's reign moves toward its fulfillment, toward the final rest of God's future:

> For from him and through him and to him are all things. To him be glory forever. Amen. (Rom. 11:36)

The second describes the reign of Christ in, with, and under God's universal history, as that history is ultimately to be consummated:

> For he must reign until he has put all enemies under his feet. The last enemy to be destroyed is death. . . . When all things are subjected to him, the Son himself will also be subjected to him who put all things under him, that God may be everything to everyone. (I Cor. 15:25-28)

Then, third, a text that envisions the landscape and the soulscape of the consummated future of God:

> Then I saw a new heaven and a new earth; for the first
> heaven and the first earth had passed away, and the sea was
> no more. And I saw the holy city, new Jerusalem, coming
> down out of heaven from God. (Rev. 21:1-2)

The paradigm of hope that emerges when these texts are
allowed to interact with one another in our imagination has a
number of general characteristics which I want to identify at the
outset in order to set the stage for some historical analysis and
some constructive reflection.

First, the paradigm of hope moves us toward a vision of
reality that is fundamentally *temporal* rather than static. The
dynamism of the Hebraic world view, which was somewhat
eclipsed as early Christianity established itself in the world of
Hellenistic culture, here comes to the fore self-consciously and
unashamedly. Ultimate reality is not some unchanging,
timeless eternity. Ultimate reality is history. So we can readily
think in terms of God's universal history with all things.

Second, the scope of this universal history is, indeed,
universal, not just historical in the narrow sense of that word.
The whole cosmos, not just the human family, is on a
pilgrimage with God from alpha to omega, and God is on a
pilgrimage with the cosmos, not just humanity, from the very
beginning to the very end. We gain this insight, if for no other
reason, when we lift our eyes to see God's future and see a new
heaven and a new earth, not only a new Jerusalem.

Third, the movement of God's universal history with all
things—and, analogously, the life of humanity with nature—is
holistic, rather than monistic or deistic. God is God and the
world is world, as Karl Barth used to say: God and the world are
fundamentally distinct. God is not identical with the world.
Nor is the world God's body. The world is created by God *ex
nihilo;* it has a beginning and an ending, however difficult that
may be to conceptualize. On the other hand, the world is not
separate from God: it is through God and to God. God's
presence permeates, embraces, and governs the world,
majestically and intimately. God is the circle, whose center is
everywhere and whose circumference is nowhere. The world is
therefore charged with the glory of God, and it will be even
more so at the end, when God will be all in all.

Likewise, the human creature's relationship with the cosmos is neither monistic nor deistic in character. Created in the image of God, the human creature transcends cosmic life. Human life, we can say with Teilhard de Chardin, is evolution conscious of itself. It is nature emerging beyond itself. So, at the end, when God will be all in all, the distinctness of human life will be reaffirmed and consummated. God will call forth a new Jerusalem, not only a new heaven and a new earth. At the same time, humanity has its life in, with, and under the cosmos. Human life is unthinkable apart from our embodiedness, apart from our deep roots in the earth and its history. So, at the end, when humanity will be gloriously transfigured in the new Jerusalem, and when the whole cosmos will be born again, humanity will be blessed with a glorious new corporality and radically transformed relationship with nature generally. The wolf shall dwell with the lamb, and a little child shall lead them.

Fourth, the paradigm of hope moves us toward a vision of reality that is finally *theocentric* rather than Christocentric. This will sound like a scandal to some of our contemporaries, who grew up at Karl Barth's knee. But Paul seems to say quite clearly, nonetheless, that the reign of Christ is subordinate to the reign of God.[4] Perhaps we should try, accordingly, to hear Paul afresh at this point, before we quickly run off to reread the *Church Dogmatics*. Systematic, dogmatic Christocentrism as we know it today, it is worth noting here, is a relatively recent phenomenon in the theological tradition. It emerged probably for the first time in Schleiermacher, in the early nineteenth century. Prior to that time the church's theologians surely always exalted the name of Christ, but virtually always in the context of a trinitarian theocentrism, as reflected in the classical creeds.

Fifth, the paradigm of hope shows us a God whose universal will is to embrace all things, to unify all things, in perfect harmony in the perfected kingdom of God, when God will be all in all. The underlying, eliciting divine *telos* of the universe is, then, *ecological and communitarian*, rather than anarchic or individualistic. As we look to the things that are to come, particularly focusing our eyes on the human future, this ecological and communitarian shape of things is especially visible. We see neither a congeries of glorified individuals alone in eternity, nor a collection of transfigured human families alone. Rather we see a newborn *city*, a newborn human community, rooted in its own renewed cosmic home. The world moves forward to the consummated Jerusalem of God in the new heaven and the new earth. It does not move toward some kind of anarchic or individualistic acosmic eternity.

The Anthropocentric–Soteriocentric Trajectory

With this fundamental theological paradigm of hope before us, we can instructively note some contrasting features of certain major trends in the theological tradition, down to our own century.[5] I want to identify these trends, in a preliminary way, by raising a question. We have two creation narratives in the book of Genesis. Which does one interpret in terms of which? The paradigm of hope that I have just identified would, as a matter of course, prompt us to see Genesis 1, the Priestly narrative, as being first, and Genesis 2–3, the Yahwistic account, as being second. But highly influential trends in the theological tradition have tended to reverse that order, in exegetical emphasis.

The temporal, universal, and holistic story of God's creative activity with the world, which we encounter in Genesis 1, has been seen by more than a few theologians *not* so much as the theater for the universal manifestation of God's glory and the arena for the cosmic expression of his goodness, in the midst of which Adam and Eve are given the choice of life or death, but more as the mere prologue to what is "really essential": the creation of the human creature, subsequently the fall, and then the foreshadowing of human salvation. The static and parochial image of the garden, rather than the dynamic and universal image of creation-history, has tended to dominate large sections of the traditional theological consciousness, at least from the time of Augustine.

Indeed, this fascination with the human story depicted in Genesis 2–3 spilled over, as it were, and influenced interpretation of Genesis 1. Thus we find Ambrose, in commenting on Genesis 1:31—which states that God looked at *everything* he had made, and behold it was very good—observing that God looked at *Adam alone*, not at all things he had made as the text says, when God saw that everything was "very good." For Ambrose the human creature is clearly the whole point of the creation narrative in Genesis 1. For him, Genesis 1 is an anthropocentric narrative and more. Congruent with his anthropocentric reading of the creation narrative, he identifies Adam's special significance in creation with the fact that the eternal Son of God would become incarnate in Adam's progeny, in the Second Adam. In this sense, then, for Ambrose the whole point of the created order is human salvation. Anthropocentrism and soteriocentrism, if I may use that term, are thus intimately related in his reading of the Genesis accounts.

This anthropocentric-soteriocentric hermeneutic of creation was given an impressive systematic statement in the thirteenth century by Thomas Aquinas. He argues that the very *raison d'être* of the whole creation is the coming into being of the rational creatures, and that the *raison d'être* of the rational creatures, in turn, is their final beatific vision. That is to say, teleologically considered, the cosmic order is a kind of stage constructed by God for the sake of the human drama of salvation (and for the angels); and it has no enduring meaning apart from that instrumentality. Thomas makes this point quite explicitly and with sobering clarity. Although he qualifies the matter in a number of ways, he finally ends his argument by saying that in the end-times, with the exception of human bodies, the whole biophysical world will fall away into nothingness. Why should it do anything else, since its only essential meaning was instrumental? We see, then, that the famous Thomistic principle that "grace perfects nature" does not in fact apply in his thought to the biophysical world generally. On the contrary, in this context, grace *destroys* nature! As for Ambrose, only much more systematically, for Thomas the whole creation is viewed anthropocentrically and soteriocentrically, that is, in terms of Genesis 2–3. And that leads to the final abnegation of nature as a whole.

This medieval theological perspective is alive and well in our own time. It has been represented by thinkers as diverse as Karl Barth and Pierre Teilhard de Chardin. For Barth the Garden scenario is, as it were, pushed back into eternity where, in effect, the salvation of humanity happens in Jesus Christ. For Barth, creation as depicted in Genesis 1 then becomes the external stage for the enactment or the realization of God's covenant with humanity in Jesus Christ. For Teilhard, the Garden is not, as it were, pushed back into the eternity prior to the creation of the world, as it is for Barth. Rather, for Teilhard the Garden is, so to speak, pushed forward into the eternity that follows the end of the world. For him the whole point of Genesis 1 is to set the stage so that the law of complexity-consciousness can run its course, so that the many cosmically scattered elements of consciousness can be gathered into greater and more intense spiritual constellations, until the universal history makes its last great leap into a world of pure spirit, at which time the whole of material reality (presumably with the exception of human bodies, as for Thomas) will fall back into nothingness, whence it came. For all his attention to cosmic evolution, cosmic drift, cosmic energies, and the cosmic Christ, the whole point of the biophysical world, for Teilhard, is the unification and the final consummation of consciousness, in and through the human creature. The natural world, for Teilhard, is actually only a passing stage in the greater scheme of things, much as it seems to be for Barth.

In my judgment, this anthropocentric-soteriocentric trajectory of the tradition offers us no viable, positive way to come to terms with the future of the whole cosmos theologically, no way to draw out the fullness of meaning given in the New Testament expectation of a new heaven and a new earth in which righteousness dwells. It can only have the effect, finally, of reinforcing the anti-cosmic, even nihilistic tendencies of modern culture, which also teach us that nature has *no future*, or nothing worth looking forward to. That means, in turn, that this anthropocentric-soteriocentric trajectory in the tradition is also ill-equipped to deal with the questions of cosmic despair and spiritual anomie, which go hand in hand with such negative cosmic expectations.

A Dynamic Creation-History

Instead of that anthropocentric-soteriocentric line of theological reasoning, I propose—prompted by the paradigm of hope—that we read Genesis 2–3 in terms of Genesis 1, not vice versa; that we see Genesis 1 not merely as a prologue, but as *the* story, which then, with regard to its human dimensions especially, is further explicated in Genesis 2–3 and beyond.[6] Genesis 1 then becomes the narrative of the universal matrix, from first things to last things. Genesis 2–3 is the story that specifically depicts the initial details of human existence. I am therefore envisioning a dynamic, comprehensive creation-history, embraced and governed by God throughout, which gives humanity a place of special significance, but not the only place. This is the premise of all that follows.[7]

We can think of the universal divine economy, then, as an integrated history and two dimensions: the all-embracing ecological and the particular sociological dimensions. The older dogmaticians were accustomed to speak of *providentia generalis* and *providentia specialis* in this connection. Human history, the city of God, surely has its own meaning in the greater scheme of things. But it is not the exclusive meaning of everything. Cosmic history, the household of God, is first and foremost the theater of God's glory, as Calvin was wont to say. Its meaning is not exhausted when it offers humanity a congenial place to live and to grow in grace. As I have argued elsewhere, nature has its own integrity in the greater scheme of things.[8]

I want to examine now the relationship between the sociological and the ecological, the human and the natural, in some detail, since it is in the context of this discussion that we can see how a theology of hope for the cosmos as a whole can also bring with it an impetus toward the renewal of the church's life with nature. This will mean dealing first with two critical theological themes, sin and salvation, then concluding with a discussion of the calling of the church.

Sin, Salvation, and Consummation

Clearly, creation-history is not as God intends it to be. Here is where the narrative of Genesis 2–3 gives its special explication of Genesis 1. The history of humanity is a fallen history. And I take that fall to be thoroughgoing and overwhelming. But now a crucial point emerges. *There is no cosmic fall*. The earth is cursed because of humanity's sinfulness. That is to say that the judgment of God rests on all the elements of human identity, on the self as embodied and embedded in the whole of nature. But nature in itself is not fallen. The notion of a cosmic fall is essentially extrabiblical.[9]

Further, although human sin is radical, the underlying intentionality of creation-history is unaffected by sin. Sin does not stop God from being the Creator and Lord of all things. God still rules and still blesses the whole creation, the just and the unjust. The principalities and powers of death, to be sure, strike out at the goodness of God's created realm, and to that degree God's providence is fought and obscured. But God remains faithful to his original intentionality, his original covenant with the whole creation. God still elicits new life everywhere, both in the cosmic household of God and in the human city of God. From the songs of the morning stars to the hymns of joy raised by the oppressed when they leave the land of Egypt, from the bursting forth of one bud of spring to the steadfast refusal of Rosa Parks to move to the back of the bus, God is incessantly at work to renew the face of the earth, notwithstanding the incursions of human sinfulness and the havoc wrought by the collective expressions of human sin.

I surely do not want to suggest some kind of simplistic, optimistic reading of human history and its radical evil at this point; for clearly, from our perspective the just cause all too infrequently triumphs. The powers of death abound in human history, as well as in nature. But like the poor woman who lost a coin and searched diligently until she found it, the people of God are "prisoners of hope," as Zechariah said. Our identity constantly prompts us to search diligently for signs of God's creative rule, both in natural and human history. A theology of hope as a matter of course seeks to articulate that hopeful preoccupation of our souls.

It is at this point that we can appropriately begin reflecting about the meaning of human salvation, as it pertains to our life with nature. I have deliberately taken a long time before addressing this topic. For there is a tendency in the theology of our era, and in the piety of many of our churches, to make human salvation everything, without question, the alpha and omega of the world, the alpha and omega of the church, the alpha and omega of our own personal existence. This is understandable; but it is an inflation. It reflects the hegemony of Genesis 2–3 over Genesis 1, and the underplaying of the kind of New Testament texts I cited earlier, with all the liabilities attendant on that theological emphasis.

In the universal history of God with all things, we are better instructed to say that salvation is one facet of the divine activity, however decisive it is in fact for us humans. Salvation is the restoration of the city of God to its intended role in the universal history of God with all things. Salvation is the outflowing of that deep potency in the heart of God that was ready from before the foundation of the world to go forth to heal human history, should the experiment of human history go awry. Salvation is the Creative Spirit of God going the extra mile, seeking out those who have gone astray, calling them back to their originally intended life with their Creator and the Creator's universal history, as a shepherd seeks out the lost sheep.

Consummation, then, is the larger term. It refers to the originally intended goal of God's history with all things, both cosmos and polis, both natural and human history. Salvation is the smaller term. It refers to the divine strategy that operates to bring human history back on course, back in phase with everything else in the created universe, as all things move, elicited by God, toward the new heaven and the new earth, and the new Jerusalem.

This allows us, then, to think of the mission of Jesus Christ as being twofold in character, as it relates to salvation and consummation. We can first look at Jesus Christ as the climax of salvation history, which can be called *providentia specialissima*, using the older dogmatic language. In this context he can be called the Restorer, the One in whom humanity is reestablished in its originally intended location in creation-history. This is effected chiefly through the cross. At the same time, we can say, Jesus Christ is also the Perfector, the proleptic inflowing, of human and cosmic history as it will be consummated at the end, when the *providentia generalis et specialis* are finally vindicated. This is effected chiefly through the resurrection. In this respect, Christ is the foretaste or the firstfruits of the end-times. Christ, then, is not only the body and blood, broken and shed for us, he is also the Lord of the banquet, that Messianic feast promised for the human community from the beginning, when the Lord said, "Be fruitful and multiply."[10]

The Church's Calling

The logic of all this leads us to this observation about the calling of the church in general, and the church's life with nature in particular: in the life of the church, when it is faithful to its calling, we can see adumbrated the originally intended relationship between humanity and nature, and also a new element, the fragmentary exemplification of the life of the end-times, when God will be all in all. As the community that walks the way of the cross and lives by the resurrection, the church, by the grace of God, lives as the royal priesthood of God, as the embodied, congregated testimony of both the restoration and the foretaste that God has brought forth in Christ. Perhaps I can invoke an old word in this connection, drawing on both its connotations of self-sacrifice and joyful celebration of the future of God—martyr. The calling of the church, we can say, is to manifest both the love of the cross and the power of the resurrection. What does it mean, then, for the renewal of the church's relationship with nature? I think we can see the life of the church with nature as having four aspects, three of which pertain to the restoration effected by salvation and the last of which pertains to the anticipated consummation proleptically given in Jesus Christ.[11]

First, as redeemed creatures we can enter into a new life of *righteous cooperation* with nature. The word "dominion" can also be used here, if we do this self-consciously and cautiously. All too often "dominion" is read out of its biblical-theological context. Then it readily becomes will-to-power, or domination. This is one of the liabilities of the anthropocentric-soteriocentric trajectory in the theological tradition. It really has no way to keep the construct of human dominion over nature from becoming, in preaching and in practice, a notion of a master-slave relationship since, according to its premises, nature has no meaning or value in itself; nature only has meaning in relationship to human affairs and human destiny. Dominion, then, rightly construed, must always mean righteous cooperation with other creatures, who belong to God and not to us.

That implies two things: using the earth, yes, but doing so respectfully, attentive to its own God-given structures and attentive to the causes of social justice. One middle axiom in this respect, for example, might be: never overwork the land or underpay the laborer. The land deserves its rest. The laborer is worthy of his or her hire. In this connection, it seems to me that the whole modern notion of private property and capital accumulation, predicated as it is on the continued exploitation of nature, is highly suspect from a theological perspective, and therefore the church should eschew it. Righteous cooperation means using the earth as God's good commonwealth in a communitarian mode, not abusing it for the sake of individual gain or class aggrandizement.

Second, as redeemed creatures we can also enter into a new life of *sensitive care* of the earth. This is care for nature, for nature's sake, an idea that may sound odd, if not scandalous, to some who have only heard the Bible interpreted in anthropocentric, soteriocentric, or secular terms. But, nevertheless, we have been created to till the garden and keep it. And this means not only for the sake of food production, and so on, but also for our own well-being. It means the whole garden, the so-called useless plants and animals, as well as the productive ones. Recall that Noah took all the animals with him into the ark; presumably if his role had been only to take along animals for food, he might well have righteously seized on the opportunity to leave the unclean and the wild animals behind.

I take it that sensitive care for nature implies three kinds of engagement with nature, pertaining to what we can think of as its three dimensions—wild nature, cultivated nature, and fabricated nature—with varying degrees of effective involvement. We cannot do a great deal about caring for wild nature, nor should we, but at least we can seek to preserve it, with due attention, of course, to the canons of social justice (obviously one does not rightly seek to save the whales, let us say, oblivious of the needs of hungry children). Wild nature is good, created so by God, and deserves to be preserved. I see no indication whatsoever in the Bible—indeed many indications to the contrary—that God would smile on an earth covered with blacktop and geodesic domes. With regard to cultivated nature, which is the interface between the wilderness and the city, we can properly intervene, by definition, more extensively. Farmlands and other sensitively managed natural reserves seem to me to be a divinely intended datum of our existence together as human beings. In the area of fabricated nature, clearly, we can legitimately intervene even more extensively and thoroughly. I can express what I mean here by saying that in my judgment architecture and city planning are divine sciences. Since our identity as God's creatures is rooted in the whole earth, moreover—not just in the city, not just in the farm—our urban existence will be appropriately designed with signs of cultivated nature here and there, and our life in cultivated nature will be appropriately managed to allow occasional incursions of the wild, as well.

Third, as persons whose lives have been restored to our authentic roles in creation-history, we not only live lives of righteous cooperation and sensitive care; we can also live new lives of *blessed wonder*. This means seeking opportunities to contemplate both the beautiful and the sublime aspects of the cosmos, standing in awe of both the sunset and the lion roaring for its prey, seeing the glory of God refracted in both the elegance of a Mies van der Roe building and in the terror of molten steel. As guides to this wonder, perhaps Psalms 104 and 29 are among the most helpful. The first is reminiscent of the Egyptian hymn to the sun; it celebrates the gloriously harmonious diversity of the creation. The second is reminiscent of a more Babylonian-type apperception of nature, celebrating the terrible presence of Yahweh in the storm and in the pangs of birthing.

Yet as members of the church, our lives have been touched by more than salvation, which restores us to our rightful relationship with nature. The gospel we celebrate and proclaim to the world is not only the good news of our salvation, but also the good news of the consummation of the world. So there is a fourth element in our renewed relationship with nature: *joyful anticipation*. We are in touch with the reality of God's future, we are embraced by it, in and through Christ. With him and through him, therefore, the church joins with the choirs of angels who celebrate the new heaven, the new earth, and the new Jerusalem which is to come. And so the life of the church is transfigured, however imperfectly, by the eschatological glory of God, in and through Christ.

If I read Romans 8 correctly, I think I am right—with Oscar Cullman—in concluding that a special kind of bodily renewal, anticipating the final resurrection, may be found in the life of the church in this world.[12] This reading of Pauline theology then has implications for our understanding of the church's ministry of healing today. I also wonder whether some kind of heightened spiritual relationship with nature more generally may not be possible in the context of the sacramental life of the church, prefiguring the kind of intimate communion with the whole earth that will be ours in the consummated kingdom of God. Perhaps as we raise such questions and think such thoughts more regularly than we have in the past, our eyes will be opened to possibilities that many of us may have hitherto ignored.

At the same time, however, we know that the powers of death are still reigning and will continue to reign until the end-times come, and that therefore our life as the martyr church must always be lived, as the word "martyr" suggests, under the sign of the cross. Each of these elements—righteous cooperation, sensitive care, blessed wonder, and joyful anticipation—will be regularly contested and often undercut, in our hearts as elsewhere, by the powers of this age. This is why a balanced, biblical theology of hope for cosmic history, and for our engagement with that history, must always be, until the Eschaton, what a theology of hope is for human history and the history of salvation, more particularly, a theology of "the Crucified God" (Moltmann). We see through a glass darkly. And we live with all the ambiguities of a sinful world. But we do see and we do live, with hope: for the future of the cosmos and for our own relationship with nature.

NOTES

1. The pioneering work of this movement—still a study that merits exposure, especially in our theological schools—is Jürgen Moltmann, *Theology of Hope: On the Ground and the Implications of a Christian Eschatology* (New York: Harper & Row, 1967). Perhaps the most accessible work of substance in this area is Carl E. Braaten, *The Future of God: The Revolutionary Dynamics of Hope* (New York: Harper & Row, 1969).
2. Some discussion of the theology of nature appears in Jürgen Moltmann's essay, "Creation as an Open System," *The Future of Creation: Collected Essays* (Philadelphia: Fortress Press, 1979), and in Carl E. Braaten's chapter, "Toward an Ecological Theology," *Christ and Counter-Christ: Apocalyptic Themes in Theology* (Philadelphia: Fortress Press, 1972).
3. For a general discussion about "the theology of nature" in the last two decades, see my article, "Toward a New Theology of Nature," *Dialog* 25:1 (Winter 1986): pp. 43-50.
4. First Cor. 15:28. For an analysis of the centrality of this point in Paul's thought, see J. Christiaan Beker, *Paul the Apostle: The Triumph of God in Life and Thought* (Philadelphia: Fortress Press, 1980).
5. For an extensive discussion of the points touched on briefly in the following paragraphs, see my study, *The Travail of Nature: The Ambiguous Ecological Promise of Christian Theology* (Philadelphia: Fortress Press, 1985).

6. From Irenaeus through Augustine, it was a theological commonplace to interpret the history of the world—creation-history—as having six periods, as an interpretation of the six days of creation in Genesis 1. On this, see my work cited in the previous note.

7. I have developed a similar kind of schema at some length in an earlier study, albeit with less emphasis on the category of hope. See *Brother Earth: Nature, God, and Ecology in a Time of Crisis* (Nashville: Thomas Nelson, 1970).

8. Ibid.

9. See ibid., "Appendix."

10. On the twofold character of the mission of Jesus Christ, cf. Jürgen Moltmann, *The Trinity and the Kingdom: The Doctrine of God* (New York: Harper & Row, 1981), p. 116: "According to Paul, Christ was not merely 'delivered for our offences' but was also 'raised for our justification' (Rom. 4:25). Reconciling sinners with God through his cross, he brings about the new righteousness, the new life, the new creature through his resurrection. The justification of the sinner is more than merely the forgiveness of sins. It leads to new life: 'Where sin increased, grace abounded all the more' (Rom. 5:20). This is the way Paul expresses the imbalance between sin and grace, and the *added value* of grace. The surplus of grace over and above the forgiveness of sins and the reconciliation of sinners represents the power of the new creation which consummates creation-in-the-beginning. It follows that the Son of God did not become man simply because of the sin of men and women, but rather for the sake of perfecting creation."

11. A number of the following points I have discussed at length, in a slightly different form, in *Brother Earth*.

12. Oscar Cullman, *Immortality of the Soul or Resurrection of the Dead? The Witness of the New Testament* (London: Epworth Press, 1958), pp. 44 ff.

INDEX

Alexander, Samuel, 168
Altruism, 216, 221, 222, 224, 228, 230
Ambrose, St., 272, 273
Anderson, Bernhard, 123, 256
Angels, 167
Anthropic Principle,
  and argument from design, 129, 131, 141, 196-99
  and chance, 19
  meta-anthropic principle, 199
  and transformation of universe, 204
Anthropocentrism, 272, 274, 278
Anthropology, Christian, 213, 224
Anaximenes, 165
Apocalypse, 266-68
Aquinas, Thomas, 34, 80, 83, 84, 109, 125, 142, 273
Archonic Principle, 61, 65, 72, 90, 97, 103, 105
Argument from design, 130, 131, 135, 197-200
Aristotle, 80, 165, 166, 169
Atoms, Era of, 118
Augustine, 33, 60, 125, 170, 272
Asimov, Isaac, 110

Barbour, Ian, 18, 19, 21, 79-85, 181
Barrow, John, 197, 204
Barth, Karl, 109, 156, 186, 269, 270, 273
Baur, F. C., 214
Berkson, William, 157, 164, 166, 170
Beth, Karl, 142
Biblical Faith: an Evolutionary Approach (Theissen), 214
Big Bang Theory,
  and contingency, 100, 205
  and creation from the future, 88, 89, 108
  and Doctrine of Creation, 16-18, 46, 77, 78, 82, 105-7, 127
  and eschatology, 204, 205
  explanation of, 47-53, 116-19
  and Genesis account, 58, 122
  and historiogenesis, 65
  and many worlds theory, 132

opposition to, 54-57, 78, 79
  theological implications of, 184-88, 120, 121, 131
Big Bounce, 52, 53, 106, 187
Big Crunch, 52, 53, 121, 132
Black Holes, 121
Brief History of Time, A (Hawking), 55
Borman, Frank, 115
Bosons, 50, 117, 135
Bretschneider, Karl Gottlieb, 155
Brunner, Emil, 103
Bryan, William Jennings, 247
Buddeus, J. F., 154
Bultmann, Rudolf, 109
Burhoe, Ralph W., 214, 218, 220, 224

Calvin, John, 274
Campbell, Donald, 218, 224
Carr, B. J., 130
Carter, B., 131, 196
Catastrophe, 265-67
Causality, 86, 91, 126, 237-42
Center for Religion and Science, 21
Center for Theology and the Natural Sciences, 17, 19, 20, 28
Chance, 39, 148
Chardin, Teilhard de. *See* Teilhard de Chardin, Pierre
Chew, Geoffrey, 138
Christianity, evolutionary approaches to, 212-16
Christocentrism, 270
Church, calling of, 277-81
Church Dogmatics (Barth), 156, 271
Clement of Alexandria, 109
Conservation, 16, 104, 159
Consonance, 11, 12, 46, 107, 141
Consummation, 276, 280
Contingency (dependence),
  and argument from design, 201
  and Big Bang Theory, 105, 205
  and Doctrine of Creation, 21, 126, 127, 143, 159, 180, 181, 201, 205
  and faith, 102
  and finitude, 192-94

Contingency (*continued*)
 levels of, 199, 200
 meaning of, 62, 63, 201
 in process theology, 144
 in scientific theory, 20, 31, 135, 137-39, 161, 175, 191, 205
Copernicus, Nicolaus, 21, 22, 146
Cosmological constant. See *Lambda*
Covenant, 276
Coyne, George V., 111
Cox, Harvey, 40
Creation,
 biblical accounts of, 256, 261
 continuous (*creatio continua*)
  and contingency, 143, 181
  opposition to, 99
  in process theology, 146
  through Logos, 124, 148
  and scientific theory, 16, 18-22, 34, 37, 78-85, 186
  as theological concept, 95, 96, 104, 124, 126, 180, 227
 distinct from "generation," 75
 doctrine of, 21, 33, 46, 58, 109, 110, 137, 257
  effect of scientific theory on, 141
  and animal rights, 260
 from the future, 87-89
 Genesis account of, 172, 174, 254-58, 260, 271
 goodness of, 123, 125, 127, 180, 227, 257, 279
 history, 274, 275
 models of, 137, 144-46
 myths, 58, 122, 123, 146, 253-55
 orders of (Schöpfungsordnungen), 102-4, 158
 out of nothing (*ex nihilo*)
  and Bible, 122-26
  and Big Bang Theory, 16, 46, 47, 105-8
  and contingency (dependence), 137, 141, 179-81, 226
  and finitude, 204
  importance of doctrine, 18-21, 74-79, 85-87, 109
  opposition to, 56, 83
  and scientific creationism, 249
  and vacuum fluctuation theory, 134
 sequence of, 171, 172, 213
Creationism,

Act 590, 14, 249, 250
 biblical, 249
 evolutionary, 261
 and First Amendment to Constitution, 248, 250-53
 scientific, 13, 27, 92, 158, 248-50
 See also Evolution
Creationism on Trial: God and Evolution at Little Rock (Gilkey), 14
Creeds, 73, 124
Critique of Pure Reason (Kant), 168
Cullman, Oscar, 280
Currents in Theology and Mission, 22

Darrow, Clarence, 247
Darwin, Charles, 146, 155, 212
Davies, Paul, 10
Dawkins, Richard, 222
Day After, The, 267
De Chardin, Teilhard. See Teilhard de Chardin, Pierre
Deism, 56-59, 90, 126, 139, 160, 244
Democritus, 174
Descartes, Rene, 154, 160, 163, 168
Determinism, 90-92, 138, 243, 244
Demiurge, 69, 179
Disturbing the Universe (Dyson), 196
Dobzhansky, Theodosius, 173
Doctrine of Creation. See Creation, doctrine of
Dualism, 62, 74, 106, 125, 127, 142, 179
Duns Scotus, 171
Dyson, Freeman, 10, 131, 196, 202-4

Ecumenical Dogmatics (Schlink), 173
Einstein, Albert,
 Attitude toward religion, 14, 137, 138
 and Grand Unified Field Theory, 49, 167, 182, 187-89
 and relativity theory, 116
Electromagnetic force, 116
Electrons, 117
Electroweak Era, 48, 49, 118
Eliade, Mircea, 64, 68, 69, 128
Emergent Evolution (Morgan), 173
Energy, 33, 35, 48
Enlightenment, 11, 126, 153
Entropy, 52, 121

Enuma Elish, 58, 122, 123, 253
Epigenesis, 16, 19, 61, 65, 72, 97, 173
Eschatology, 71, 72, 97, 203, 204, 224, 230-32, 270, 280
Evolution,
  biological and cultural interrelated, 217, 218
  and Christian faith, 156, 173-75, 219, 223
  as God's action, 219, 261
  -"ism", 253
  mechanism of, 38
  teaching of in public schools, 247-53
  as theory, 251, 252, 261
  See also Darwin, Charles; and Natural Selection
Everett, 132
Exodus, Book of, 256

Faith, 109, 11, 219, 223
Fall, The, 22, 271, 275
Faraday, 20, 163, 164, 166
Finitude, 191-94, 204
First Three Minutes, The (Weinberg), 201
Forgiveness, 267
Forsyth, P. T., 244
Freedom, 91, 92, 220, 222, 229, 230

Galatians, Letter to the, 268
Galileo, 146
Gamow, George, 45
Gaudium et Spes, 10
Generation, 75
Genesis,
  1:1-3, 115
  and anthropocetrism, 272, 273
  cosmology of, 17, 57, 96, 97-99, 120, 122-28, 172
  and thelogy of hope, 274-76
  See also Big Bang Theory, and doctrine of creation; Creation, doctrine of; Creation, *ex nihilo;* Creation, Genesis account of
Gifford Lectures, 19
Gilkey, Langdon,
  and contingency, 181
  and doctrine of creation, 73, 81-85,
  and scientific creationism, 14, 15, 98

Gish, Duane, 98
Gleick, James, 10
Gnosticism, 125, 179
God,
  feminine imagery for, 32, 36, 41
  goodness of, 40, 257
  future of, 268, 269
  ideas of, 214, 215
  image of, 213, 216, 228, 229, 254, 255, 258, 270
  immanence of, 33-37, 41, 42, 81, 93, 143, 144, 256
  incarnation of, 43
  involvement in created order, 38, 43, 76, 181, 269
  models of creative work, 144, 145
  -"of the gaps", 33, 34, 37, 55, 121
  transcendence of, 41, 42, 61, 81, 93, 94, 122, 125, 127, 256
    overemphasized, 143
    in process theology, 144
  as Uncaused Cause, 80, 125
  will of, 224, 271
Gospel,
  and doctrine of creation, 46, 47, 58, 60, 72, 94, 109
  role of in eschatology, 77, 99, 267, 280
Gospel According to John (Luther), 265
Gould, Stephen Jay, 98
Graduate Theological Union, 17, 19, 20, 28
Grand Unified Field Theory (GUT),
  and cosmology, 49, 50
  explanation of, 116-19, 135
  and quantum theory of gravity, 54
  theological significance of, 137, 164-67, 176
Gravitational Force, 116, 135, 196
Gray, Asa, 219

Hardy, Alister, 175
Harnack, Adolf von, 214
Hawking, Stephen, 54-57, 60, 131
Hefner, Philip, 181, 203
Heidegger, Martin, 169, 170
Heim, Karl, 156
Heisenberg uncertainties, 119
Hesiod, 253, 254
Hesse, Mary, 65

Hick, John, 220
Historical-critical method, 155
Historiogenesis, 61, 65, 67
Historiomachy, 66, 67, 90, 97
Homo erectus, 213
Homo sapiens, 28, 31, 32, 213
Hot Quark Era, 135
Hoyle, Fred,
    attitude toward religion, 55, 78-80,
        84, 121
    steady state model, 45, 82, 186, 190
Hubble, 183
    constant, 116, 195
Humanity,
    as created co-creator, 212, 225-29
    as exploiters of creation, 258, 259
    as stewards of creation, 255, 258,
        261, 278, 279
    relationship with cosmos, 270
    salvation of, 276
    two natures of, 221, 223
Hume David, 130
Hyers, Conrad, 112, 145

Immanence. *See* God, immanence of
Inertia, Principle of, 154, 160
Institute for Creation Research, 98
Irenaeus, 75
Isham, C. J., 56
Issues in Science and Religion (Bar-
    bour), 83

Jacob, Edmund, 82
Jaki, S. L., 111
Jammer, Max, 163, 165
Jastrow, Robert, 46, 120, 185
Jawist, 70
Jesus Christ,
    and evolution, 219, 229, 230
    as New Adam, 229, 272
    as telos of cosmos, 273
    as climax of salvation history, 277,
        278, 280
John of Damascus, 75
John Paul II, Pope, 10
Justification by Faith, 267, 268
Justin Martyr, 111

Kant, Immanuel, 168-70
Katz, Solomon, 218
Kaufman, Gordon, 94, 95

Kelsey, David, 128
Kepler, Johann, 34
Kingdom of God, 94, 108
Kummer, H., 221

Lambda (cosmological constant), 189,
    192
Lash, Nicholas, 112
Laws of Nature, 100-102, 139, 163
Leibnitz, 168, 196
Lemaitre, G., 186
Leslie, John, 133
Liedtke, Gerhard, 259
Life,
    effects of on universe, 204
    on other planets, 147
Lightman, Alan, 10
Logos, 41, 124, 139
Love Principle, 224, 228
Luther, Martin, 73, 109, 153, 265,
    268

McMullin, Ernan, 79, 107, 141, 188,
    192, 204
Matter, 33, 35, 48, 53
Mathematics, 31, 34, 139, 183
Melanchthon, Philip, 153
Milky Way, 51
Moltmann, Jürgen, 112, 181, 281
Monism, 74, 142, 179
Monotheism, 63
Morgan, A. Lloyd, 173
Morris, Henry, 112
Morrow, Lance, 46
Murphy, Nancey, 212
Mutations, 39
Myth, role of, 62, 64. *See also*
    Creation myths

Naturalism, 12, 79, 90
Natural Law, 102
Natural Selection, 38, 220, 249
Neutrinos, 52, 121
Neutrons, Era of, 118
New Jerusalem, 269-71, 277
Newton, Sir Isaac
    force theory of, 154, 163, 182
    religious beliefs of, 34, 163, 168
Niebuhr, H. R., 236
Nihilism, 108, 266, 273
Nihil negativism, 76
Nihil privatism, 76

Orders of Creation. *See* Creation, orders of
Origen, 111

Panentheism, 35, 93
Pennenberg, Wolfhart, 19, 20, 177, 181, 182
Pantheism,
  and creation *ex nihilo*, 74, 75, 125, 127, 142, 179
  in post-modern theorists, 93, 94, 139
  in work of Spinoza, 138, 238
Particles, Era of, 49
Paul, St., 256, 270, 280
Peacocke, Arthur R.,
  and Big Bang cosmology, 108, 120, 178
  and creation *ex nihilo*, 181
  and metaphors for God, 145, 146, 198, 219
  and reforming approach, 213, 243
Pelikan, Jaroslav, 126
Penzias, Arno A., 78, 116
Peters, karl, 218
Peters, Ted, 263, n.22
Pius, IX, Pope, 10
Pius XII, 46, 120, 185
Planck, Max, 153
  constant, 195
  time, 49, 50, 106
Plasma, Era of, 49
Plato, 51, 69, 74, 76, 179
Plotinus, 169, 170
Pneuma, 165
Polanyi, Michael, 174, 175
Polkinghorne, John, 31, 139
Polytheism, 63
Pontifical Academy of Sciences, 46, 185
Popper, Karl, 157
Prayer, 21, 22, 235-45
Preservation. *See* Conservation
Prigogine, Ilya, 52
Process theology, 143, 146
Prophets, 33
Protons, Era of, 118
Providentia, 274, 277

Quantum Theory, 54, 131, 132, 133, 138

Quantum Theory of Gravity, 54, 55, 106, 117, 135
Quantum Vacuum Fluctuations, 133
Quarks, Era of, 49, 118, 135

Rahner, Karl, 182
Rees, M. J., 131
Reign of God. *See* Kingdom of God
Relativity, Theory of, 88, 116, 182, 187-89
Resurrection of Jesus, 61, 72, 108
Ritschl, Albrecht, 214
Rubbia, Carlo, 117
Russell, Bertrand, 12, 108, 201
Russell, J. K. fellow, 17, 19, 21
Russell, Robert John, 16, 20, 21, 139

Sacraments, 31, 36
Sagan, Carl, 55
Salam, Abdus, 117
Santmire, H. Paul, 22
Schleiermacher, Friedrich, 270
Schlink, Edmund, 103, 104, 172, 173
Scientific Creationism. *See* Creationism, Scientific
Scientism, 12
Scopes, John Thomas, 247
Second Vatican Council, 10
Secular Humanism, 12, 248
Selfish Gene, The, 222
Simpson, G. G., 38
Sitter, Wiliem de, 116
Smith, Houston, 253
Smyth, Newman, 219
Social Darwinism, 219
Soteriocentrism, 272-74, 277
Space-time, 182, 183, 189
Spinoza, Baruch, 138, 154, 237, 238
Spirit (Holy), 124, 165
Steady State Theory, 45, 78, 79, 82, 121, 186, 190. *See also* Hoyle, Fred
Stengers, Isabelle, 111
Stevens, Anthony, 215
Stewardship. *See* Humanity, as stewards of creation
Stoeger, William R., 111
Stoicism, 165
Strong Nuclear Force, 116
Supergravity, 135
Superstring Theory, 117, 135

Supersymmetry Theory, 117-19, 135, 136
Syllabus of Errors, 10

Table Talk (Luther), 153, 265
Tatian, 111
Teilhard de Chardin, Pierre, 147, 174, 213, 215, 224, 270, 273
Theissen, Gerd, 214-18, 220, 224, 225
Theodicy, 220
Theogony (Hesiod), 253
Theology
  of the earth, 267
  of hope, 267-70, 274, 276, 281
  of liberation, 268
Theophilus of Antioch, 74
Theory of Everything (TOE), 135, 136, 140
Thermodynamics, Second Law of, 39, 52, 88, 121
Tillich, Paul, 112, 182, 186, 194
Timaeus (Plato), 69, 179
Time,
  Augustinian view of, 33, 125, 170
  infinite, 141, 142
  and myth, 64, 65
  linear, 45, 86, 89, 127
  Plotinian view, 169
  in relativity theory, 33, 182, 187
  $= 0 \, (t = 0)$, 47, 65, 184-88, 121, 205
Timm, Roger E., 22
Tipler, Frank, 197, 204
Torrance, Thomas, 137, 198
Toulmin, Stephen, 110
Tracy, David, 112, 140
Trefil, James, 50, 51, 52, 137, 197, 198
Turner, Victor, 215

Unified Field Theory. *See* Grand Unified Field Theory

United Church of Christ, *Statement of Faith,* 128
Universe,
  age of, 147
  closed, 52, 121, 135, 188-90, 201, 203
  expanding, 52, 116, 130, 147, 183, 202, 203
  flat, 52, 53, 135
  freeze of, 48
  future of, 59, 201, 202, 268, 271. *See also* Eschatology
  many universes theory, 197, 198, 201
  only possible, 135, 199
  open, 52, 53, 121, 135, 184, 188-90, 201-3
  oscillating, 121, 188
  rationality of, 137, 138
  at $t = 0$, 184, 188
Voegelin, Eric, 63, 68
Von Rad, Gerhard, 67, 70, 71

Weak Nuclear Force, 116
Weber, Renee, 54
Weinberg, Stephen, 53, 117, 203
Wheeler, 132, 183, 190
Whitehead, Alfred North, 144
White, Lynn, 258
Wholism, 89-93, 169
Wilson, Robert W., 78, 116
Wisdom,
  figure of, 145
  literature, 33, 123
Word and World, 18, 22, 45
Word of God, 96, 109, 122, 139
Works and Days (Hesiod), 254

Zygon, 19